Free Speech on America's K–12 and College Campuses

Lexington Studies in Political Communication

Series Editor: Robert E. Denton, Jr., Virginia Tech

This series encourages focused work examining the role and function of communication in the realm of politics including campaigns and elections, media, and political institutions.

Titles in the Series

Free Speech on America's K–12 and College Campuses

Legal Cases from Barnette *to* Blaine

Randy Bobbitt

LEXINGTON BOOKS
Lanham • Boulder • New York • London

Published by Lexington Books
An imprint of The Rowman & Littlefield Publishing Group, Inc.
4501 Forbes Boulevard, Suite 200, Lanham, Maryland 20706
www.rowman.com

Unit A, Whitacre Mews, 26-34 Stannary Street, London SE11 4AB

British Library Cataloguing in Publication Information Available

Library of Congress Cataloging-in-Publication Data Available

ISBN 978-0-7391-8647-3 (cloth : alk. paper)
ISBN 978-0-7391-8648-0 (electronic)

∞™ The paper used in this publication meets the minimum requirements of American National Standard for Information Sciences Permanence of Paper for Printed Library Materials, ANSI/NISO Z39.48-1992.

Printed in the United States of America

Contents

Preface

In 1981, as a reporter for *The Tampa Tribune*, I wrote an article titled "Lou Grant in Sweat Socks" for the paper's features section. It profiled the student-run newspapers at the University of South Florida, University of Tampa, and Hillsborough Community College and was based on interviews with both student editors and faculty advisers. The title was based on a popular television series of the day, *Lou Grant*, which was one of the most successful programs to ever deal with the world of journalism.

"Way, way, way too long," my editor said of the 3,500-word first draft. "You weren't assigned to write a book." After hours of self-editing, I cut the story down to 2,000 words, and by the time the article was published, it had been cut to 1,300.

Thirty-five years and two careers later, I actually have written a book on the subject of student media. But instead of focusing only on college newspapers, this one deals with both college and high school campuses and addresses free speech in a broader sense. While cases involving student media are usually the most dramatic, this book also deals with issues such as dress codes, free speech zones, and one of the most controversial issues affecting colleges in the twenty-first century—hate speech.

While I did write for two student newspapers during my undergraduate years, the articles I wrote seldom generated controversy. My first experience with administrative angst over the content of a student newspaper came in 1992, shortly after I accepted my first tenure-track appointment in the journalism school at Marshall University. Two newspaper staffers had decided, without consulting their faculty adviser, to include the name of the accuser in a story dealing with an alleged case of sexual assault that occurred near campus. Identifying the alleged victim by name violated commonly accepted rules of journalism ethics. The result was a three-way conflict among the newspaper staff, the faculty of the journalism school, and the university president that nearly caused the director of the journalism school—my boss and mentor—to lose his job. At the height of the controversy, while still publicly defending the student journalists, he privately expressed disappointment in the decision by saying, "Just because you can, doesn't mean you have to." Twenty-four years later, I often use that quote in my own class discussions when legal and ethical issues arise. The Marshall case is discussed in more detail at the opening of chapter 3.

This book covers the fifty-year period from 1965 through 2015. There are a few cases outside of that time period, however, including the 1943 case of *West Virginia Board of Education v. Barnette*. The purpose of the research was *not* to produce an exhaustive list of *every* case involving the free speech rights of K-12 and college students. A quick glance of the archives of the Student Press Law Center, Foundation for Individual Rights in Education, and the American Civil Liberties Union indicates that such a list would require a multivolume set. Instead, the purpose was to produce a representative catalog of cases, scattered across the five decades, and representing five areas—high school media, college media, religious issues, political correctness, and alleged disruption.

The title was taken from two cases—one from early in the history of campus free speech debates and another from one of the most recent. "Barnette" refers to the case mentioned above—a case set against the backdrop of World War II in which the U.S. Supreme Court dealt with the legality of forcing school students to salute the flag and recite the Pledge of Allegiance. "Blaine" refers to a 2001 case in which a high school student in Washington was suspended for writing a disturbing poem as part of an extra credit English assignment. Like many cases of that decade—many which are discussed in chapter 6—it was argued against the backdrop of the 1999 Columbine tragedy, in which two troubled students killed a dozen of their classmates, one teacher, and themselves after teachers and guidance counselors missed "red flags" about the perpetrators' behavior.

Chapter 1 provides an overview of the topic, including a brief discussion of some recent trends on college campuses that have not yet produced court cases. It also discusses the work of three advocacy groups (mentioned above) that support students whose First Amendment rights are at risk.

Chapter 2 covers some of the most important cases in the history of high school journalism, with an emphasis on the 1988 Supreme Court case of *Hazelwood East School District v. Kuhlmeier*, which allowed principals the right to exercise "prior review" of student newspapers. With no similar cases reaching the Court since, *Hazelwood* is still the standard for resolving conflicts between the competing rights of students and administrators.

Chapter 3 deals with major cases in college journalism, including a 2007 case, *Hosty v. Carter*, which was decided at the appeals court level and in favor of college administrators. When the Supreme Court declined to hear the students' appeal, it left in place an appeals court ruling that provided college administrators the right to control the content of student newspapers—but only among colleges within the Seventh Circuit.

Chapter 4 deals with religious cases, including school prayer, recitation of the Pledge of Allegiance, and the rights of faith-based student organizations on high school and college campuses.

Chapter 5 deals with the trend of college campuses establishing "speech codes," "free speech zones," and other rules to discourage speech that is not "politically correct."

One of the newest and more troubling trends involving campus speech is that of college students and faculty members acting collectively to demand their institutions "uninvite" commencement speakers and other campus visitors based on those individuals' controversial or (allegedly) offensive ideas.

Chapter 6 covers the role of high school administrators (and a few of their college counterparts) in reacting to student speech in the form of provocative dress, social media postings, or disturbing writings submitted in class. The earliest case in this area was *Tinker v. Des Moines Independent Community School District* (1969), which began when three students attending separate schools wore black armbands to protest the Vietnam War. The case was decided in favor of the students, prompting Supreme Court Justice Abe Fortas to write in his majority opinion that students "do not shed their Constitutional rights to freedom of expression at the schoolhouse gate."

In subsequent cases, courts at several levels of the legal system have attempted to apply the *Tinker* standard in cases involving speech that takes place off campus in the form of social media or other online venues. While free-speech-minded judges tend to rely heavily on *Tinker*, those claiming to be pragmatists support the judgment of school administrators in regulating threatening speech in light of the Columbine tragedy.

This book is the culmination of four years of research, much of it done while holding down a full-time teaching assignment at the University of West Florida. During that time, I received a considerable amount of support from colleagues Kurt Wise and Bruce Swain in the Department of Communication Arts, as well as Leslie Bradley, our administrative assistant. I thank the staffs of the Student Press Law Center and Foundation for Individual Rights in Education for their research assistance. I also thank my editor at Lexington Books, Nicolette Amstutz, for her encouragement and support.

This book is dedicated to the memory of my mother, Betty C. Bobbitt, who passed away a few months before it was published. Her love and support has always been a source of inspiration.

Chapter One

The Schoolhouse Gate

THE BEST OF TIMES

For many outside of the fields of education and journalism, the history of free speech on campus goes back to the 1969 Supreme Court case, *Tinker v. Des Moines Independent Community School District*. In that case, three students attending adjacent schools in Iowa had challenged school rules prohibiting them and their classmates from wearing black armbands to protest the Vietnam War. The Court ruled in favor of the students, and the case has long been considered the landmark decision involving free speech at K-12 schools. The famous quote emerging from the majority opinion in the case was that "it can hardly be argued that either students or teachers shed their Constitutional rights to freedom of speech expression at the schoolhouse gate"[1] (the *Tinker* case is discussed in more detail in chapter 6).

But *Tinker*'s anointment as the first Supreme Court dealing with student free speech is erroneous. The history of Supreme Court cases dealing with campus free speech issues actually goes back to 1943 and the case of *West Virginia Board of Education v. Barnette*.[2] In that case, the parents of three public school students challenged a school district rule requiring all students to begin the day by reciting the Pledge of Allegiance. In that case as well, the Supreme Court ruled in favor of student free speech rights; or more precisely, the right of the students *not to speak* (the *Barnette* case is discussed in more detail in chapter 4).

Prior to the *Barnette* case reaching the Supreme Court, the only precedent in this area of law was a little-known case, *State v. District Board of School District No. 1*, in which the Supreme Court of Wisconsin ruled in favor of school officials who suspended two students for ridiculing the principal in a poem published in a local newspaper. The court wrote that "such power is

1

essential to the preservation of order, decency, decorum, and good government in the public schools."[3]

THE WORST OF TIMES

The *Tinker* case dealt with a form of speech not sanctioned by the school, yet
for the next fifteen years the "schoolhouse gate" concept was applied in cases
involving both sanctioned and non-sanctioned activities, and in the majority
of cases, students retained their free speech rights. The landscape changed in
the mid-1980s with two Supreme Court cases in which the justices chipped
away at student free speech rights based on two concepts deemed to take
priority over that of the "schoolhouse gate."

In *Bethel School District v. Fraser* (1986), the Court ruled in favor of a
local school district that suspended a student for using inappropriate language while speaking at a school assembly. The new terms coined were
"captive audience" (because students were required to attend) and "disrupting the educational process" (because the school district claimed the speech
interfered with the orderly operation of the school). Instead of confirming
student rights based on *Tinker*, which the students' attorneys expected the
justices to do, the Court ruled that students' constitutional rights were not
"co-existent" with the rights of adults in other settings and that a school
"does not have to tolerate speech which is inconsistent with its educational
mission."[4]

Two years later, the Court further struck down student rights in the case
of *Hazelwood v. Kuhlmeier*. A high school principal in suburban St. Louis
used the "disruption" standard from *Bethel* to censor the school newspaper,
objecting to two stories—one about teen pregnancy and birth control and the
other about the effect of divorce on children when they were of high school
age. The principal objected to the first story because of its sexual nature and
the second because he believed the privacy of specific families was at risk,
even though none were specifically identified.

Students on the newspaper staff sued the principal, and the case eventually reached the Supreme Court. The Court ruled in favor of the principal,
determining that censorship was acceptable if it (1) served the educational
mission of the school; (2) was done in a reasonable manner; (3) was related
to pedagogical concerns; and (4) served a valid purpose. Civil libertarians
and others concerned about student free speech rights saw the vagueness of
the four-part *Hazelwood* standard as giving school administrators a "blank
check" to censor student newspapers not only for stories that were legitimately disruptive, but also those that were simply critical of the school, its teachers and administrators, or its policies[5] (the Hazelwood case is covered in
more detail in chapter 2).

While the *Bethel* and *Hazelwood* cases have weakened the rights given to students by *Tinker*, the latter case is still relevant to cases argued today. What begin as a ruling dealing with the specifics of three students using symbolic speech to passively object to an unpopular war has been used for nearly five decades as a precedent to argue—sometimes successfully and sometimes not—for students' rights in cases involving dress codes, school uniforms, restrictions on slogans and symbols appearing on clothing, the content of student newspapers and literary magazines, drama club productions, and most recently, student expression that takes the form of Internet and social media rants.[6]

The *Tinker* case was decided in the final session in which Earl Warren presided over the Court as chief justice. With both Warren and Associate Justice Abe Fortas—the author of the majority opinion in *Tinker*—leaving the Court, the ideological makeup of the court shifted from liberal to conservative.

Supreme Court historian Erwin Chemerinsky points out that as Warren and Fortas were replaced by Warren Burger and Harry Blackmun, the Court's dramatic shift had a major impact on the law in a number of areas, including how the First Amendment would be applied on high school campuses over the next three decades. In fact, Chemerinsky wrote in a journal article, between 1970 and 2000 school administrators won nearly every court case involving student free speech rights at the high school level.[7] In his surprising dissent in *Tinker*, Justice Hugo Black stressed the need for judicial deference to the authority and expertise of school officials. Chemerinsky pointed out that in the three decades since, Supreme Court decisions seemed to resemble Black's dissent more than Fortas's majority opinion.[8] Since 1999, many administrators at K-12 schools have justified their crackdowns on all forms of free speech by citing the Columbine massacre in which two troubled students killed twelve classmates, one teacher, and themselves at their high school in the upscale Denver suburb of Littleton, Colorado. Analysis of the case revealed that teachers, administrators, and guidance counselors missed "red flags" in the students' schoolwork and behavior, creating a climate in which the slightest aberration in student discourse or demeanor was cause for suspicion (the connection between the Columbine tragedy and administrative censorship is discussed in more detail in chapter 6).

"School administrators' response to these legitimate fears often has been to clamp down on student expression deemed different or unusual," wrote First Amendment attorney David L. Hudson, Jr. in a 2003 report on student free speech published by the First Amendment Center. "Many schools have enacted 'zero tolerance' policies that impose harsh penalties for first-time student offenders. School districts have controlled language, censored students' personal websites, established dress codes, banned controversial symbols, tossed out books, and required uniforms. But if students are to learn the lessons of democracy, such as the importance of exercising the right to freedom of speech, they must live in an environment that fosters the free exchange of ideas."[9]

One example of administrative overreaction occurred in 2007, when administrators at a high school in Blaine, Washington, were concerned about the writings of a high school student who was reflecting on Columbine and subsequent school shootings in the Northwest. Despite submitting to a psychological evaluation and convincing experts that he was not a threat to himself or anyone else, had no access to weapons, and had no thoughts of carrying out any of the actions he had described in his writing, the student was suspended. The family appealed to the Federal District Court, which ruled in favor of the school, and on appeal to the Ninth Circuit, that ruling was upheld[10] (this case is discussed in more detail in chapter 6).

THE MARKETPLACE OF IDEAS

The idea of free speech in society did not begin with the First Amendment to the Constitution, but rather the writings of English poet and philosopher John Milton (1608-1674), who believed that societies should allow their citizens the greatest possible access to the greatest diversity of ideas. Milton, and other philosophers of his time, believed that everyone should be free to openly discuss controversial social and political issues, even if it meant challenging the views of authority figures or anyone else. In the battle between truth and falsity, Milton believed, truth would always win if the audience carefully evaluated the competing ideas. Three centuries later, the U.S. Supreme Court paraphrased the idea when it coined the term "marketplace of ideas."[11]

Milton and other libertarians of the day believed that individuals should have absolute rights of free expression, and that it was the responsibility of the populace to determine what was true and what was false, and what was important and what was trivial. That belief ran counter to the prevailing authoritarian philosophy of the time, which held that only the English monarchy and other government officials were qualified to determine the value of ideas and who would be allowed to express them. Milton added that the danger of suppressing falsehoods was that some truths might also be lost in the process. And for those who disagreed about the value of including falsehoods in the public debate, just the intellectual exercise of separating truth from falsehood was worth the effort.[12] Whether high school and college campuses are true "marketplaces of ideas" (many cases discussed in this book used the term "public forums") is not settled law. There are so many factors involved—the ages of the students, the political leanings of campus administrators, the political climate of the times, and the culture of the surrounding community—that attempting to predict the outcome of cases is nearly impossible.

STRANGE BEDFELLOWS

At the forefront of the fight for speech rights on campus are four nonprofit organizations: the American Association of University Professors, which protects the rights of faculty members; the Foundation for Individual Rights in Education, which protects the rights of students and student groups on college campuses; the Student Press Law Center, which defends the rights of student journalists and advisers; and the American Civil Liberties Union, which defends the free speech rights of all citizens.

AAUP, based in Washington, DC, and FIRE, based in Philadelphia, have taken particular interest in campus speech codes (discussed in more detail in chapter 5).

The SPLC is an Arlington, Virginia-based nonprofit organization that receives more than 3,000 requests for help each year from students and faculty advisers. The most common cause for complaints is attempts at prior restraint by high school principals and university administrators. At the university level, the fastest-growing area of SPLC work is in the area of access to information, as student journalists often find it difficult to obtain information regarding university budgets and campus crime statistics, even though much of the information is required to be made public by state laws.

The ACLU is a Washington, DC-based organization that advocates adherence to the Constitution, including the First Amendment, in all areas of American life. While the SPLC would be the primary organization involved in conflicts involving campus media, the ACLU would be more likely to get involved in free speech conflicts other than those involving media, such as dress codes.

Both FIRE and the ACLU are run mostly by attorneys and other professionals interested in free speech issues and other civil rights issues. While their leaders are admittedly liberal in their political leanings, they often find themselves working with unlikely partners in free speech issues, including conservative Christian groups such as the Alliance Defense Fund (when students' religious freedoms are threatened by campus administrators), the National Rifle Association (defending the rights of students to wear clothing featuring the NRA logo or images of guns), and the Sons of the Confederacy (defending the rights of students to wear clothing featuring the Confederate flag).

There is some First Amendment-related good news happening in American education today, however. In a 2014 study titled "The State of the First Amendment," the Nashville-based First Amendment Center found more support today than in past years for K-12 student journalism. More than two-thirds of Americans agreed that journalism students in public schools should be allowed to report on controversial issues without the approval of school administrators. In 2001, less than one-half of respondents supported that idea.[13]

DECIDING FACTORS IN CAMPUS SPEECH CASES

Despite court rulings that have established that the First Amendment applies to speech and press on high school and college campuses, administrators often attempt to limit speech and exercise editorial control over campus media. And because of the students' limited legal resources, many are either unwilling or unable to challenge those administrators in court.

When cases do reach the legal system, the courts take many factors into consideration, including:

1. Speech that takes place on a high school campus can be controlled to a greater degree than speech that takes place on a college campus. The courts' rationale for this disparity is two-fold. First, college students are older and assumed to be more mature than high school students, rendering them more capable of processing complex or controversial information and making appropriate judgments regarding its validity. Second, the college campus is often a venue for debating conflicting political ideas and opinions, thus making many campus activities (including student media) the equivalent of public forums; the same cannot be said about the high school environment.
2. Sanctioned activities such as student newspapers, yearbooks, literary magazines, drama club productions, and halftime entertainment at athletic events can be controlled to a greater degree than nonsanctioned activities such as informal gatherings and extemporaneous speeches.
3. Communication involving a captive audience, such as a class activity or assembly for which attendance is required, can be controlled to a greater degree than communication to a noncaptive audience, such as a gathering on the school grounds for which attendance is voluntary. Because of the captive audience concept, the courts acknowledge school administrators' authority to regulate speech that may be disruptive to the educational process. Therefore, the courts typically side with school leaders and allow them to enforce dress codes and other regulations that would not apply to adults or children off school grounds.
4. Students at private schools are more subject to speech and press limitations than their counterparts at public schools. Administrators at

private schools are given more leeway to censor campus media than their counterparts at public schools because public schools are considered agencies of the state government, and the courts seldom allow agencies of government to infringe upon speech. At private schools, however, the courts generally allow administrators to control campus media and are reluctant to interfere, especially at church-run schools, because of the doctrine of separation of church and state. If the catalog or other recruiting materials at a private university makes a promise of free speech, however, a student who believes that right was violated might prevail in a breach-of-contract lawsuit. [14]

THE K-12 CAMPUS

In siding with the students in *Tinker*, the Court ruled that the armbands were a form of "passive" protest that did not interfere with the educational mission of the school. The court placed the burden of proof on school administrators to prove the armbands were disruptive, rather than on the students to prove that they were not. [15] In *Tinker*, the Court used the words "conclaves of totalitarianism" to characterize what public schools might become if administrators had complete authority to regulate the speech of their students.

"Surveys of scholastic journalism indicate that censorship and punishment for constitutionally protected student expression are common and that some school administrators are insensitive to constitutional values," wrote the authors of a popular media law textbook. "It is not uncommon for college editors to be required to submit copy for review to a faculty adviser. In high schools, administrators are often the censors." [16] In both *Bethel* and *Hazelwood*, the Court seemed to agree to some extent with the contention of school administrators that it was important that the public did not perceive that the objectionable message was endorsed by the school. In *Tinker*, with the speech being part of a nonsanctioned activity, that was not a factor. [17]

Today, both K-12 and college students find themselves subject to administrative censorship in their choice of clothing, spoken opinions, and work published in student media. Many observers believe that growing concerns over student safety and a growing national concern over diversity and political correctness have resulted in the erosion of student rights once thought to be untouchable.

"Parental fears, administrative dictates, curriculum demands, and state-imposed standards crowd out the sort of lessons that prepare young people to fully function as informed citizens in the real world," wrote First Amendment scholar Paul McMasters in a 2000 SPLC publication. He then posed the question, "How does a teacher coax from the principal the latitude to teach the Bill of Rights when the principal is being told by the school board and parents to keep things simple, cheap, and non-controversial?"[18]

In the introductory chapter to its primer on student press rights, *Law of the Student Press*, the SPLC argues that the free speech and free press rights of students should be protected as strenuously as those of the professional media and citizens in general.

"Many young people today are woefully uninformed about the most important issues affecting their lives, from drug abuse to AIDS, from college financial aid to school budgets," the chapter stated. "The student press should be free to address these types of issues. In addition, schools are where most students are exposed to the fundamentals of democracy, including values embodied by the Constitution. What is a student to believe when taught about the First Amendment in a social studies or government classroom, only to have free expression in a student newspaper or yearbook suppressed by school officials?"[19] The chapter cites an essay by former *New York Times* editor Tom Wicker, who wrote in 1974 that "All too many of these high school editors and reporters may well conclude, from hard experience, that freedom of the press is as bad a joke as the ones school boards would like them to print in place of news and opinion; and holding that cynical view they are far more likely to become doctors, engineers, or politicians rather than reporters. If they do become reporters, having felt the knife so early, they are not likely to stick their necks out in the name of the First Amendment."[20]

Textbook authors Don R. Pember and Clay Calvert concur. "For centuries, students were presumed to have few constitutional rights," wrote Pember and Calvert in their 2015 textbook, *Mass Media Law*. "They were regarded as second-class people and told it was better to be seen and not heard. Parents were, and still are, given wide latitude in controlling the behavior of their offspring, and when these young people moved into schools or other public institutions, the government had the right to exercise a kind of parental control over them: in loco parentis, in the place of the parent."[21]

Added Chemerinsky: "School officials—like all government officials—often will want to suppress or punish speech because it makes them uncomfortable, is critical of them, or just because they don't like it. The judiciary has a crucial role in making sure that this is not the basis for censorship or punishment of speech. Yet, subsequent cases rarely follow this approach. Instead, they proclaim the need for deference to authority and expertise of school officials."[22]

One high school media adviser who claimed her job was threatened for not "reining in" her students was perplexed by the lack of interest on the part of local media. "Why are they (local media) so anxious to see us fail?" she asked in an interview with SPLC executive director Mark Goodman. "They highlight what they perceive are our students' mistakes and are never willing to defend our right to be less than perfect. Would they really like to be held to the same standard?"[23]

That adviser was not alone. Other advisers quoted in Goodman's 2001 essay on the future of the student press expressed similar frustration with not being able to interest the professional media in their plight, "A growing number (of advisers) believe that the commercial media is only interested in the First Amendment and press freedom when its rights are being threatened and have little concern about how those rights apply to others," Goodman wrote. "If we care about the future of journalism, we have to show student journalists that we care about them, too. Professionals who fail to defend student press freedom will have only themselves to blame when young journalists they hire are one day as indifferent to the First Amendment as many working journalists are now to the problems confronted by the high school press."[24] Goodman added that student journalists should aspire to the same ideals as their professional counterparts, even if they never work in the field at that level. These counterparts, journalism teachers and publication advisers, work to implant in students a ceaseless dedication to presenting the public with the truth. This work, however, is challenged by the overwhelming censorship teen journalists and those who work with them face, and Goodman warns of harmful consequences if this continues.[25] Textbook authors Kent R. Middleton and William E. Lee agree. "The First Amendment rights of students at public high school students are weak," they wrote in their 2013 textbook, *The Law of Public Communication.* "Some courts are extending the authority of high school officials to speech that students post off campus on websites and social media."[26] In a 2000 article about the future of free speech on high school campuses, Chemerinsky reminded readers of Fortas's opinion in *Tinker* and hoped it could be applied in the future without delineating between sanctioned and non-sanctioned speech. Citing Justice William Brennan's opinion in a 1967 case, Chemerinsky wrote that "the vigilant protections of constitutional freedoms are nowhere more vital than in the community of American schools."[27] In 2012, the Supreme Court declined to review several high school cases regarding speech taking place online and in other off-campus settings, thus missing the opportunity to clarify the high school administrators' role in controlling students' off-campus speech.

THE COLLEGE CAMPUS

The history of free speech on college campuses can be traced back to the early 1960s and the work of Mario Savio, a political activist who was one of the founders of the free speech movement at the University of California at Berkeley. While Dr. Martin Luther King Jr. was advocating nonviolent social change in his quest for equality for black Americans in the Southeast, Savio was advocating voting rights and employment opportunities for blacks and immigrants in California.

As a student at Berkeley, Savio became well-known to administrators and campus police, at one point in 1963 being arrested for advocating higher pay and better benefits for workers in the hospitality industry in northern California. In the summer of 1964 he took time away from his studies to join the Freedom Summer protests in Mississippi.

When he returned to Berkeley that fall, he discovered that while he was away, but due largely to his expected return, the administration had enacted a new rule prohibiting all political speech on campus as well as fund-raising for political causes.

Instead of complying with the new rule, Savio was even more motivated to speak out in favor of civil rights, including freedom of speech. Multiple confrontations with UCB administrators followed, as did arrests. He gave his most famous speech, titled "Operation of the Machine," on December 2, 1965. It drew a crowd of more than 4,000 listeners, mostly students and faculty, and resulted in his arrest, along with that of about 800 members of the audience who refused to disperse. He was sentenced to 120 days in prison.

Savio's advocacy for civil rights caught the attention of Federal Bureau of Investigation Director J. Edgar Hoover, who assumed that Savio, like others involved in the free speech and civil rights movements, must have communist connections. From the early 1970s until his death in 1996, Savio lived a mostly non-controversial life—earning advanced degrees in mathematics and physics and becoming a college professor in those fields—but he remained on the FBI's watch list through the tenure of nine of Hoover's successors.[28] A half century after Savio's work set the precedent for free speech rights on college campuses, issues that he could have never imagined are providing ongoing challenges for the First Amendment as students, professors, and even visitors to campus find their speech rights are at risk.

In their 2015 essay in *The Atlantic*, civil rights attorneys Greg Lukianoff and Jonathan Haidt explained two new terms related to the political correctness trend—*microaggressions* and *trigger warnings*.

"Microaggressions," they reported, are small actions or word choices that "seem on their face to have no malicious intent" but are thought of as a kind of violence nonetheless. Something as innocent as asking a Latino student "Where are you from?" might be inferred as questioning that person's citizenship, or saying to an Asian student, "I bet you're good at math" might be interpreted as making an assumption based on a stereotype.

During the 2014-2015 academic year, administrators within the University of California system circulated to faculty a list of statements to be avoided in lectures, such as "America is the land of opportunity" and "I believe the most qualified person should get the job."[29]

"Trigger warnings" are alerts that professors at some schools are expected to issue if something in the reading material, a video, or a topic discussed in class might be upsetting to some students. Under the principle of trigger warnings, students have a right to know in advance (and in some cases, be excused from a class meeting or class assignment) if topics such as sexual assault, domestic violence, or drug addiction might bring about emotional distress based on events in that student's past. Even classic works of literature such as Chinua Achebe's *Things Fall Apart* (racial violence), F. Scott Fitzgerald's *The Great Gatsby* (domestic violence), and Virginia Woolf's *Mrs. Dalloway* (suicide) have become examples of materials subject to trigger warnings on some campuses.

Advocates of trigger warnings trace their origin to the study of post-traumatic stress disorder in military personnel following their exposure to dangerous situations in wartime. In 2014, Oberlin College in Ohio issued instructions to its faculty to include warnings on course syllabus and to avoid potential "triggering topics" in class discussions. The instructions defined a trigger as "something that recalls a traumatic event to an individual" and explains that "anything could be a trigger—a smell, song, scene, phrase, place, person, and so on." A trigger warning, the policy further advised, "shows that the school cares about their safety."[30] While some students believe trigger warnings are unnecessary and condescending, a surprising number support them. One tenured professor of political science at Oberlin, Marc Blecher, told a *New York Times* reporter that he feared for his untenured colleagues who might "look at the trigger-warning policy while putting together a syllabus and be terrified."[31]

At George Washington University and Rutgers, where trigger warnings caused considerable discussion, student-written op-ed pieces called them a "preventive measure, because many politically charged classes explore controversial social issues and literature classes often examine works with grotesque, disturbing, and gruesome imagery within their narratives."[32] At Barnard College in New York, President Judith Shapiro endorsed trigger warnings by telling faculty in the early 2000s that "no Barnard student should ever feel uncomfortable in class."[33] Critics of trigger warnings, however, dispute the connection and claim that avoiding important material simply because it is potentially upsetting is part of the trend of "coddling" students by protecting all students from material from which few actually need protection. One critic analogizes trigger warnings to "trying to teach a medical school student training to be a surgeon but who fears that he or she will be distressed at the sight of blood." The American Association of University Professors added that "the presumption that students need to be protected rather than challenged in a classroom is at once infantilizing and anti-intellectual."[34] Adds

Lukianoff and Haidt: "The current climate is largely about emotional well-being. It presumes an extraordinary fragility of the collegiate psyche, and therefore elevates the goal of protecting students from psychological harm. The ultimate aim, it seems, is to turn campuses into 'safe spaces' where young adults are shielded from words and ideas that make some uncomfortable."[35]

Agreeing with Lukianoff and Haidt's "fragility" comment is political columnist George F. Will, who ridicules speech codes and labels today's college students as "delicate little snowflakes" who melt at the slightest exposure to ideas that challenge them. "We've created a new entitlement," Will wrote in a 2016 column. "Today's college students feel they should be entitled to go through their entire lives without ever being offended."[36]

Political columnist Rem Reider agrees. "College should be a time and place for a freewheeling exchange of ideas, for exploration, for putting views to the test," he wrote in a 2015 column in *USA Today*. "Not for hunkering down in a safe cocoon."[37] Lukianoff believes trigger warnings are antithetical to the purpose of a university education and may actually cause more problems than they solve. "Some institutions believe it is their responsibility to shield students from unpleasant material, while many others believe that college should be the place where students are encouraged to think the unthinkable, discuss the unmentionable, and challenge the unchallengeable," he wrote.[38] He further claims that trigger warnings might encourage students to file complaints against faculty members as an alternative to seeking counseling or other assistance for the underlying conditions that caused the reaction in the first place.[39] Who is to blame for the decline of free speech on college campuses? Lukianoff and other civil libertarians point to the general climate of political correctness and the erroneous belief of some administrators that students need the "comfortable learning environment" provided by speech codes, speech zones, and trigger warnings. He also claims that some universities have simply "lost their way" concerning their role in producing good citizens.

"On college campuses today, students are punished for everything from mild satire, to writing politically incorrect short stories, for having the 'wrong' opinion on virtually every hot-button issue, and increasingly, simply for criticizing the university's administration," Lukianoff wrote in his 2012 book, *Unlearning Liberty: Campus Censorship and the End of American Debate.* "And all of this happens at the very institutions that rely most on free speech, open exchange, and candor to fulfill their mission. At the same time, we are paying more and more for higher education, which, perversely, expands the very campus bureaucracy that fosters this anti-free-speech movement."[40] In a later book, Lukianoff wrote, "Higher education deserves profound criticism for maintaining illiberal and unconstitutional speech codes and punishing students and faculty for what they say. However, I believe the even greater failure of higher education is neglecting to teach the intellectual habits that promote debate and discussion, tolerance for views we hate, and genuine pluralism."[41]

Some observers believe that the lack of concern among students for the potential loss of their free speech rights is due in part to their lack of knowledge of past events and the importance that free speech plays in democracy. "For today's students, the historic link between free speech and the protection of dissenters and vulnerable groups is outside their direct experience, and too distant to affect their feelings," wrote Chemerinsky and Howard Gillman in a 2016 essay in *Chronicle of Higher Education*. "This generation has a very strong and persistent inclination to protect others against hateful, discriminatory, or intolerant speech, especially in educational settings."[42] In June of 2015, an anonymous professor posted an online essay titled, "I'm a Liberal Professor, and My Liberal Students Terrify Me." Much like faculty members who opt to take early retirement rather than adjust their teaching styles to be politically correct, many comedians popular on college campuses, including Chris Rock, Bill Maher, and Jerry Seinfield, announced in 2015 they would no longer perform on college campuses because "too many students can't take a joke."[43]

The issue of free speech on college campuses, especially on issues such as microaggressions, trigger warnings, and speech codes (discussed in more detail in chapter 5), have generated public comments from a variety of the country's top civil libertarians.

Ken Paulson, executive director of the First Amendment Center, wrote in 2001 that "Universities have historically been places where people could express views openly in the hopes of building a better society. Sometimes these viewpoints come in the form of speeches or articles; sometimes they come in the form of ads. Sometimes these views refresh, sometimes they repel."[44]

Political columnist A. Barton Hinkle adds that, "One of the truly delightful things about college is that it allows earnest young people to try out all sorts of ridiculous ideas without causing much harm. After graduation, most will grow up and learn how to laugh at their prior selves. The rest will become professors. Let's hope the undergrads and grad students involved in some recent controversies become part of the former group."[45]

Nadine Strossen, professor at New York University Law School and general counsel to the American Civil Liberties Union, believes that the "marketplace of ideas" concept should be applied no differently on a college campus than it is anywhere else in the culture. "One longstanding rationale for the view that speech must be protected, regardless of its content, is the belief that we need a free marketplace of ideas, open even to the most odious and offensive ideas and expressions," she wrote in a 1990 article in *Duke*

Law Journal. "Because truth ultimately will triumph in an unrestricted marketplace."[46]

Kirsten Powers, a political commentator whose libertarian opinions often put her at odds with both liberals and conservatives, agrees with Strossen. "Campuses should be places where students are able to make mistakes without fear of retribution," she wrote in her 2012 book, *The Silencing: How the Left is Killing Free Speech.*[47] "If there is no margin for error, it is impossible to receive a meaningful education."

In *Unlearning Liberty*, Lukianoff offered an anti-microaggression and anti-trigger warning snippet that now appears on the syllabi for many college courses in communication, political science, sociology, and other subject areas where class discussion is an integral part of the learning experience. "Being offended is what happens when you have your deepest beliefs challenged," he wrote. "And if you make it through four years of college without having your deepest beliefs challenged, you should ask for your money back."[48] At the University of California Irvine in 2015, two professors used a free speech exercise in a freshmen class of communication majors. At the beginning of the term, the professors offered a hypothetical scenario similar to the incident that happened the previous year at the University of Oklahoma, which resulted in a fraternity being expelled from campus after its members were caught on video reciting a racist chant. The fifteen students in the free speech seminar voted unanimously in support of the university and against the fraternity. When the same scenario was repeated at the end of the semester, the class was evenly split.[49]

UNCIVIL DISOBEDIENCE

At Northern Kentucky University, in 2006, Professor Sally Jacobsen invited her students to assist her in destroying the display of Northern Right to Life, the school's pro-life organization. The display consisted of hundreds of tiny white crosses that represented children lost to abortion. Jacobson, a professor of literature and coordinator of the school's Women's Studies program, attempted to justify their actions by claiming they were exercising their First Amendment rights in destroying the display.

"Any violence perpetrated against that silly display was minor compared to how I felt when I saw it," she told local media. NKU saw things very differently and placed Jacobsen on leave; she was eventually charged with criminal solicitation for the incident and left the university at the end of the semester.

According to the NKU student newspaper, *The Northerner*, Jacobsen also entered mediation with NKU, Northern Right to Life, and the student government. As a result, Jacobsen agreed to pay $270 in restitution for the stolen and damaged goods and donate $1,000 to Madonna House, a nonprofit organization that helps single pregnant women. The six students who were charged were ordered to do community service and write an apology and have it published in "Viewpoints" section of *The Northerner*.[50] A similar incident took place at the University of Wisconsin-Stevens Point in 2008, when a student government representative tore down crosses that were part of a pro-life display. According to media reports, he shouted, "since abortion is a right, you don't have the right to challenge it."[51]

But the story wasn't over at Northern Kentucky. Even without Jacobson there to lead them, similar incidents occurred at NKU in 2010 and 2012. The format for the 2010 protest was again a field of white crosses, while in 2012 it took the form of hundreds of sets of baby clothes hanging on a clothesline with red X's through every fourth one. Without a faculty member to prompt them, students attempted to destroy the displays and were charged with vandalism and disorderly conduct.[52] At the University of California, Santa Barbara, in 2014, a professor of feminist studies objected to a student staging a peaceful pro-life protest on campus. When she spotted the women carrying a sign that included a graphic image of an aborted fetus, Mereille Miller-Young reportedly tore the sign from the woman's hands and then shoved another protestor who attempted to retrieve it.[53]

WHAT'S HAPPENING NOW

In the 2005-2006 Supreme Court session, the justices took on the controversial issue of university administrators who refused to allow military recruiters to operate on their campuses. The universities had done so because of their objections to the military's "don't ask, don't tell" policy of dealing with gay service members. Lower courts had ruled in favor of universities that sued the federal government for withholding funds, but the Court reversed and ruled in favor of the government, determining that it could withhold funding without violating the school's free speech rights in opposing the policy.[54]

The debate over the future of free speech on college campuses reached the halls of Congress in May 2015, when a House of Representatives subcommittee heard a number of speakers expressing concerns about the spate of news stories indicating that students had lost, not gained, rights in the previous decade. "Policies that limit free speech limit the expression of ideas," said Representative Bob Goodlatte, a republican from Virginia. "And no one can be confident in their own ideas unless those ideas are constantly tested through exposure to the widest variety of opposing arguments. This is especially crucial in democracy."[55]

Lukianoff was there to speak out about the proliferation of speech codes and free speech zones. He suggested that as an alternative, Congress should enact more specific and narrowly drawn anti-harassment laws that would make speech codes and free speech zones unnecessary.[56]

When President Obama gave his commencement speech to the graduates of Rutgers University on May 15, 2016, he addressed the issue of political correctness on campus, specifically the trend of "uninviting" commencement speakers. Pointing to the example of former Secretary of State Condoleezza Rice, with whom he had public disagreements over foreign policy, he nonetheless chastised Rutgers for withdrawing her invitation to speak at the 2014 Rutgers commencement because of student complaints.

"That was misguided," Obama told the gathering. "I don't believe that's how democracy works best, when we're not even willing to listen to each other."[57] In the past decade, FIRE has collected anecdotes of hundreds of cases in which commencement speakers and other dignitaries were "uninvited" as a result of student and faculty protests (discussed in more detail in chapter 5).

The public debate over removing the Confederate battle flag from the grounds of public buildings in the southeastern United States led to related discussions about the possible relocation of statues of Confederate generals and political leaders. From there, the discussion moved to the renaming of college campus buildings that had originally been named in honor of individuals such as President Woodrow Wilson and various Civil War generals.

At numerous universities across the country, the issue of free speech surfaced amid the backdrop of racial tensions affecting college campuses. At the University of Missouri, years of alleged racial discrimination came to light in 2015 only after the university's football team threatened to stop practicing and competing midway through that fall's season. The team's threat was never carried out, but it did draw attention to years of unaddressed racial strife on campus and resulted in the resignation of several top administrators. One of the highlights of the conflict was an on-campus protest, covered by the national media, during which media studies professor Melissa Click attempted to stop student journalists from interviewing students and photographing the event.

The irony of a professor who taught classes in First Amendment principles attempting to stop student journalists from gathering news was lost on Click, but not on school administrators, who, after months of negative publicity, fired her the following spring.[58]

During the 2016 presidential campaign, students supporting republican candidate Donald Trump used chalk to post political messages on campus sidewalks. Messages such as "Trump 2016," "Stop Islam," and "Build the Wall" showed up on numerous campuses.

Administrators were annoyed but not overly concerned, based on the temporary nature of the postings (most disappeared following the next rainstorm) that did not rise to the level of vandalism. They also recognized the free-speech values at stake, claiming that "Trump 2016" was not that different than "Feel the Bern" (in support of Democratic candidate Bernie Sanders) or "Vote Cruz" (in support of Republican candidate Ted Cruz).[59] Students sympathetic to the feelings of Muslim and Latino students disagreed, however. At the University of Alabama, University of Missouri, University of Michigan, University of Kansas, Emory University, and more than a dozen other institutions, offended students claimed the chalkings represented "hate speech" and made their displeasure known to school administrators.

At Emory, more than forty students protested outside the office of President James W. Wagner, demanding that he publicly condemn the messages, which he refused to do. Senior Vice President Jay McNair also declined to do so, but did hint that he was glad to see the free speech debate that resulted. "Some students are using their own free speech rights to speak out on what Trump symbolizes to them," he said.[60] Harvey E. Klehr, professor of political history, agreed that the chalkings did not rise to the level of hate speech because they did not represent acts of aggression and did not target specific students. Klehr added the dustup was overblown by student groups and local media and suggested that the proper response to the students should have been, "We understand that you're unhappy and angry and maybe even afraid of Trump, but you need to grow up. You have the right to protest Donald Trump, but don't ask the university to shut down other students' speech."[61]

The scenario was somewhat different at the University of Florida, where pro-Trump messages—in permanent ink rather than removable chalk—appeared on the doors of the building housing the school's African American studies program. Ibram X. Kendi, a professor in that program, took offense and asked that university officials to investigate.

Gregory P. Magarian, professor of law at Washington University in St. Louis, sees both sides as having valid points. "If we decide that 'Trump' is equal to hate speech, we run into a problem in determining what that means," Magarian said. "But there's certainly a context in which Trumpism takes the form of an aggressive attack on certain people."[62]

At Dartmouth College, a "Blue Lives Matter" display erected by a conservative student group as part of a National Police Week celebration in May 2016 was vandalized, allegedly by black students upset about the deaths of black citizens in the custody of or in conflict with white police officers.[63]

NOTES

1. *Tinker v. Des Moines Independent Community School District*, 393 U.S. 503 (1969).
2. *West Virginia Board of Education v. Barnette*, 39 U.S. 624 (1943).
3. *State v. District Board of School District No. 1*, 116 N.W. 232 (1908).
4. *Bethel School District v. Fraser*, 478 U.S. 675 (1986).
5. *Hazelwood School District v. Kuhlmeier*, 484 U.S. 260 (1988). See also: Randy Bobbitt, *Exploring Communication Law*. Boston: Allyn & Bacon, p. 85-87.

6. Erum H. Shahzad, First Amendment Constraints of Public School Administrators to Regulate Off-Campus Student Speech in the Technology Age. Doctoral dissertation, University of North Texas, 2003. p. 1.

7. Erwin Chemerinsky, "Students Do Leave Their First Amendment Rights at the School-house Gates: What's Left of Tinker?" *Drake Law Review*, vol. 48 (2000), pp. 527-46.

8. Ibid.

9. David L. Hudson Jr. *The Silencing of Student Voices: Preserving Free Speech in America's Schools*. Nashville, TN: The First Amendment Center, 2003, p. 5.

10. LaVine v. Blaine School District, 257 F.3d 981 (2001).

11. Randy Bobbitt, *Decisions, Decisions: Case Studies and Discussion Questions in Communication Ethics*. Dubuque, IA: Kendall-Hunt, 2015, p. 27.

12. Ibid., p. 27.

13. "The State of the First Amendment 2014." The First Amendment Center, 2014.

14. Bobbitt, *Exploring Communication Law*, p. 84. See also: Robert Trager and Donna L. Dickerson, *Freedom of Expression in the 21st Century*. Thousand Oaks, CA: Pine Forge Press, 1999, p. 146

15. Hazelwood School District v. Kuhlmeier. See also: Bobbitt, *Exploring Communication Law*, pp. 85-87.

16. Donald M. Gillmor, Jerome A. Barron, Todd F. Simon, and Herbert A. Terry, *Mass Communication Law: Cases and Comment*. St. Paul, MN: West Publishing Company, 1990, p. 635.

17. Chemerinsky.

18. Paul McMasters, "Teaching Freedom Where it Does Not Exist." *SPLC Report*, Spring 2000, p. 2.

19. *Law of the Student Press*, second edition. Arlington, VA: Student Press Law Center, 1994, p. 13.

20. Ibid.

21. Don R. Pember and Clay Calvert, *Mass Media Law*. New York: McGraw Hill, 2015, p. 85.

22. Chemerinsky.

23. Mark Goodman, "Freedom of the Press Stops at the Schoolhouse Gate." *Nieman Reports*, Spring 2001.

24. Ibid.

25. Ibid.

26. Kent R. Middleton and William E. Lee, *The Law of Public Communication*. Boston: Pearson, 2013, p. 64.

27. Chemerinsky.

28. Seth Rosenfield, "How the Man Who Challenged the Machine Got Caught in the Gears of J. Edgar Hoover." *San Francisco Chronicle*, October 10, 2004.

29. Greg Lukianoff and Jonathan Haidt, "The Coddling of the American Mind." *The Atlantic*, September 2015.

30. Kirsten Powers, *The Silencing: How the Left is Killing Free Speech*. Washington, DC: Regnery Press, 2012, p. 85-6.

31. Lukianoff, *Freedom from Speech*. New York: Encounter Books, 2014, pp. 50-51.

32. Ibid., p. 39.

33. Ibid.

34. Lukianoff and Haidt.

35. Ibid.

36. George F. Will, "A Freedom From Speech." Syndicated newspaper column, November 14, 2015.

37. Rem Reider, "Campuses Need First Amendment Training." *USA Today*, November 29, 2015, p. 7-A.

38. Lukianoff, *Freedom from Speech*, pp. 39-40.

39. Ibid., p. 51.

40. Lukianoff, *Unlearning Liberty: Campus Censorship and the End of American Debate*. New York: Encounter Books, 2012, pp. 1-4.

41. Lukianoff, *Freedom from Speech*, p. 13.

42. Erwin Chemerinsky and Howard Gillman, "What Students Think About Free Speech." *Chronicle of Higher Education*, April 8, 2016, p. 4-B.

43. Lukianoff and Haidt.

44. Ken Paulson, "How Free is Campus Speech?" Syndicated newspaper column, April 24, 2001.

45. A. Barton Hinkle, "The Death of Free Speech on College Campuses." *Reason*, March 18, 2015.

46. Nadine Strossen, "Regulating Racist Speech on Campus: A Modest Proposal." *Duke Law Journal*, 1990, pp. 484-573.

47. Kirsten Powers, *The Silencing*, p. 77.

48. Lukianoff, *Unlearning Liberty*, p. 50.

49. Chemerinsky and Gillman, "What Students Think About Free Speech."

50. Lukianoff, *Unlearning Liberty*, pp. 200-201.

51. Ibid., p. 230.

52. Ibid.

53. Powers, *The Silencing*, pp. 69-75.

54. Rumsfeld v. Forum for Academic and Institutional Rights, 547 U.S. 47 (2006).

55. Lydia Wheeler, "Colleges Are Restricting Free Speech on Campus, Lawmakers Say." TheHill.com, June 2, 2015.

56. Ibid.

57. Rem Reider, "Obama's Support for Free Speech on Campus Welcome." *USA Today*, May 27, 2016, p. 2-B.

58. "A Year of Protest." *USA Today*, February 28, 2016, p. 1-A.

59. Sarah Brown, "Trump Chalkings Open New Debate Over Speech and Sensitivity." *Chronicle of Higher Education*, April 15, 2016, p. 6-A.

60. Ibid.

61. Ibid.

62. Ibid.

63. Steve Annear, "Blue Lives Matter Display Removed at Dartmouth College." *Boston Globe*, May 17, 2016. See also: Anjani Bhat, "Black vs. Blue: Dartmouth Activists Spark Controversy Over 'Blue Lives Matter' Display." *USA Today College*, May 20, 2016.

Chapter Two

High School Media

DISAGREE WITHOUT BEING DISAGREEABLE

In 1968, the American Civil Liberties Union published a report titled "Academic Freedom in Secondary Schools," in which it proposed a policy regarding freedom of the high school press. "Generally speaking, students should be permitted and encouraged to produce publications as they wish," the report stated. "Faculty advisers should serve as consultants on format and suitability of the materials, but neither they nor the principal should prohibit the publication or distribution of material except when the health and safety of students or the educational process are threatened, or the material might be of a libelous nature. Such judgment, however, should never be exercised because of disappointment or disagreement with the article in question."[1] Five decades later, most journalism experts believe that high school newspapers should be learning laboratories where students learn all aspects of the journalism business—sometimes the hard way.

"Students make mistakes," wrote Robert Dardenne, a professor of journalism at the University of South Florida in a 1996 book, *A Free and Responsible Student Press*. "Preventing them by prior review or other strict controls is much more of an injustice to the educational goals of both the school system and the student press than training students to make sound decisions and holding them responsible for those decisions."[2]

HAZELWOOD SCHOOL DISTRICT V. KUHLMEIER: STUDENT NEWSPAPERS ARE NOT PUBLIC FORUMS

Throughout the turbulent era of the 1960s and early 1970s, there were few widely publicized conflicts between high school journalists and administra-

21

tors. That was partly because principals honored the "schoolhouse gate" concept established by the *Tinker* case and partially because most student newspapers tended to "play it safe"—sticking to routine topics such as favorite teachers, upcoming events, and the successes and failures of the schools' athletic teams.

That changed in the 1980s, as student journalists became more aggressive in covering topics such as drugs, sex, and school budgets. While the Supreme Court case of *Bethel School District v. Fraser*[3] set the standard for student expression in general, the first case to deal specifically with the student press began in 1983 at Hazelwood East High School in suburban St. Louis, Missouri.

Hazelwood East was one of three public schools in the district, which was operated by a six-member board of education. The school offered two journalism classes: Journalism I, which covered the basics of writing, editing, and design; and Journalism II, which produced the student newspaper, *Spectrum*. The content of both courses were approved by the board.

Spectrum was published six times per academic year and was funded by board of education dollars as well as advertising sales. School policy established that the content of the paper would be produced largely by students enrolled in Journalism II, although articles submitted by non-staffers could be published if they met editorial guidelines. According to media accounts, faculty adviser Robert Stergos selected the editors and closely supervised their work, including approving or disapproving the paper's content and design.

In early 1983, after *Spectrum* published numerous articles on controversial topics, Hazelwood East principal Robert Reynolds began requiring Stergos to submit the content to him—or, in his absence, an assistant principal—for approval. Stergos complied until he left the school on April 29 of that year, and upon leaving notified his replacement, Howard Emerson, about the rule.

The first issue produced under Emerson's supervision was scheduled to be published on May 13. Before cleaning out his desk the previous month, Stergos had approved two articles: one concerning teenage pregnancy and another on the effect of divorce when a couple's children were of high school age.

Emerson submitted the uncorrected galley proofs to Reynolds on May 10. The principal objected to those two articles, but realized there would not be enough time to sufficiently edit them to address his concerns. Instead, he ordered them deleted.

The articles did not carry bylines, but had been edited by staffers Cathy Kuhlmeier, Lee Ann Tippett-West, and Leslie Smart. The pregnancy article was an anonymous discussion among three female students and their reactions to becoming pregnant, their relationships with their parents and boyfriends, birth control practices, and sexual behavior. The divorce story quoted a student who spoke of her parents' divorce and the father's subsequent neglect of her and her family.

Reynolds was later quoted in court documents as saying that despite the anonymous presentation of the girls' comments in the pregnancy article, it included enough personal details by which their classmates or other readers would likely be able to identify them and that the topic was "too sensitive for an audience of immature readers." In the case of the divorce article, he said that the clear identification of the parents by the student quoted would result in a violation of the family's privacy.

The students did not know about the principal's deletions until the paper arrived from the printer. Kuhlmeier, Tippett-West, and Smart filed suit against the principal and school district in Federal District Court. During a preliminary hearing, the school district introduced an expert witness, a former high school newspaper editor and college journalism instructor, who supported the principal's assertion that the articles were not appropriate for a high school audience. Reynolds added that "no student's grade was affected by reason of the incident involved and no journalism student was deprived of class credit."[4]

The court ruled in favor of the principal and school district, concluding that the newspaper was a school-sponsored laboratory activity rather than a public forum and the principal's actions did not deny the students their First Amendment rights. They distinguished the case from *Tinker*, which involved student expression in non-sanctioned activities. The court cited precedent in a 1982 case, *Nicholson v. Board of Education*, in which a court upheld the right of a high school principal to exercise prior review over the student newspaper.[5] The students appealed the case to the Eighth Circuit in 1986, which agreed with the students' claim that *Spectrum* was a public forum. In reversing the ruling of the lower court, the justices of the appellate court determined that the newspaper's policy statement that it represented "the viewpoint of staff members and not of the school" meant the responsibility for controversial material lay with the students, not the principal.

The school district appealed that ruling to the U.S. Supreme Court, which agreed to hear the case during its 1987–1988 session. The Court reversed the ruling of the Eighth Circuit, reverting to the original trial court's viewpoint that the *Tinker* standard did not apply and that the paper's status as a laboratory activity took priority over the "viewpoint" concept stated by the Eighth Circuit. The Court described the laboratory model as pertaining to "school-sponsored publications, theatrical productions, and other expressive activities that students, parents, and members of the public might reasonably perceive to bear the imprimatur of the school . . . these activities may fairly be characterized as part of the school curriculum, whether or not they occur in a traditional classroom setting, as long as they are supervised by faculty mem-

bers and designed to impart particular knowledge or skills to student participants and audiences."[6]

In *Hazelwood*, the Court drew a distinction between newspapers that were
part of a formal curricular activity (i.e., operated on the laboratory model)
and a newspaper that was extracurricular in nature and therefore open to any
students who wished to contribute articles. The former was not a public
forum, the Court ruled, while the latter was.[7]

The *Hazelwood* ruling established that high school newspapers were not
public forums, and therefore students could not claim their First Amendment
rights were infringed. In essence, it replaced the *Tinker* ruling and became
the new standard for judging free speech cases at high schools—not only
those involving student newspapers, but those involving all forms of student
expression.[8] "The standard is consistent with our oft-expressed view that the
education of the nation's youth is primarily the responsibility of parents,
teachers, and state and local school officials, and not of federal judges," the
majority opinion stated.[9]

More specifically, the Court determined that censorship was acceptable if
it:

1. serves the educational mission of the school;
2. was done in a reasonable manner;
3. was related to pedagogical concerns; and
4. serves a valid purpose.[10]

"Educators do not offend the First Amendment by exercising editorial
control over the style and content of student speech in school-sponsored
expressive activities so long as their actions are reasonably related to pedagogical concerns," Justice Byron White wrote in the majority opinion.[11]
White paraphrased a line from *Bethel* when he reminded the Court that "the
determination of what manner of speech in the classroom or in school assembly is inappropriate properly rests with the school board." Later in his opinion, White added that, "Educators are entitled to exercise greater control over
student expression to ensure that participants learn whatever lessons the activity is designed to teach, that readers or listeners are not exposed to material
that may be inappropriate for their level of maturity, and that the views of the
individual speaker are not erroneously attributed to the school."[12] Advocates
of high school journalism contend that in *Hazelwood*, the Supreme Court
"dramatically lowered the First Amendment hurdle that lower courts had said
school officials had to overcome before they could legally censor student
media."[13]

LESS PEDAGOGY, MORE PUBLIC RELATIONS

Some critics of the *Hazelwood* decision believe that for censors of high school newspapers, the primary commitment "is not to teach students the values of a democratic society, but to ensure that their school is portrayed in a positive light, no matter how unrealistic that portrayal may be," wrote Mark Goodman, executive director of the SPLC, in a 2001 essay published after a series of court rulings supported the censorship rights of principals and other administrators.[14]

Goodman's view was further supported by the comments of a school superintendent involved in a 1988 conflict with student journalists. When fourteen-year-old middle school student Dan Vagasky of Ostego, Michigan, attempted to publish a story about the arrest of a fellow student accused of shoplifting during a school field trip, the principal at first ordered the story spiked, then put the student paper out of business altogether.

"I view any piece of information that comes out of our schools as our opportunity to put our best foot forward," Ostego school superintendent James Leyndyke told local media. "We should not pay to show what we do poorly."[15] For his efforts, Vagasky won the Courage in Student Journalism Award from the Newseum, an Arlington, Virginia, free speech think tank, and a $5,000 college scholarship.

The concern for how schools are perceived in the public became an even bigger factor in the late 1990s as student newspapers created parallel web-sites that were designed to be "edgier" in nature and where information was published with less supervision from faculty advisers.[16] In the decade following the Hazelwood ruling, school administrators took advantage of the precedent. At high schools across the country, high school newspapers were shut down by principals and other administrators for publishing articles on birth control, sexually transmitted diseases, sexual assault, tattoos, drugs, gay rights, and ironically, complaints about administrative censorship. Some well-publicized cases include the following:

- A high school principal in Texas refused to allow the student newspaper to publicize students' plans to hold an "alternative prom," prompted by the school's warning that it planned to administer breathalyzer tests to those attending the official prom.[17] In Alaska, administrators at a high school confiscated copies of a student newspaper that contained an editorial that criticized the school for recognizing cheerleading as an "official sport."[18] In Chicago, a student was suspended after writing an editorial criticizing the school's decision not to allow students to wear shorts.[19]
- In Washington state, after a student newspaper published a commentary criticizing the food in the school cafeteria, the principal prohibited the

publication of any material "that is critical or might be perceived as critical of any staff member or program."[20]

Each of the above cases either failed to make it to court were dismissed early in the process, leaving the decisions of the principals in place and reinforcing the *Hazelwood* decision.

High school journalists across the country have seen their work products subject to prior restraint after attempting to publish or broadcast stories dealing with sensitive issues such as teenage sex and pregnancy, sexually transmitted diseases, drug abuse, body piercing, youth violence, or race relations at the school. While many such examples would be found by the courts to fall within the guidelines of the *Hazelwood* ruling, some other prior restraint decisions are harder to justify. For example, in 1997 a high school principal in Alabama permitted the student newspaper to publish a story about safe-sex practices, but a few weeks later prohibited a story critical of cafeteria food.[21]

One "unintended consequence" of the *Hazelwood* ruling was the trend of state legislatures proposing laws to prohibit high school administrators from censoring student newspapers. In the first three years after the ruling, twenty-nine states and debated such legislation, but only six passed the laws. But in those states—Colorado, Arkansas, Iowa, California, Massachusetts, and Kansas—the courts have not been consistent in supporting those rights. When seeking to have those rights verified in court, many students instead are frustrated to see the courts apply the *Hazelwood* standard.[22]

Before and after the *Hazelwood* case, legal scholars debated whether high school journalists merited the same level of editorial leeway and First Amendment protection as their college counterparts. In response to numerous cases of administrative overreaction that resulted in the censorship of high school newspapers and yearbooks, *USA Today* editorialized that principals should limit their interference to cases involving material that is libelous or obscene. "A major function of schools is to prepare students for life in a democracy," the editorial read. "And one of the cornerstones of democracy is the free exchange of ideas. Lessons in bowing to life under censorship shouldn't be part of the curriculum." In response, a spokesperson for a consortium of high school principals responded that principals are "stewards of our children while they're at school, and also of the public funds that pay for classroom instruction, including journalism."

The response also claimed that high school journalists should not enjoy the same level of freedom as that enjoyed by reporters at *USA Today*.[23] A study found that high school principals with degrees or professional experience in journalism were more likely to kill stories on controversial topics such as teen sex and pregnancy than their counterparts without such degrees or experience.[24] "Censorship is the fundamental cause of the triviality, innocuousness, and uniformity that characterizes the high school press," concluded a national study by the Robert F. Kennedy Memorial Center in 1974. "It has created a high school press that in most places is no more than a house organ for the school administration."[25] To stay out of trouble, many faculty advisers are telling their students: "Don't criticize principals, teachers, coaches, or cafeteria food, and don't try to be funny."[26] Today, many courts justify their support for high school administrators in allowing them to censor the student paper by pointing to their responsibility in preventing the school from being sued for libel or invasion of privacy. Advocates of a robust student press are skeptical of that position, however, pointing to the Student Press Law Center's claim that "there has never been a published court decision reporting a successful libel claim against a high school publication."[27]

ALL THE NEWS THAT FITS, WE PRINT

Prior to the *Hazelwood* ruling, the Journalism Education Association's policy on administrative review of high school publications stated that the adviser's duties included "advising, counseling, and editing." Following the ruling, attempting to put more control in the hands of the students, it replaced the term "editing" with "supervising the editing process." The revised statement added that prior review by administrators (or any school employee other than the faculty adviser) was "illogical, journalistically inappropriate, and educationally unsound." An earlier policy statement claimed that censorship was appropriate only in cases of content that was "libelous, malicious, or obscene," but it did not specify who was responsible for such decisions.[28]

One problem with prior review, the SPLC contends, is that it creates a delay in the publication process as busy principals and assistant principals treat review of student publications as low-priority tasks, as page proofs sit in their in-box for days or are inadvertently lost under piles of other documents on their desks. In other cases, administrators may simply "sit on" controversial material until it becomes no longer timely.[29] In perhaps the most outrageous case of prior review uncovered by the SPLC, a high school principal in Illinois used the threat of allowing the publication of a negative article about the school's tennis coach to force him to resign. The pending story about the coach's theft of money from the team's account was timely and accurate, but was killed by the principal after the coach quit.[30]

"It's no surprise that the turnover rate among publication advisers is remarkably high," wrote Mark Goodman, executive director of the SPLC, in a 2001 essay. "Those who stand up for the rights for their students are the real heroes."[31] The "laboratory" approach to producing a high school newspaper, combined with a "hands off" policy by administrators, often means that papers are published with numerous spelling and grammatical errors as well as photographs and cartoons of dubious news value. Despite administra-

tors' belief that tighter supervision—by either administrators or adviser—
would lead to a higher degree of professionalism, experts in the field believe
that allowing students to make non-libelous errors—as well as errors in judgment—and learn from such mistakes is part of the laboratory process.
"Whereas a free press can be professional, a press that is required to be
professional cannot be called a free press," wrote Tom Dickson, a journalism
professor at Southwest Missouri State University, in a 1997 journal article.[32]
While the courts generally uphold the rights of school administrators to exercise prior review, there are no school districts in the country where school
boards or other officials require them to do so. The SPLC, however, cautions
administrators against it, as doing so increases the likelihood they would be
held responsible for allegedly defamatory or other controversial material.[33]

In 1990, high school newspaper adviser Judith Watson sued the school
district where she worked after her contract was not renewed. She claimed
the principal at Eagle Valley Middle School in Eagle, Colorado, refused to
renew her contract in retaliation for her allowing the students to publish
controversial articles, refusing to retract articles that were accurate but "did
not show the school in a positive light," and advising students of their First
Amendment rights. A state trial court ruled in favor of Watson.[34]

CENSORSHIP BY CONFISCATION

In the late 1990s, high school principals reluctant to implement a preemptive
policy of "prior review" found themselves acting after the fact by confiscating copies of the newspaper after they were delivered to the school, and in
some cases, already placed on racks.

As the 1997-1998 school year dawned at Northeast High School in St.
Petersburg, Florida, Principal Mark Miller confiscated all 1,000 copies of the
student newspaper, the *Nor'easter*, when the "welcome back" issue contained what he called "serious factual errors."

At the time of the controversy, Northeast and other area high schools
were facing court-ordered busing aimed at achieving long-term desegrega-
tion goals. Against that backdrop, many schools were considering declaring
themselves "traditional schools" that would involve higher academic standards and greater involvement of parents. The school's library information
specialist announced that 95 percent of the faculty were in favor of the
"traditional school" approach, but parents of NHS students claimed the two
goals were incompatible. Student journalists noted the philosophical conflict
and wrote about it in the first newspaper issue of the year. When Miller saw
the article, he ordered the papers locked in the adviser's closet. He declined,
however, to specify what parts of the story were erroneous, claiming only

that if distributed, the issue containing that article "would upset a lot of parents."[35]

When student journalists at Hatboro-Horsham High School published a satirical article about the effects of "overactive intestinal bacteria" on the human body—specifically the problem of excessive flatulence—the principal of the school didn't find it particularly funny. She confiscated all 1,200 copies of *Hat Chat* and fired the paper's faculty adviser.

The school paid $800 to have the issue reprinted, showing a black box in place of the deleted article. "We don't want Beavis and Butthead to take over," said Principal Connie Malatesta.

Ironically, the article about the connection between bacteria and farting was a replacement for two commentaries for and against abortion that Malatesta ordered deleted. It's unclear why she did not review the replacement articles before the paper went to press.

The student editors complained to the school board, which sided with the principal, citing a Pennsylvania law that permits principals to exercise prior review but does not allow them to delete material simply because it is critical of the school or its leaders.[36]

In the 2003 case of *Draudt v. Wooster City School District*, a Federal District Court in Ohio overturned a principal's confiscation of the December 20, 2002, edition of the Wooster High School newspaper, *The Blade*. The issue included articles about the punishment of students caught drinking and claiming that athletes breaking those rules were given less severe penalties. The principal believed the article was potentially libelous.

The students filed suit against their principal in January 2003, asking the court for an injunction compelling the school to release the paper. The judge denied that request and instead ordered the two sides to work out a compromise. The compromise allowed the paper to be reprinted with the controversial article deleted. But in a rare post-*Hazelwood* victory for high school journalists, the Court ruled that *The Blade* was a public forum—under the control of the students—and that the principal's new rule of "prior review" could not be enforced.[37]

In 2005, a principal at a Tennessee high school confiscated all 1,800 copies of the student newspaper because of articles on birth control and body art. The birth control article contained accurate information from a local physician about the failure rate of various birth control methods. But what most irked the principal the most was a quote from the doctor indicating that students need not have parental permission to obtain birth control products.[38]

At Timberland High School in Wentzville, Missouri, in 2009, Principal Winston Rogers was so convinced that tattoos were harmful to the learning environment that he banned any mention or image of them in the school's newspaper, the *Wolf's Howl*. After the paper inadvertently published a small photograph of a student wearing a tattoo image of a breast cancer awareness ribbon to honor a family friend who had recently died, the principal confiscated all copies of the paper and ordered that future editions had to be reviewed and approved by him before they could be distributed.

To show support for the student journalists at Timberland, the National High School Journalism Association printed 2,000 temporary tattoos bearing the phrase, "Tattoos are temporary—ignorance is permanent" at its annual convention the following year.[39]

WE NEVER MET AN AD WE DIDN'T LIKE

Just like their counterparts at college newspapers (see chapter 3) and community daily newspapers, the advertising staffs at high school newspapers often create controversy by either accepting or rejecting ads associated with questionable products, services, or ideas.

In the fall of 1967, students at New Rochelle High School in New York, led by Richard Orentzel, formed the Ad Hoc Student Committee Against the War in Vietnam. The group attempted to purchase advertising in the school newspaper, *The Huguenot Herald*, offering to pay the standard rate for student organizations. Editor Laura Zucker approved the ad, but before that edition could go to press, principal Adolph Panitz learned of the ad and ordered it deleted.

When Zucker and her father sued the school, claiming it violated the student editors' First Amendment rights, the principal defended his deletion of the ad by claiming the newspaper was not a "newspaper in the traditional sense," but rather a "teaching tool for the benefit of the students who compile, edit, and publish it," and therefore was not subject to First Amendment freedoms. The principal also claimed that because the Vietnam War was not a school-related activity, it had no place on the pages of a high school newspaper. The students refuted the principal's first position by citing a statement on its masthead that its purpose was to "provide a forum for the dissemination of ideas by and to the students of New Rochelle High School." They refuted his second position by pointing out the paper had previously published student-written articles about the war and the military draft; the material for one article came from the principal himself. A Federal District Court rejected both of the principal's points and ruled in favor of the students, allowing them to publish the advertisement in a subsequent issue.[40]

In Lexington, Massachusetts, in 1994, community activist Douglas Yeo attempted to place an advertisement promoting abstinence in the student newspaper at Lexington High School. Student editors rejected the ad, prompting Yeo to sue the school district in Federal District Court, claiming the school had violated his First Amendment rights. Yeo claimed that public funding of the school paper made it a public forum that should be required to accept all advertisements that were in acceptable taste. A trial court ruled in favor of Yeo's public funding claim, but the First Circuit Court of Appeals reversed that decision, determining that as long as all editorial decisions were made by the students rather than school administrators, no First Amendment issues were at stake. In 1998, the U.S. Supreme Court declined to hear Yeo's appeal.[41]

In 2005, the student newspaper at Kearsley High School in Flint, Michigan, ran a controversial advertising insert from a local anti-abortion group that included graphic descriptions of partial-birth abortions. The previous year, the local school board had passed a rule prohibiting newspaper inserts in order to conform to the Michigan Association of School Boards' statewide ban on distributing fliers in schools.

Cody Perkins, editor for the school year 2004-2005, worked to have the ban overturned, but was unsuccessful. Perkins and other students working on *The Eclipse* agreed to accept the insert without checking with their adviser, Darrick Puffer.

The students were not punished for their decision, but the case did generate a great deal of public discussion in the town of Flint, where controversies involving local schools were rare.

Early the following school year, Puffer, 2005-2006 editor Sara Stogner, and other *Eclipse* staffers were successful in having the ban lifted. "Paid advertising in the newspaper is not the same as passing out fliers," Puffer said. Perkins, by then a college freshman, added, "It was a long time coming. I didn't understand why we had to fight for it."[42]

In November 2005, a school superintendent in Pennsylvania ordered an ad for a support group for gay and lesbian students removed from a newspaper and the issue that carried it reprinted. Common Roads was a well-established support group operating chapters across central Pennsylvania, and it had never met opposition from any school administrators to its small ad published in a number of school publications. But when Superintendent Robert Frick learned it had been printed in a yet-to-be distributed copy of *Limelight*, the student paper at Lampeter-Strasburg High School in Lancaster, Pennsylvania, he ordered those papers confiscated and locked away. *Limelight* Editor Evan Macy said the faculty adviser and principal had both approved the ad. Frick told local media that he "did not have any problem" with the gay lifestyle, but he had concerns about an ad "inviting students to meetings that we know nothing about." Macy said he was not as concerned about the fate of the ad as he was the double standard the superintendent demonstrated. "There's no way he (Frick) would have ordered an ad for a meeting of a Christian support group pulled from the paper," he told local media.[43]

LITERARY MAGAZINES AND YEARBOOKS

Although not as controversial as student newspapers, student-run literary magazines and yearbooks are occasionally in the news because of unusual material and photographs.

Early in 2006, the San Diego Union High School District in California rejected a $1.5 million claim filed by the parents of a sixteen-year-old girl who posed in her underwear for photos in a high school publication. The lawsuit sought damages for defamation, invasion of privacy, inadequate supervision, and sexual harassment. The photos were published in the previous spring's edition of *Dialogue*, the prestigious literary magazine at Torrey Pines High School.

Monterey Salka and two friends posed in combinations of underwear and flesh-colored tank tops. In two images, Monterey appeared to be topless, but her hair was covering her breasts. No breasts or genitals were shown in any of the photographs.

Family attorney Daniel Gilleon claimed that Monterey regretted posing for the photos and the parents were basing the suit on the school's failure to seek their permission. But Dan Shinoff, attorney for the school district, responded that despite Salka's status as a minor, she had already done some professional modeling and was fully aware of what she was doing. "She's already all over the Internet," Shinoff told local media. "For someone who has already sought notoriety for her own image, suing over someone using those images is very interesting."[44]

In 2012, seniors at Wheatmore High School in Trinity, North Carolina, were allowed to include a "prop of their choice" in their senior yearbook photographs that were taken a few weeks before the school year started. The only direction they received was to choose "something that represents you and helped you achieve something." For Caitlin Tiller, that meant bringing her three-month-old son Leelin. "I picked my son because he's helped me become a better person," she told local media.

Nearly the entire school year passed with no discussion of the photo. But on April 12—two days before the yearbook went to press—Tiller was told by the yearbook's adviser that her photo would need to be retaken because the one with her son "promoted teen pregnancy." Tiller told the adviser that the photo of her and her son "met all stated requirements" and if that Leelin couldn't be in the photo, she wouldn't be either. "That's your choice," the adviser reportedly said before hanging up the phone.

Tiller and her mother appealed the case to the Randolph County School Board, and when the appeal was denied, they took the case to the local media. Responding to media inquiries, school superintendent Donald Andrews claimed Tiller was offered an alternative—a paid advertisement in which Tiller could appear with her son. Tiller claimed no such offer was made.[45]

In 2013, transgender teen Jeydon Loredo, born female but identifying as male, wanted to wear a tuxedo in his high school yearbook photo. Administrators at La Feria High School in Houston, Texas, said no, offering no explanation beyond its opinion that the photo "violated community standards." Jeydon's mother took her son's case to the office of the school superintendent, who backed up the principal. Attorneys for the Southern Poverty Law Center stepped in to help, claiming the school had violated Jeydon's rights under the First and Fourteenth amendments as well as Title IX, which prohibits gender discrimination in public schools. Under the threat of legal action, the school backed down and allowed the tuxedo photograph to be published.[46]

UNOFFICIAL, ALTERNATIVE, AND UNDERGROUND NEWSPAPERS

Before the Internet and social media made it easy for students to mock their teachers and administrators in cyberspace (see examples in chapter 6), students resorted to print products to express their displeasure with the school environment or simply entertain themselves and their friends. While annoyed at the nature of alternative publications, principals found themselves with little ability to control their content or limit their distribution because the papers were not produced as part of any formal academic program.

The 1969 case of *Sullivan v. Houston Independent School District* began when the administration of a public school claimed it had met the "disruption" standard in banning distribution of an underground newspaper because students were reading it in class. A Federal District Court, however, ruled that students reading a newspaper in class might be a disruption, but not a "substantial disruption." Teachers would be justified in such a situation by having a rule banning outside reading in class and then punishing students who disobeyed it, and that was a constitutionally preferred measure to banning the paper altogether. [47]

In 1972, two students at Lane Technical School in Chicago were suspended for distributing 350 copies of *The Cosmic Frog*, an alternative newspaper they published. The controversy occurred about the same time that a student at nearby Bowen High School was suspended for circulating a petition calling for "teach-ins" to protest the Vietnam War. The court consolidated the cases under the case name *Fujishima v. Board of Education*. In both cases, students had been charged with violating Section 6-19 of the Chicago Board of Education Rules, which prohibited the distribution of "any books, tracts, or other publications that had not been approved by the General Superintendent of Schools."

A Federal District Court ruled that Section 6-19 violated the students' First Amendment right of free speech. The following year, the school board appealed the ruling to the Seventh Circuit, but the appellate court upheld the lower court's ruling. [48]

Overshadowed by the *Hazelwood* ruling was another 1988 case, *Burch v. Barker*, in which the Ninth Circuit Court of Appeals sided with students who sued their school for prohibiting their distribution of an underground newspaper. The appeals court believed that *Tinker* was a better case for comparison than *Hazelwood*, as Tinker involved non-sanctioned speech while *Hazelwood* involved speech that was produced by a journalism class that was structured as part of the curriculum. [49]

In 1998, three seniors at Huntington High School in West Virginia were suspended for producing a five-page underground newspaper titled *HHSucks*, which administrators labeled as "profane." Distributed the last day of the school year, the paper was filled with vulgar humor, a fictional interview with Principal Charlie Buell, and sexual references to students, teachers, and administrators who were identified by name. The three students responsible for the paper were allowed to graduate the following week but were not allowed to participate in the commencement exercises or the academic awards banquet. "I'm sure it was intended as humor, but it was callous and raunchy," said math teacher Paul Beahrs. "They hurt some kids' feelings pretty bad. I think some of the teachers were hurt as well and some of them took it with a grain of salt. But all of the teachers thought it was beyond cruel for the kids involved." Teachers and administrators told local media they were surprised by the paper, considering its three editors were honors students with no disciplinary history. "We're all glad to see that this will not become some type of tradition," said Camelia Hale, faculty adviser to the school's official student newspaper. "It was vicious. It was a bad way to end the year. I'm sure those kids were raised with better values and I really feel for their parents."

Parents of students suspended indicated plans to sue the school, claiming their children's First Amendment rights had been infringed; while parents of students identified in the paper threatened to sue for defamation. But over the summer, hurt feelings had been resolved on both sides and the following school year began with little memory of the controversy. [50]

In 2000, a teacher at Palisades High School in Los Angeles sued the the school district after a student-produced satirical underground newspaper, *The Occasional Blow Job*, identified her as "porn star" and used a photograph showing her head superimposed on the body of a nude model.

The court initially awarded Janis Adams $4.35 million, and the school banned the publication from the campus and suspended eleven students on its staff. On appeal, the school district was successful in having the damage award reduced, although the final amount was not disclosed. [51]

HAVE YOUR PEOPLE CALL OUR PEOPLE

In the fall of 2005, journalism professors at Ball State University in Indiana began offering an interesting new course. Titled "The Administrator and the First Amendment," the course was sponsored by the Department of Educational Leadership. The online course was intended not for the BSU student body, but rather principals and other administrators at the state's high schools. Topics covered included the function of journalists, court cases involving students and the First Amendment, and the role of principals and advisers in supervision of student media. Today, the content of the course has been incorporated into a course in academic leadership. [52]

BEST OF THE REST

In 1977, student journalists at Hayfield Secondary School in Virginia were told by the school's administration that they could not publish an article about birth control in the school newspaper, *The Farm News*. When Gina Gambino and Lauren Boyd sued the Fairfax County School Board over the censorship, a Federal District Court ruled in their favor. On appeal to the Fourth Circuit, the school board claimed (1) the newspaper was not a public forum but rather a laboratory-based activity, (2) the readership of the paper was a captive audience because the paper was distributed during school hours, and (3) the article in question was ineligible for First Amendment protection because it dealt with a subject (birth control) that was not part of the approved school curriculum. The court discounted all three points and upheld the ruling of the District Court.[53]

At Osceola High School in Kissimmee, Florida, the student newspaper published an editorial in May 1990 that questioned the legitimacy of scholarship programs for minority students, calling them "reverse discrimination." The piece in *The Chief Edition* stated that students "should not be given money just because of the color of their skin or their heritage." After weeks of controversy and complaints from parents, the newspaper's faculty adviser was fired and the school's principal instituted a new policy of prior review. A column in the *St. Petersburg Times* chastised the school and parents for relying on censorship instead of encouraging students to debate the issues.[54]

In the late 1990s, after a Florida student wrote a column criticizing the rap music industry for the role models it creates, her principal said it "lacked racial sensitivity" and prohibited her from writing any more articles—despite the fact that race was never mentioned in the column.[55]

In May 2002, the student newspaper at Whiteland Community High School in Whiteland, Indiana, published a satirical story ridiculing senior Heide Peek. Peek, the article in *Smoke Signals* claimed, wanted to work at a zoo after graduation because her ambition was to be "raped by a monkey." It also listed her favorite song as "Underneath Your Clothes."

Peek sued the Clark-Pleasant Community School District over the article, claiming it caused her emotional distress, in part because she had been sexually assaulted the previous year. The case took nearly two years to be heard in a Johnson County Superior Court, which ruled in Peek's favor. The school district appealed the ruling to the Indiana Court of Appeals, which took another two years before reversing the lower court, determining that the comments were published inadvertently when the newspaper's adviser failed to remove them.[56]

In 2002, Katy Dean, a staff writer of *The Arrow*, the student newspaper at Utica High School in Michigan, interviewed a local couple who lived near the school district's garage. Rey and Joanne Frances claimed that diesel exhaust from the buses entering and leaving the garage exacerbated Rey's lung cancer and the couple was suing the school district.

The administration of the school ordered the resulting article deleted, citing support from the 1988 *Hazelwood* ruling. Administrators claimed that the article included "numerous errors" (none were ever found) and cited statistics from *USA Today*, which administrators claimed was an "unreliable source."

One of the key issues to be determined was whether the paper was a curricular (laboratory model) or extracurricular (adviser model) activity. If it was the latter, it would be considered a "limited public forum" and therefore not subject to the Hazelwood rule.

Based on the definitions provided earlier in this chapter, it had features of both. The paper was part of a class activity, for which students received academic credit and grades, which partially supported the administrators' position that it was operated under the laboratory model. However, the faculty adviser's role was limited to advice and light editing; student editors still had the final say on which stories would be published, which supported the students' view that it was an extracurricular activity.

After nearly two years of litigation, U.S. District Court Judge Arthur Tarnow ruled in favor of Dean, claiming the paper was indeed a "limited public forum" and that the *Hazelwood* precedent did not apply. He added that his ruling took into consideration the importance of the topic, the thoroughness of Dean's reporting, and his position that the school could not restrict publication of the article simply because it was potentially embarrassing to the school system.

SPLC executive director Mark Goodman called the ruling "the most important student newspaper censorship case since *Hazelwood*." The school district declined to appeal.[57]

In 2003, administrators at Morehead High School in Eden, North Carolina, took control of the student newspaper after parents complained about articles covering topics such as teen pregnancy and students who were practicing Wiccans. Principal Andy Thacker appointed an assistant principal to sit in on the paper's editorial meetings and work with adviser Laurie Wilson to eliminate "controversial" content from the paper.[58]

As the 2004-2005 school year neared its end at East Bakersfield High School in California, student editors at the school newspaper, *The Kernal*, wanted to publish a package of five articles supportive of the school's gay and trans-gendered students. Labeling the articles as "too controversial," Principal John Gibson ordered the articles deleted. Even though the students inter-viewed for the articles consented to being identified, the principal told local media he was concerned for their privacy and safety.

The local American Civil Liberties Union office helped the students take their case to court. After a month of hearings, Superior Court Judge Arthur Wallace sided with the principal and refused to order the publication of the articles to go forward.[59]

In early 2006, two student editors at Everette High School in Washington sued the school district after their principal demanded to review the student newspaper before it could be printed. Seniors Claire Lueneburg and Sara Eccleston said newly hired Principal Catherine Matthews was angry over a story in the *Kodak* claiming she was the third choice of students on the search committee, suggesting that student input was ignored.

Matthews clamed that in insisting on prior review of the paper, she was merely adhering to a district policy that required principals to approve school publications.

But the students and their lawyer claimed the rule, in place since 1998, had never been enforced at Everette.

In a subsequent issue, the students inserted a statement on its editorial page that labeled the paper a "student forum." They hoped that would lay the groundwork for undoing the principal's prior review plan, but Matthews ordered the reference deleted.

That's when the students decided to sue the principal in Federal District Court. After eighteen months of preliminary hearings and just a few days before the case was set to go to trial, the two sides reached an out-of-court settlement. Lueneburg and Eccleston were already sophomores in college by that time, but had continued pursuing the case in order to establish the prece-dent for editors who would follow them. According to the agreement, school officials could review the newspaper prior to publication but could not dic-tate content unless they found material that was inaccurate or libelous. Finan-cial terms of the settlement were not disclosed, but as in many similar cases, according to news reports, "both sides claimed victory."[60]

In 2007, three high school students in Knightstown, Indiana, produced a movie titled "The Teddy Bear Master," that showed evil teddy bears attacking and killing a teacher they disliked. The students were expelled by school officials, but following a well-publicized court case, the students agreed to write letters of apology to the teacher and his wife. They were also awarded $69,000 and saw their expulsions erased from their permanent records. The teacher sued the students for emotional distress, but that case was dismissed in 2011.[61]

NOTES

1. George E. Stevens and John B. Webster, *Law of the Student Press*. Ames, IA: University of Iowa Press, 1973, pp. 110-11.

2. Robert Dardenne, *A Free and Responsible Student Press*. St. Petersburg, FL: The Poynter Institute for Media Studies, 1996, p. 60.

3. *Bethel School District v. Fraser*, 478 U.S. 675 (1986).

4. *Kuhlmeier v. Hazelwood School District*, 607 F.Supp. 1450 (1983) and *Hazelwood School District v. Kuhlmeier*, 484 U.S. 260 (1988).

5. *Nicholson v. Board of Education*, 682 F.2d 858 (1982).

6. Grace Wigal, "Hazelwood School District v. Kuhlmeier: The Death of No Prior Restraint in an Official High School Newspaper." *West Virginia Law Review*, vol. 91, (1989), pp. 635-663.

7. Don R. Pember and Clay Calvert, *Mass Media Law*. New York: McGraw Hill, 2015, p. 90.

8. Tom Dickson, "Preparing Scholastic Press Advisors for Roles After Hazelwood Decision." *Journalism & Mass Communication Educator*, Winter 1997, pp. 4-15.

9. *Hazelwood School District v. Kuhlmeier.*

10. Ibid.

11. Ibid.

12. Ibid. See also: *Bethel School District v. Fraser.* In *Bethel*, the Court ruled in favor of the school's punishment of a student who allegedly disrupted the operation of a school with a vulgar speech at a school assembly, determining that the administration of a school was not required to "tolerate speech that is inconsistent with its educational mission."

13. Mark Goodman, "Freedom of the Press Stops at the Schoolhouse Gate." *Nieman Reports*, Spring 2001.

14. Ibid.

15. Susan Philips, "Student Journalism: Are Free Speech Rights in Danger?" *CQ Researcher*, June 5, 1998, pp. 481-504.

16. Goodman, "Freedom of the Press Stops at the Schoolhouse Gate."

17. Philips.

18. Ibid.

19. Ibid.

20. Goodman, "Freedom of the Press Stops at the Schoolhouse Gate."

21. Randy Bobbitt, *Exploring Communication Law*. Boston: Allyn & Bacon, 2008, p. 87.

22. Goodman, "Freedom of the Press Stops at the Schoolhouse Gate."

23. "Schools Fail Free Speech 101," and "Keep Principals Involved." *USA Today*, February 12, 2007.

24. Dickson.

25. Jack Nelson, *Captive Voices: The Report on the Commission of Inquiry into High School Journalism*. New York: Schocken Books, 1974.

26. Philips.

27. *Law of the Student Press*. Arlington, VA: Student Press Law Center, 1994, p. 104.

28. Tom Dickson, "Preparing Scholastic Press Advisors for Roles After Hazelwood Decision." *Journalism & Mass Communication Educator*, Winter 1997, pp. 4-15.

29. *Law of the Student Press,* Arlington, VA: Student Press Law Center, 1994, p. 41.

30. *Death by Cheeseburger: High School Journalism in the 1990s and Beyond.* Washington, DC: The Freedom Forum, 1994. p. 70.

31. Mark Goodman, "Freedom of the Press Stops at the Schoolhouse Gate." Nieman Reports, Spring 2001.

32. Dickson.

33. *Law of the Student Press*, Arlington, VA: Student Press Law Center, 1994, p. 79.

34. *Watson v. Eagle County School District* (797 P. 2d 768 [1990]). See also: *Law of the Student Press*, Arlington, VA: Student Press Law Center, 1994, p. 91-92.

35. Jim DeBrosse, "Principal Says Paper Has Errors, Seizes Issue." *The St. Petersburg Times*, August 23, 1997, p. 1-B.

36. "Students Say Principal's Decision to Confiscate Newspapers Stinks." *SPLC Report*, Spring 2000.

37. *Draudt v. Wooster City School District*, 246 F. Supp. 2d 820 (2003). See also: Frank D. LoMonte, Adam Goldstein, and Michael Hiestand, *Law of the Student Press.* Arlington, VA: Student Press Law Center, 2013, p. 47.

38. "Principal Censors Newspaper Over Articles on Birth Control, Tattoos." *SPLC News Flash*, November 29, 2005. See also: Frank D. LoMonte, Adam Goldstein, and Michael Hiestand, *Law of the Student Press*.

39. Steve Parker, "High School Principal Explains Decision of Tattoos," *St. Louis Post-Dispatch,* November 5, 2009. See also: Pember and Calvert, p. 96.

40. *Zucker v. Panitz*, 299 F. Supp. 102 (1969). See also: George E. Stephens, and John B. Webster, *Law and the Student Press*. Ames, IA: The Iowa State University Press, 1973, pp. 64-5.

41. "Court Refuses to Hear Advertiser." *SPLC Report*, Fall 1998, p. 31.

42. "Michigan Students Win Fight to Overturn Restrictive Ad Policy." *SPLC LegalAlert*, April 2006.

43. "Superintendent Orders Pennsylvania High School Newspaper to Remove Ad for Gay Support Group." SPLC *LegalAlert,* January 2006.

44. "California High School Rejects Parents' Claim over Unauthorized Photos." *SPLC LegalAlert*, January 2006.

45. Elise Sole, "Teen Mom's Banned Yearbook Photo." *Yahoo News*, May 3, 2013.

46. Juan A. Lozano, "Transgender Student's Tuxedo Pic Banned." Associated Press report, November 16, 2013.

47. *Sullivan v. Houston Independent School District*, 307 F. Supp. 1328 (S. D. Texas, 1969). See also *Law of the Student Press*, p. 29.

48. *Fujishima v. Board of Education,* 460 F.2d 1367 (1972).

49. *Burch v. Barker,* 861 F.2d 1149 (Ninth Circuit, 1988).

50. Mark Truby, "Students Suspended for Publication." *Herald-Dispatch*, June 3, 1998, p. 1-A.

51. *Adams v. Los Angeles Unified School District*. Case No. B159310, Los Angeles County Superior Court No BC235667 (2000).

52. "Indiana School Offers New Course to Teach High School Administrators About Students' Rights." *SPLC LegalAlert*, October 2005.

53. *Gambino v. Fairfax County School Board*, 564 F.2d 157 (1977).

54. Dardenne, p. 78.

55. Goodman, "Freedom of the Press Stops at the Schoolhouse Gate."

56. *Peek v. Whiteland Community High School*, Case 41-D-01-04060CT-00081, Johnson County Superior Court (2005).

57. *Dean v. Utica Community Schools*, No. 03-71367 (E.D. Michigan, 2004). See also: "Michigan Court Releases Written Opinion in High School Censorship Case," *SPLC LegalAlert*, November 2004.

58. "Administrator Will Oversee High School Newspaper." Associated Press report, January 20, 2003.

59. "Judge Refuses to Order Distribution of Articles in California High School Paper." *SPLC LegalAlert,* May 2005.

60. "Washington State Student Editors Sue School District Over Prior Review Policy." *SPLC LegalAlert,* January 2006. See also: Jim Haley, "Everett Schools Settle with Student Editors." *Everett Herald,* August 31, 2007.

61. "Student Filmmakers Reinstated After Lawsuit Brought to Bear." Associated Press report, March 22, 2007.

Chapter Three

College Media

MARSHALL MESS

On the evening of September 13, 1992, Charles Plymail and Kathy Young, both twenty-eight, met at the Calamity Café, a popular restaurant and bar across the street from the main entrance to Marshall University in Huntington, West Virginia. Plymail was a Marshall student; Young was not. After dinner and drinks, they went to Plymail's nearby apartment. That's where their stories diverge. Plymail said they engaged in consensual sex, but Young claimed she was raped, and she said so to the Huntington Police Department. Plymail was arrested the next day and taken to the Cabell County Jail.

A few days later, Bill Gardner, the managing editor of *The Parthenon*, Marshall's student newspaper, found the report during a routine visit to police headquarters. Under West Virginia law, the names of complainants in sexual assault cases can be redacted, and while it was the HPD's policy to do so, it's not clear why it was not done in this case. Gardner wrote the story for *The Parthenon* that would be published on the front page on September 22. Gardner and editor-in-chief Kevin Melrose decided the story would be more complete if they fully identified both Plymail and Young by their names, ages, and home addresses. The decision violated the paper's own editorial policy as well as generally accepted ethical guidelines of most media organizations. Anticipating the controversy the story would start, Melrose and other staffers collaborated on an editorial titled "Why Our Story Named Names" that ran in the same issue. The editorial claimed the staff's decision was based on two factors. First, it claimed, alleged sexual assault victims should not be treated differently from the victims of other crimes, in which case both the alleged victim and alleged perpetrator were named. Second, withholding the names of alleged rape victims perpetuated the belief that victims in such cases were partially to blame. The editorial also pointed out that the paper did not publish any information that was not available to anyone conducting a public records search.[1]

Despite the explanation, the decision outraged the university's president and the majority of students, faculty, and the surrounding community. Members of the school's counseling staff said that identifying rape victims traumatized them for a second time and would discourage future victims from filing charges. For weeks after the story, Marshall students and faculty members filled the paper's editorial page with letters denouncing the decision, while fewer than 5 percent agreed with it.

Student Government Association president Taclan Romey said students were outraged that *The Parthenon*, funded partially by student activity fees, could so blatantly disregard student opinion in its editorial decisions. "If people don't agree with what the *New York Times* prints, they can stop buying the paper," Romey said. "But here, we're forced to pay for it."[2]

Marshall alumni, many of them holding degrees from the journalism school, penned letters criticizing the story. Even Huntington residents with no connection to the university—including one employee of the county prosecutor's office—lambasted the paper. A woman who had been identified against her wishes by the local daily newspaper, the *Herald-Dispatch*, following her 1987 rape also weighed in, claiming that Young was "raped twice" as a result of being named and concurred with the opinions of other letter-writers that being publicly identified would discourage future victims from coming forward.[3]

Young's mother, a Marshall alumna, wrote her own letter to the editor, claiming she was "appalled and disgusted" by the paper's "lack of integrity and sensitivity." Pat Young added that the paper "violated my daughter's control of her life as surely as her alleged assaulter did . . . perhaps the day will come when a rape victim's name can be printed with same aplomb that a burglary's victim is, but that day is not here yet."[4]

The Parthenon has a long history at Marshall, having been published for nearly two-thirds of the university's 155-year history. Housed within the university's prestigious W. Page Pitt School of Journalism and Mass Communications, the award-winning publication is published four times a week based on a successful adaptation of the laboratory model, with students in advanced reporting and editing classes doing the majority of the work. Although structured differently today, at the time of the rape story the paper had a full-time adviser and advertising director and two faculty members teaching the advanced classes that produced the paper. A student-run FM radio station, WMUL, also runs on the laboratory model.

Professor Ralph J. Turner, a Marshall alumnus and thirty-year veteran of the journalism school, defended the paper and disclosed in his own editorial that when interviewing for the editor's job the previous spring, Melrose had indicated that he planned to overturn the long-standing policy of not identifying alleged rape victims. "The editors' decision is not unlike the practice of our court system in which both the accused and accuser are identified," Turner wrote. "Journalists are playing judge and jury if they print names of the accused and not those of the persons bringing charges." Turner added that the responsibility of removing the stigma of rape belongs more to counselors than journalists. "Sexual assault counselors know the importance of working with victims to help them through the trauma and feelings that they did something wrong," Turner wrote. "Treating sexual assault openly might be one step in that direction."[5]

The majority of the journalism school's seventeen-member faculty said they understood the staff's decision as a matter of law, but disagreed with it on ethical grounds. While publicly defending (along with other faculty members) the students' First Amendment right to make editorial decisions, journalism school director Harold C. Shaver privately expressed disappointment in the students' original decision. "Just because you can, doesn't mean that you have to," he told the students and faculty members. But he also pointed out in his own letter published in *The Parthenon* that the issue of whether to identify alleged rape victims should be open to discussion. He cited Geneva Overholser, editor of the *Des Moines Register*, as saying that journalists "should not be afraid of telling it like it is in sex crimes."[6]

The week after the story's publication, Marshall President J. Wade Gilley condemned the paper in a letter to Melrose, accusing the paper of being "insensitive to women's issues" and disclosing "lurid details" of the incident that went beyond the paper's First Amendment freedoms. "While we do not question the 'right' of a newspaper to publish such information, we do believe such situations require the exercise of responsibility, compassion, and mature judgment, as is the case with most reputable newspapers," Gilley wrote. "Obviously, those characteristics are missing from The Parthenon's laborious and convoluted rationale for printing rape victims' names and addresses."[7] The letter was co-signed by Robert Sawrey, president of the Faculty Senate; Sharon Noble, president of the Classified Staff Council; and Romey. In a subsequent interview with a *Parthenon* reporter, Gilley was quoted as saying that as he read the original story, he "thought about somebody in the bathroom masturbating . . . that's how crude and vulgar it was. Should you print how long—how many inches the man's penis was?"[8] Gilley later backtracked and claimed he was only quoting what he heard from the parents of rape victims.

The university's Committee on Student Conduct and Welfare then passed a resolution prohibiting student media from identifying sexual assault victims by name. Claiming that the First Amendment "does not protect a student newspaper from censorship, and any arguments to the contrary are fallacious," the resolution stated that withholding the names of rape victims was "standard journalist practice across the nation" and that "student journalists have no right to differ from the policy." Melrose fired back: "No resolution from any committee can supersede the First Amendment . . . if it comes down to a conflict between the Student Conduct and Welfare Committee and the Constitution, we'll stand by the First Amendment."[9]

The resolution came to the attention of Mark Goodman, executive director of the Student Press Law Center, who denounced the resolution and said "it was obvious that the committee has not read any cases related to student publications."[10] Art Professor Susan Jackson, who drafted the resolution, then backpedaled and said the resolution was "meant more to send a message to The Parthenon than to establish a new policy."[11]

The following week, Gilley issued "Executive Policy Bulletin No. 3" that disbanded the "Board of Student Publications" that had overseen student media and replaced it with a "Student Media Board." The new group would function as publisher of the newspaper and be comprised of eleven members, representing a variety of constituent groups—students, current and emeritus faculty, classified staff, and alumni. The Faculty Senate would appoint current faculty members (with one being from the journalism school) while the Student Government Association would appoint three students (one being a journalism major). Gilley would appoint one staff member, one emeritus professor, a member of the journalism school's alumni association, and two other students, giving him control of five of the eleven seats. The committee's purpose, Gilley announced, was to "set editorial policy," but he denied that the formation of the board was directly related to the rape issue.[12] The committee would oversee not only *The Parthenon*, but also the school's yearbook and radio station.

What bothered Melrose and journalism faculty members most was that only three of the positions would be filled by those with a journalism background, as opposed to the previous board, comprised mostly of journalism students and faculty. They accused Gilley of using the issue as an excuse to seize control of the paper and turn it into a "public relations tool for the university."[13]

Gilley claimed that the group was patterned after one at West Virginia University and was "no different from the real world, where you have publishers who aren't journalists . . . right now, there's absolutely no one to provide oversight. The students can do whatever, to the wildest limits of their imagination." Shaver claimed the takeover "took him by surprise" and that he was "not allowed to tell anyone what he thought of it."[14]

While Marshall's non-journalism alumni and the community as a whole backed Gilley, the move was strongly criticized by the local newspaper, the *Herald-Dispatch*, and the *Charleston Gazette*, the state's other large daily newspaper. The *Herald-Dispatch*, many of whose editorial writers were Marshall alumni, called Gilley's move a "dark day" for freedom of speech that would "set back Marshall journalism for years."[15]

The editorial echoed the concern of faculty members and journalism alumni who worried that the publicity generated by the case might harm the school's recruiting efforts. "Why would a high school senior contemplating a career in journalism come to Marshall, knowing that freedom of the press here is just a theory?" asked one editorial.[16] Columnist Dave Peyton worried that if Gilley were allowed to control the content of the student paper, he might next attempt to dictate which plays the school's theater program could stage, determine which musical pieces the band could play at halftime of football games, and ban the use of live nude models in art classes.[17]

In an October 18 editorial titled "Marshall Mess," the *Gazette* added that it was "wrong for the university president to seize the paper to silence the student writers who wouldn't obey him" and that "the students acted in good faith, trying to prove that rape is nothing but a violent crime, and the victim has no cause to feel guilty. . . . The First Amendment gives Americans the right to speak their views—and Gilley is revoking that right for student editors."[18] Goodman added, "We have the president of a major university who seems to be completely oblivious of what the First Amendment is about."[19]

Despite claiming they were told not to do so, Shaver and other faculty members publicly opposed the plan. A week after the announcement of the board, Shaver met with Gilley, dean of liberal arts Deryl Leaming, university attorney Layton Cottrill, and university public relations officer C. T. Mitchell. Shaver later claimed that Gilley threatened his job—a charge corroborated by Leaming but denied by Cottrill and Mitchell. Gilley later claimed that he did not threaten Shaver with the loss of his job, but merely reminded him that as part of the administrative team, he should not publicly criticize university policy.[20]

One journalism faculty member made his opposition more public than his colleagues. Broadcasting professor Dwight Jensen—who taught courses in media law, media theory, and media history—went to Cabell County Court and asked for an injunction to stop the formation of the board. Claiming that Gilley's actions violated the students' rights of free press and due process, Jensen requested subpoenas to require Gilley, Mitchell, Romey, and athletic director Lee Moon to appear at a preliminary hearing. The first three had been directly involved in the issue, but it was never clear why Moon was called to testify. Gilley was successful in having the subpoenas quashed, and only Shaver and other members of the journalism faculty testified at the hearing. Judge John Cummings said that Gilley's decision was "probably not the wisest thing to do" but eventually ruled against the request for injunction, determining that Jensen had failed to prove the new board caused any harm.[21]

The following week, however, Gilley and Shaver squared off again, this time at a tense Faculty Senate meeting. Sensing that faculty support was waning and the community was tiring of the issue, Gilley agreed to compromise. Shaver proposed a fifteen-member board that would include more journalism students, fewer non-journalism faculty members, and—most importantly—fewer presidential appointments. After the meeting, both Gilley and Shaver told reporters that both sides came away pleased with the compromise. "I think everybody wins in this situation," Gilley said. "Hal Shaver deserves a lot of credit for coming up with this plan." Added Shaver: "Our major concern was to maintain the integrity of the program. We wanted to make sure that the board had a majority people who understood journalism."[22]

THE STUDENTS' RIGHT TO KNOW

Across the country, college media have had a long and colorful history. Unlike the Marshall case, which was partly decided in a local courtroom, the more famous cases were settled in federal courts, with some even reaching the U.S. Supreme Court. And while student newspapers created controversy almost from their beginnings in the late 1800s, the first conflicts to reach the court system did not do so until the 1960s and 1970s.

In nearly every case from 1967 through the mid-1990s, cases were decided quickly and in favor of the students. Judges typically sided with student journalists based on their age and presumed maturity level (as compared to high school students) and the fact that in most cases, newspapers are funded by student fees and advertising revenue. Except for providing the newspapers with office space and electricity, most institutions provide little financial support for student newspapers, and as a result, have no say in the content of those publications.

In many of those late twentieth-century cases, administrators claimed that because a student newspaper was housed on campus and used the name of the institution, the content of the publication reflected on the school. In many cases those concerns were merely a smokescreen for the administrators' desire to not have their already public mistakes become more widely publicized. Some administrators claimed that the "people's right to know" should not be stretched far enough to include "the students' right to know."[23] Fortunately for student journalists, both state and federal courts seldom found either justification—preserving the image of the university or not publicizing administrative blunders—were valid reasons for administrative control.

Two recent cases, however, raise a troubling question: Can the administration of a university use the *Hazelwood* ruling—a case involving a high school newspaper—as a rationale for exercising prior restraint over a college newspaper? In *Kincaid v. Gibson* (1999) and *Hosty v. Carter* (2005), administrators cited the "disruption of the educational process" principle from the *Hazelwood* case. In *Kincaid*, the students were eventually victorious over administrators demanding the right to review a student newspaper's content before it was published, but it took seven years and thousands of dollars in legal fees. In *Hosty*, the students lost their case after six years of appeals, as a Federal District Court and U.S. Court of Appeals agreed with the university's use of the *Hazelwood* rationale in seizing control of the student newspaper.

The trend of college newspaper censorship is especially problematic at historically black colleges and universities (HBCUs), where administrators are reluctant to establish and fund new publications and often attempt to exercise editorial control over publications that already exist. Theories to explain the higher likelihood of administrative control of black college papers (compared to their counterparts at historically white institutions) include the concern that black students may not be capable of producing quality journalism without heavy supervision (i.e., censorship) or simply that administrators at HBCUs are less tolerant of criticism likely to come from student newspapers that are not closely supervised.[24]

As many college newspapers began publishing online editions in the late 1990s, advisers became concerned with the level of control that administrators might attempt to exercise. Most institutions have an "acceptable use policy" that prohibits the use of university-owned computer networks to transmit pornography, indecency, and other objectionable material, and advisers worried that such policies might be used to limit speech in the online newspapers. While no such cases have yet reached the courts, the Student Press Law Center issued a report in 1998 that predicted that no acceptable use policy could be used to circumvent rights guaranteed by the First Amendment.

ORGANIZATIONAL MODELS

There are three organizational models commonly found among college newspapers, and the type of model in place often dictates the degree to which administrators may feel entitled to exercise editorial control over the published product. In the *laboratory model*, the paper is produced as part of one or more classes (usually in the journalism department), and in these cases administrators might feel justified in exercising control over the paper because of its pedagogical connection. In the *adviser model*, there are no classes associated with the production of the paper, but a faculty member serves as the adviser; the administration would have less justification in claiming control. In both the laboratory and adviser models, the newspapers receive nearly all of their funding from student activity fees and advertising revenue.

In the *independent model*, there is no official relationship between the paper and the university, and in most cases the newspaper offices are located off-campus and receive no student activity fees. In the more successful cases, such as the *Independent Florida Alligator* at the University of Florida, the paper is dependent on advertising revenue and competes with the local daily newspaper for both stories and revenue.

While the laboratory model provides more structure and a wide pool of staff talent to produce the student newspapers, there are many disadvantages. Newspapers produced almost entirely by students in journalism programs become so strongly identified with those programs that it generates the perception on campus that the newspaper "belongs" to those departments. At some universities, administrators claim that the student newspaper is a vehicle for faculty members to grind personal axes against the leadership of the institution by directing student journalists to pursue negative stories that fit the faculty members' agenda (despite the fact that assignments are usually made by other students rather than faculty).

While the perceptual problem is significant, the more troubling issue is legal liability. The more closely aligned a newspaper or other media outlet is to an academic department, the greater the level of liability is for the university.

DISRUPTING THE EDUCATIONAL PROCESS, OR MAYBE NOT

The earliest known legal case involving a college newspaper was *Dickey v. Alabama State Board of Education* (1967). The case began when Ralph Adams, president of Troy State University in Alabama, was upset over negative news stories and editorials concerning university and state politics and established a rule that prohibited the student newspaper, the *Tropolitan*, from publishing editorials critical of the governor or state legislature. Informally known as the "Adams Rule," the edict clarified that editorials supporting the governor and legislature would be allowed.

At the time of the controversy, Frank Rose, president of the University of Alabama, was under fire from officials in state government for not censoring his school's lecture series, which included a number of controversial speakers. One hundred and eighty miles away at Troy State, *Tropolitan* Editor Gary Dickey wanted to publish an editorial that was supportive of the Alabama president for standing up for the First Amendment. Dickey showed a preliminary draft to his faculty adviser, who rejected it. He then took it to Adams, who rejected it as well. The faculty adviser gave Dickey an article titled "Raising Dogs in North Carolina" to run in its place. But instead,

Dickey used the headline for his original editorial, "A Lament for Dr. Rose," and left the space below blank except for the word, "censored." That happened late in the spring semester, and over the summer Dickey was told he could not attend the school in the fall because of "willful and deliberate insubordination."

Dickey sued the university, and the Federal District Court cited *Tinker*, ruling that the students' free speech rights could not be limited unless the school could prove "disruption or substantial interference" to the educational process. In this case, the school could not. The court ordered the university to readmit Dickey and also pay his attorney's fees.[25]

Three years later, in *Antonelli v. Hammond* (1970), a Federal District Court ruled that the president of Fitchburg State College in Massachusetts could not exercise prior restraint over the campus newspaper. The case began when President James J. Hammond, objecting to the student newspaper's publication of an article containing profane words, established a committee to review and approve future issues of the newspaper. One specific article at issue was one submitted by black activist Eldridge Cleaver. Editor John Antonelli objected to the new policy and sued. Even though the District Court ruled against the president, it left the door open to the possibility of censorship in the future if the material in question was "damaging to the educational process."[26]

In *Trujillo v. Love* (1971), students at Southern Colorado State University sued the school when the administration fired the editor of the student newspaper after it published a cartoon that ridiculed SCSU administrators and an editorial that was critical of a local judge. The president claimed his actions were justifiable because the paper operated on the laboratory model. A Federal District Court disagreed, however, and ruled that despite the structure of the newspaper, it was nonetheless a forum for student expression and once the school had delegated editorial responsibilities to the students, it could not interfere with their exercise of those responsibilities.[27]

In *Bazaar v. Fortune* (1973), the Court of Appeals for the Fifth Circuit ruled that University of Mississippi could not censor the school's literary magazine. The controversy began when the magazine published an article about interracial relationships that administrators said included "earthy language."

"The university here is clearly an arm of the state, and that single fact will always distinguish it from the purely private publisher as far as censorship rights are concerned," the court ruled. "It seems a well-established rule that once a university recognizes a student activity as elements of free expression, it can act to censor that expression only if it acts consistent with First Amendment constitutional guarantees."[28]

In *Joyner v. Whiting* (1973), a Circuit Court of Appeals ruled that a university president could not prove "disruption to the educational process" and could therefore not exercise editorial control over the student newspaper. The plaintiff was Johnnie Joyner, editor of the student newspaper at North Carolina Central University, a historically black institution in Durham, North Carolina. At issue was a front-page editorial that said white students were not welcome at the school, that white students could not serve on the student newspaper staff, and that the paper would not accept advertising from white-owned businesses. University President Albert Whiting, fearing that the university might be in violation of the Fourteenth Amendment's Equal Protection Clause, as well as the Civil Rights Act of 1964, withdrew funding for the paper until he could set up a process for approving the copy prior to publication.

A federal court agreed with the university president and ruled that because of the Fourteenth Amendment and the Civil Rights Act, state funds could not be used to support racial segregation, even indirectly. But the Circuit Court of Appeals reversed that decision, ruling that the president could not exercise prior restraint over the newspaper because the editorials did not disrupt the educational process and that just expressing a point of view in the student newspaper did not mean the university itself was in violation of the law. The court also stated that the university had no legal obligation to create a student newspaper, but once it did, it could not shut it down simply because it objected to its content.[29]

Two years later, in *Schiff v. Williams* (1975), the student press was victorious again. At Florida Atlantic University in Boca Raton, Florida, the university president fired the entire editorial staff of the newspaper—not because of content, but because of poor grammar, incorrect spelling, and non-libelous factual errors. The president claimed a student publication supported by state funds had no right to "reflect discredit and embarrassment upon the university." The students sued the president in Federal District Court and won reinstatement to their positions. The university appealed to the Circuit Court of Appeals, claiming that the student editors were state employees and the president was within his rights to fire them, but the appeals court sided with the students and upheld their reinstatement.[30]

In *Stanley v. McGrath* (1983), the board of regents at the University of Minnesota attempted to remove funding for the student newspaper, *The Minnesota Daily*, after it published a satirical edition which included what administrators called a "blasphemous 'interview' with Jesus on the Cross that would offend anyone of good taste." The board proposed modifying the school's student fee system to allow students to "opt out" of paying for the student newspaper.

A trial court ruled in favor of the university, determining that the students did have the right to refuse to pay the fees. When the case was appealed to the Eighth Circuit, the appeals court ruled in favor of the students, claiming the new fee structure would violate the First Amendment because it was based on the content of the paper.[31]

While advocates of a free and robust student press were no doubt pleased with the outcome of the *Dickey, Antonelli, Trujillo, Bazaar, Joyner, Schiff,* and *Stanley* cases, their long-term significance is debatable. Because none reached the U.S. Supreme Court and were instead decided at lower levels of the judicial system, they are not binding in all jurisdictions. In addition, the decisions were narrowly tailored to specific forms of speech—a student newspaper or literary magazine, for example—and failed to address the larger question of whether student journalists at public universities have the same First Amendment rights as their professional counterparts.

KINCAID V. GIBSON: THE ADMINISTRATOR AND THE ADVISER

The *Kincaid* case began at Kentucky State University in 1994 when the newspaper's faculty adviser was removed after refusing to censor articles, editorials, and cartoons that were critical of the university's administration. The controversy later expanded to include differences of opinion concerning the content of the student yearbook.

After filing a grievance with the university's judicial panel, faculty adviser Laura Cullen was reinstated but given a new job description that required her to censor the newspaper and remove materials considered "harmful to the university's image." The adviser and several students then sued the university in Federal District Court, claiming that both the adviser's new job duties and confiscation of the yearbook were illegal forms of prior restraint.

The adviser and students lost in the trial court and again in an appeals court. Both courts cited *Hazelwood*, determining that the administrators' actions were taken "in a reasonable manner." Early in 2001, the appeals court reviewed the case again and finally reversed it, ruling in favor of the students.[32]

Even before the incident, Cullen and vice president for student affairs Betty Gibson had what other university employees described as a "chilly" relationship. From 1992 to 1994, Cullen reported directly to Gibson, but beginning in 1994, a reorganization of university administrators placed Leslie Thomas, director of student life, between the two. Cullen reported to Thomas, who reported to Gibson.

According to court documents, Gibson began complaining to Cullen in the fall of 1993 about the content of the student newspaper, *The Thorobred News*, specifically editorials and cartoons critical of the KSU administration. The following fall, even though Gibson was no longer Cullen's direct supervisor, she reportedly told Cullen to stop student editors from publishing a specific letter to the editor. It was never determined how Gibson knew about the content of the letter in advance. Cullen refused, claiming the First Amendment barred her as well as Gibson from interfering with the editorial process.

The following week, Cullen was transferred to a different department on campus and demoted to "secretary." Gibson claimed the transfer was based on numerous complaints she had received from other administrators about the content of the paper and the fact that the department to which Cullen was transferred was understaffed. Cullen, however, claimed the transfer was due to her refusal to cooperate with Gibson's attempt at censorship, as well as Cullen's leadership role in an employee union.

The same day as the job transfer, 2,000 copies of the student yearbook, *The Thorobred*, was delivered to the Student Publications Office. The yearbook's $9,000 cost had been paid by student activity fees. Gibson blocked distribution of the yearbook until she could discuss it with KSU President Mary Smith. Gibson and Smith then confiscated all copies of the yearbook and had them locked in a warehouse. Their decision, according to news reports, was based on their unhappiness with its title, *Destination Unknown*, and its purple cover, which did not match the university's colors of green and gold. They also complained about the absence of captions under the majority of the photographs and what the two administrators believed were too many images showing celebrities and trivial events with little or no connection to the university.

Over the holiday break, Cullen was successful with her grievance filed against Gibson and was reinstated as student publication adviser. Gibson issued a memo outlining her "expectations" regarding Cullen's future job performance, which included a reduction in the number of spelling and grammatical errors, a preference for more positive news, a greater reflection of the school's diverse student body and faculty, and a requirement that all editions would be reviewed by the Student Publications Board before going to press.

In March 1995, Cullen filed suit in the U.S. District Court for the Eastern District of Kentucky against Gibson, Smith, and the KSU Board of Regents. Cullen's complaint included a request that the court review the prior restraint issue as it pertained to the student newspaper, order the release of the student yearbook, and address Cullen's claim that her demotion was punishment based on her union activities. By midsummer, the court had rejected the second and third components of Cullen's case, and while still waiting for a ruling on the prior review issue, Cullen resigned from her position at KSU on July 31.

When the fall semester began in August, new student newspaper editors Cari Coffer and Charles Kincaid, still loyal to Cullen, filed a motion to intervene in the case. Judge Joseph M. Hood denied their request, along with a class action suit filed on behalf of the student body. Coffer and Kincaid then filed their own suit against Gibson and Smith, arguing that the prior review requirement violated their First Amendment rights and the university's refusal to release the yearbook, which had already been paid for by student activity fees, constituted a breach of contract.

While the student editors pursued their case, Cullen appealed hers to the Sixth Circuit Court of Appeals. It was another two years before the court ruled her case was moot because of her resignation. Regarding the students' First Amendment claims, Hood determined that neither the newspaper staff nor student body had suffered any "real injury" and that "threatening to censor" was not the same as "actually censoring." Hood also used the *Hazelwood* standard of "disruption of the educational process" in ruling in favor of the university.[33]

While the students prepared to take their appeal to the Circuit Court of Appeals, the lower court's decision in favor of the university's right to confiscate copies of the student newspaper and yearbook was left in place, and the result was an atmosphere of uncertainty in college newsrooms across the country.

Student newspaper editors and advisers at other universities were outraged by the court's citation of the *Hazelwood* standard, based on the unfairness of applying the ruling from a case involving high school journalists to those involving college journalists. "It is ludicrous to assume that a thirteen-year-old is similar in judgment to a twenty-two-year-old college senior," read one editorial in *The Student*, Miami University's student paper. "Moreover, virtually all college students are adults who enjoy inherent rights and responsibilities. The judge implied that college students are no more capable than are juveniles."[34]

The University Daily, the student newspaper at Texas Tech University, took its objections a step further, publishing a special "blackout" issue that included advertisements and announcements of upcoming events, but no news. Instead, each column that would usually offer news would include just black or white space covered by the word "censored." National media organizations commended the newspaper staff for showing solidarity with its counterpart at Kentucky State, but its advertisers were not pleased. "I paid for advertising, and this makes the issue useless," said the manager of a local restaurant. Added a local retailer: "We paid for something visual to be in there, and it wasn't. . . . A lot of our customers called us because they were upset."[35]

KSU students took their case to the Sixth Circuit Court of Appeals. In 1999, a three-judge panel initially ruled against the students but allowed the case to be heard by the full court. It took another eighteen months, but the Sixth Circuit ruled in January 2001 in favor of the students.

Judge R. Guy Cole, writing for the majority, claimed "there can be no question that *The Thorobred* is a journal of expression and communication in the true sense of a public forum . . . the university's confiscation of this journal of expression was arbitrary and unreasonable."[36] The celebration of the students' win earned the attention of free speech advocates nationwide, including the SPLC and the Society of Professional Journalists' Legal Defense Fund, both of which had supported the students' efforts. "By hiding these yearbooks, the university did more damage to its reputation than it would have by releasing them."[37]

HOSTY V. CARTER: THE "THREAT OF CENSORSHIP" AND "ACTUAL CENSORSHIP"

In the fall of 2000, Margaret Hosty was a thirty-nine-year-old student at Governors State University in University Park, Illinois, a suburb of Chicago. She was studying to be an English teacher, but along the way served as managing editor of *The Innovator*, GSU's student newspaper.

Under Hosty's leadership, the paper published a series of articles critical of the GSU administration. In early November, Dean of Student Affairs Patricia Carter called Charles Richards, owner of Regional Publishing, the paper's off-campus printer, and told him not to print future editions of the paper until she or another administrator could review them. That directive was inconsistent with the policy of GSU's Student Communications Media Board, which stated that the staff of all student publications will "determine content and format of those publications without censorship or advance approval."[38]

Hosty and editor Jeni Porche were aware of Carter's edict, but nonetheless hand-delivered the artwork for the next edition directly to the printer. The manager of the print shop said later he suspected that Carter's insistence on prior review was likely unconstitutional, but he complied with it for fear of not being paid for the work.

Hosty and Porche, along with staff writer Steven Barba, filed a civil suit in Federal District Court, claiming that Carter's interference with the publishing process was a violation of the students' First Amendment rights. The initial complaint named Carter as well as sixteen other administrators, but in a preliminary hearing, all but Carter were excused from the suit due to procedural issues. Carter, represented by the Illinois Attorney General's office rather than the university's legal staff, claimed the *Hazelwood* ruling gave her the right of prior review, based on the "disruption of the educational process" concept. Much like Gibson in the case at Kentucky State, Carter claimed that the "threat of censorship" was not the same as "actual censorship" and that she never insisted on the removal of any material in the one issue of the paper that was delayed. The students, however, complained that Carter deliberately dragged out the approval process before finally giving the printer the go-ahead signal in mid-December—a full week after students had left town for the holiday break.[39]

At the onset of the case, Hosty and her two co-plaintiffs fought the battle alone. Citing her religious convictions as well as commitment to her cause, Hosty said she spent eighteen hours per day finding, reading, copying, and analyzing court decisions in previous cases involving administrative review of college newspaper content.

"My leisure time, mental energy, and spiritual endeavors all have suffered from necessarily concentrating my attention and efforts on the barrage of litigation responsibilities," Hosty told a reporter from the *Fort Worth Star-Telegram*. "We've been left to endure the tribulations of litigation without so much as any law firm, legal organization, or individual attorney stepping up to assume even an advisory role . . . not a single media organization, student group, or civil rights coalition has so much as held a bake sale on our behalf."[40] Eventually, SPLC helped out with amicus curie briefs, and doctoral student John Wilson, who was writing his dissertation on the topic of student press freedom while operating a free speech website, volunteered to help with the legal research.

The students lost the initial case when it was argued at the trial court level in 2002. In April 2003, a three-judge panel for the Seventh Circuit Court of Appeals ruled in favor of the students, claiming that applying the *Hazelwood* standard (from a high school case) "was not a good fit for students at colleges and universities." The judges cited demographics from the U.S. Bureau of the Census that reported that less than 1 percent of college students were under the age of eighteen and that 55 percent were twenty-two or older.[41]

Early in 2004, however, the full panel of the appeals court reversed and ruled in favor of the university. In his majority opinion, Judge Frank Easterbrook determined that GSU had created a "non-public forum" that was not subject to First Amendment protection because it represented only the opinions of students on the editorial staff.

When the students announced their plans to appeal their case to the U.S. Supreme Court for its 2005-2006 session, the Washington, DC, firm of Levine, Sullivan, Koch, and Schultz stepped forward to prepare the case. On February 21, 2006, however, the Court announced it had declined the students' appeal, which left the ruling of the Circuit Court in place.

Although the circuit court decision in *Hosty v. Carter* applies only to states within that circuit (the Seventh, consisting of Indiana, Illinois, and Wisconsin), organizations such as the SPLC and College Media Advisors fear it may be used in other states and open the door to new attempts at regulating student media and a timid, less aggressive student press. "We believe the nation's colleges and universities should be havens for free expression, diverse viewpoints, and controversial opinions," said CMA President Lance Speer in a statement issued after the Supreme Court's decision not to hear the case. "And student journalists should be able to enjoy the same constitutional freedoms of the commercial and private press to question or criticize those in positions of power and influence without fear or reprisal or sanction. The *Hosty* decision certainly poses a threat to that ability."[42]

The Innovator never published again, and at the beginning of the following school year it was replaced by *The Phoenix*, a student-run newspaper that was given strict editorial guidelines (i.e., no articles or editorials critical of the administration) that was still subject to prior review. Almost immediately, student editors Stephanie Blahut and David Chambers sued the university, claiming the paper's faculty adviser, journalism professor Emmanuel Alozie, had been appointed by the university and was functioning as a de facto editor because he had the authority to delete content from the paper—a privilege that most advisers at public universities did not have. Blahut and Chambers also complained that administrators restricted their access to the newspaper offices on nights and weekends and purposely delayed their requests for the repair of aging equipment and the purchase of new equipment and supplies. Administrators also refused to process the payroll for students working on the paper over the summer.

By the time the case was heard in the fall of 2004, both Blahut and Chambers had graduated, and Federal District Court Judge Robert W. Gettleman ruled that the former students lacked standing to sue on their own behalf, on the behalf of student editors who followed them, or on the behalf of the student body at large.[43]

In 2006, shortly after the *Hosty* case, California became the first state to pass "anti-Hosty" legislation that made it illegal for public universities to punish students for communication that would otherwise be protected by the First Amendment if it occurred off-campus. Illinois, the state in which the *Hosty* case took place, passed a similar law the following year.

GOING UNDERGROUND

While universities have had little success in regulating the content of student publications, they have also been prohibited from blocking the distribution of "unofficial," "alternative," or "underground" newspapers.

In 1970, for example, a court decided in *Channing Club v. Texas Tech University* that the university administration could not stop a student organization from publishing its own newsletter because it objected to profanity contained in it. The court ruled that it was not enough for the university to claim the possibility of disruption; it had to prove that such disruption was imminent, which it could not. The Court also pointed out that the language in the newsletter was no worse than language found in books at the campus library and bookstore.[44]

In *Papish v. Board of Curators of the University of Missouri* (1973), the U.S. Supreme Court ruled in favor of Barbara Papish, a graduate student at the University of Missouri who published a controversial newspaper called the *Free Press Underground.* The issue that generated the court case featured a cartoon showing police raping the Statue of Liberty and a news story featuring text that was profane but not obscene.

After Papish was suspended, she sued the university in Federal District Court. The case eventually reached the Supreme Court, which ordered Papish's reinstatement and asserted that "the mere dissemination of ideas—no matter how offensive to good taste—on a state university campus may not be shut off in the name alone of conventions of decency."[45]

JOURNALISTIC PRIVILEGE

Just as student journalists generally win the debate over the right to make content decisions, they are also successful, in most cases, when claiming the same level of reporter privilege as their professional counterparts. In *New Hampshire v. Seil* (1982), for example, a judge ruled that student reporters did not have to reveal their sources of information for newspaper stories about campus crime. Even though New Hampshire did not have laws allowing journalists to protect their sources of information, the judge ruled that the students could do so in this case because the prosecutor had not exhausted all other possible sources of information prior to seeking it from the students. [46]

Support for "journalistic privilege" was not as strong four years earlier, however. During a campus disturbance at Stanford University in which demonstrators occupied part of the university's hospital, police officers were injured in a scuffle with the demonstrators. Police could not identify the attackers, but believed that the *Stanford Daily*, the university's student newspaper, was holding unpublished pictures in which the suspects could be identified. The prosecutor obtained a search warrant to go into the newspaper office and look for them, but the search did not reveal any photos other than those already published. The newspaper then sued under the Fourth Amendment, claiming "unreasonable search and seizure." One of the points in the newspaper's argument was that search warrants were intended to be a method by which law enforcement personnel could search the property of a suspect, while in this case, the newspaper was not suspected of any wrongdoing; it was a neutral third party. A lower court ruled in favor of the students, but on appeal, the Supreme Court overturned the decision, ruling 5–3 that law enforcement officers may obtain search warrants and make surprise searches of newsrooms to confiscate notes, audio tapes, and videotapes, even though no one in the newsroom was accused of a crime.

As the Court did in the 1972 case of *Branzburg v. Hayes*, in which it found that the needs of law enforcement sometimes outweigh the professional obligations of journalists, the Court determined that the Fourth Amendment did not protect journalists from searches when authorities have probable cause to believe they can provide crucial evidence in criminal investigations. In writing the majority opinion, Justice Byron White addressed the issue of the potential abuse of search warrants by suggesting that Congress and state legislatures prevent that by passing more specific laws. [47]

Two years later, Congress did just that, passing the Privacy Protection Act of 1980, which now restricts government or law enforcement's ability to search newsrooms of all types—campus newspapers as well as professional newspapers and broadcasting outlets. [48]

On Halloween night in 1994, the annual downtown street parties in Carbondale, Illinois—within a mile of the campus of Southern Illinois University—got out of hand. Due partly to a new rule that required bars and restaurants to close at 10 p.m., unhappy partiers reacted by breaking windows of storefronts and parked cars, setting off firecrackers, overturning trash cans, and setting fire to landscaping. More than 120 individuals were arrested, nearly all of them SIU students. [49]

Law enforcement officials asked local media outlets—including the student newspaper and television station at SIU—to turn over unpublished photographs and unaired video. The city's daily newspaper and three television stations at first resisted but then complied when served with subpoenas. The SIU paper, the *Daily Egyptian*, as well as the student-run television station, WSUI, refused. "Our student newspaper is a teaching tool," said Walter Jaehnig, director of the SIU journalism program. "One of the lessons we teach is that a newspaper covers news. It does not participate in the law enforcement or prosecution process."[50] Jaehnig drew a distinction between the Halloween case, for which he believed the request for the photographs and video would constitute a fishing expedition, and a 1992 arson on campus that destroyed a building and killed five students. "That was different," he said. "Five people had been killed. It was in the best interests of the community."[51]

When university president John Guyon got involved, however, the stance of the university changed. Guyon ordered university attorneys to work out a compromise with law enforcement officials. Instead of turning over the materials in bulk, the student journalists used information from law enforcement to search through the materials to look for specific suspects and turn over only those materials. The compromise sat well with Jaehnig, but not with students, who complained that having to cooperate with law enforcement was inconsistent with what they were taught in their classes. "Now when we go out to cover a story, we don't know if we're working for the Daily Egyptian or for the cops," said one student journalist. "I don't think we should be in the business of providing evidence against students. They'll never trust us again."[52]

On April 1, 1996, the University of Kentucky men's basketball team won the championship game of the Final Four in East Rutherford, New Jersey. Seven hundred miles away in Lexington, Kentucky, students on the UK campus celebrated the win. The celebration quickly got out of control as students and other fans began destroying street signs and public phone booths, breaking windows of storefronts and parked vehicles, and setting cars on fire.

Twenty-five people were arrested based on their behavior being witnessed by officers of the Lexington and university police departments. But for crimes committed but not witnessed by police, the officers asked for the help of the local media. Two local television stations received subpoenas for unaired video footage, while the local daily newspaper, the *Lexington Herald-Leader*, and the UK student newspaper, *The Kernal*, were asked to voluntarily turn over unpublished still photographs. The television stations turned over their video without challenging the subpoenas. The *Herald-*

Leader declined to cooperate, citing a long-standing policy of not providing unpublished photos to anyone. The staff of *The Kernal* declined repeated requests for the photographs, but after weeks of pressure, referred the requests to individual photographers who had the photographs in their possession.[53]

In 2000, a California judge ruled in favor of a student editor at California State University at Sacramento who challenged a subpoena to turn over unpublished photographs of a fight that took place at a football game. The attorney for an individual involved in the fight claimed her client was the victim of excessive force on the part of the arresting officers. The judge, however, ruled that the attorney knew the identities of more than a dozen witnesses to the incident and should have subpoenaed them first, and by not doing so, had not exhausted other sources of information.[54]

ACCESS TO INFORMATION

On April 5, 1986, a student at Lehigh University in Pennsylvania was raped and murdered in her residence hall. Nineteen-year-old Jeanne Clery had chosen Lehigh over other universities because her preliminary research showed it to be safer, by comparison, to other schools on her wish list.

But the statistics were misleading. They did not show the thirty-eight violent crimes—many of them sexual assaults—that had occurred on the Lehigh campus in the three years prior to her enrollment. If she had more complete information, her grieving parents said, she would have chosen a different school.

Howard and Connie Clery began meeting with Lehigh officials and congressional representatives from Pennsylvania to see what they could do to prompt Lehigh and other universities to do a better job in making information about campus safety available to prospective students, parents, and the media. They formed Security on Campus Inc., a nonprofit organization to fight for more transparency in the reporting of crime statistics.

Congress responded by passing the Campus Security Act of 1990, which required universities to make campus crime statistics more accessible. At first, enforcement of the law was inconsistent. In 1996, members of Congress heard from the student journalists and faculty advisers in their districts that their universities were either stonewalling on the release of information or providing data that was misleading. The House of Representatives passed a resolution instructing the Department of Education to step up its enforcement of the Campus Security Act. As a result, in 1998, the law was expanded and renamed the Jeanne Clery Act. The law has been fine-tuned several times since.

Despite the law, however, many universities are still reluctant to release crime statistics for fear of frightening current and potential students and their parents. A 2006 report from the Student Press Law Center claimed that only 37 percent of colleges and universities in the country are in compliance with the Clery Act. As a result, student media outlets as well as professional journalists often file suit to obtain such information, using either the Clery Act or the state's public records law.

According to the SPLC, inquiries about access to campus crime statistics are the second-most frequent question, behind only complaints about prior restraint.[55]

Some universities have been successful in limiting negative publicity regarding campus crime by dealing with cases internally. Rather than referring cases of alleged sexual assault, hazing, and gay-bashing to local prosecutors (and by doing so allowing news to leak into the off-campus press), many universities attempt to deal with such cases as student disciplinary actions—the results of which are protected by state and federal privacy laws.

That strategy was not foolproof, however. In the late 1990s, courts began ruling in favor of student journalists, claiming that universities must turn over records of campus disciplinary proceedings to local and campus menu.

One such case took place in 1997, when the Ohio Supreme Court ruled that Miami University must release the results of disciplinary hearings. The student newspaper, *The Miami Student*, had requested four years of records from the University Disciplinary Board. The board, comprised of students and faculty members, heard cases in which students could be suspended or expelled.

The court determined that documents resulting from the proceedings were not "educational records" as defined by Family Educational Rights and Privacy Act, a federal law that governs the release of students' academic and health records. University officials had feared that if it turned over the records it would violate the federal law and might lose federal aid.

As part of the ruling, the court did allow the university to delete Social Security and student identification numbers, but not student names.[56]

In 2006, journalism students at Ohio University studied the availability of public records in their state by making formal requests at fifteen state colleges and universities. Those requests, which dealt only with records that were clearly public under Ohio law—faculty salaries, campus crime, and the names of major donors—were met with refusals in 60 percent of the cases.

The project involved twenty-five members of the OU Chapter of the Society of Professional Journalists. The students then fanned out across the state to follow up in person during their six-week winter break. They visited the appropriate university offices during regular business hours and without identifying themselves or the reasons behind their requests. In most cases, including at their own university in Athens, the students were referred to the schools' legal affairs offices. The students eventually determined that the denials were not the result of conspiracies, but rather a lack of understanding of the state law.

That same year, the Massachusetts Supreme Court ruled that Harvard University was exempt from state public records laws because it was a private institution. The Clery Act applies to both public and private institutions, but it was not a factor in the case because it deals primarily with more generalized statistical data, whereas the student newspaper at Harvard was interested in specific incident reports covered under the state law. The newspaper argued (unsuccessfully) that because the university police department had many of the same powers given to city and county law enforcement agencies in the state, it should be held to the same standards in terms of disclosure of information.[57]

For college journalists, the pursuit of news often results in a conflict between access to information (based on public records laws in effect in their states) and student privacy (based on FERPA).

For example, when a student is the victim or alleged perpetrator of a well-publicized crime or a university athlete has been suspended from competition, journalists often ask university officials for information regarding that student's mental or physical health, academic performance, or disciplinary history. Under FERPA (as well as a university's own student records policy), most of that information cannot be released to the media and is available to other university officials on a need-to-know basis.

While police reports and other documents that overtly identify alleged perpetrators or victims are protected under FERPA, documents related to campus crime on a more general basis must be available under the Clery Act.

College journalists also have difficulty gaining access to university budgets, strategic planning documents, student government activities, faculty evaluations, and athletic department procedures. Some administrators claim such documents are exempted under state public records laws, and university attorneys often stonewall requests in hopes that journalists will eventually either lose interest in the story or graduate.

One well-publicized conflict between public records laws and FERPA took place at North Dakota State University in 2008. The student newspaper, *The Spectrum*, was developing a story on a string of anti-Semitic incidents on campus. The NDSU administration denied staff writers access to the disciplinary records. When the student journalists filed a public records request, the university intentionally dragged out the process until after the paper had published its last issue of the year. The students continued the process, however, and the state's attorney general eventually ruled that the university should have provided the requested information with the names of students redacted, thus complying with both the public records law and FERPA.[58]

The same year, the attorney general of Kentucky ruled that administrators at Eastern Kentucky University redacted far more information than necessary from campus police reports before releasing them to student journalists. The university claimed that it was merely protecting student privacy, but the attorney general determined that much of the information redacted did not identify students and was therefore unrelated to their privacy.[59]

SOMETIMES A STAGECOACH, SOMETIMES NOT

Editors of student newspapers face three issues related to advertising: (1) their right to accept advertising related to controversial products, services, or issues; (2) their right to deny space to such advertisers; and (3) the authority of administrators or state officials to make such decisions for them.

As a matter of tradition, supported by the First Amendment, newspapers have the right to reject advertisements without explaining their reasons. Under the concept of "editorial control," newspapers and magazines (and in most cases, broadcasters) cannot be compelled to accept advertising to which they object. The principle goes back to the 1933 case of *Shuck v. Daily Herald*, in which an Iowa state court expressed concern that "if a newspaper were required to accept an advertisement, it could be compelled to publish a news item."[60]

A 1969 case established a similar standard for college newspapers. The case of *Lee v. Board of Regents* began when students at the University of Wisconsin Whitewater wanted to run paid "advertorials" in the school's newspaper, *The Royal Purple*, on three topics: one promoting the agenda of a labor union representing university employees, one condemning discrimination in employment and housing, and one in opposition to the Vietnam War. The newspaper staff rejected all three, claiming its advertising pages were limited to non-controversial topics.

The students sued the university in Federal District Court, where attorneys for the school's board of regents defended the advertising policy as a "reasonable means of protecting the university from embarrassment and the staff from the difficulty of exercising judgment as to material which may be obscene, libelous, or subversive."[61]

Judge James E. Doyle, however, ruled in favor of the students, finding the newspaper's funding by student activities fees as grounds for it being a public forum that must be open to all students and viewpoints. In their 1973 book, *Law of the Student Press*, authors George E. Stevens and John B. Webster wrote that the Lee case set the precedent that a college newspaper's advertising space "must be open to anyone who is willing to pay to have his views published therein."[62]

In the 1986 case of *Sinn v. Daily Nebraskan*, the Eighth Circuit Court of Appeals ruled in favor of student journalists at the University of Nebraska, determining that any attempt by the university's administration to set advertising policy would violate the First Amendment.[63] The case began when two individuals attempted to place roommate advertisements in the student newspaper. The text for the proposed ad mentioned the individuals' sexual orientation, causing the staff of the paper to reject the ad because they perceived it as discriminating against renters who were not gay or lesbian. The staff also feared the ad might violate the Fair Housing Act.

The two individuals sued the newspaper, claiming it violated their First Amendment rights. Both the Federal District Court and Eighth Circuit Court of Appeals disagreed, determining that because the decision was made by the newspaper staff and not university officials, there was no First Amendment claim.

Much like other newspapers, many student papers cite the First Amendment tradition of accepting or rejecting advertisements—a tradition that dates back to the country's founding. ("My newspaper is not a stagecoach with seats on it for everyone," quipped eighteenth-century publisher Benjamin Franklin.)[64]

Studies have determined that college newspapers reject advertisements at a greater rate than commercial newspapers. Policies that support their right to reject ads provide the following rationale: hints of racial bias, poor taste, related to services provided by spiritualists or fortune tellers, suspected fraud, or ads that might be harmful to the reputation of the school.[65]

Harvey Gotliffe, a professor of journalism at San Jose State University, surveyed 140 college newspapers and found that slightly more than half had formal policies regarding advertising content, and that most overtly stated that editors had the right to accept or reject advertisements. [66]

Early in 2001, political activist David Horowitz attempted to place an ad in college newspapers across the country—the content of which many of the papers found objectionable but published nonetheless. The ad, titled "Ten Reasons Why Reparations for Blacks is a Bad Idea for Blacks—And Racist Too," outlined his view of the public debate over slavery reparations. Of the newspapers that received the ad, many rejected it outright. Other newspapers published the ad but elsewhere in the same issue denounced its message while explaining their First Amendment right to publish it. Other papers published the ad without explanation and later apologized to their readers.

Horowitz was an individual whose political ideology had moved from the far left to the far right of the spectrum. One of the more controversial points within the ad was that, "If slave labor created wealth for Americans, then obviously it has created wealth for black Americans as well, including the descendants of slaves." Critics of the Horowitz ad took specific offense to its claims that black Americans are "indebted" to the United States for freeing them from slavery and that they had already been compensated for slavery in the form of welfare programs and affirmative action.

Ken Paulson, executive director of the First Amendment Center, was uncertain as to Horowitz's motive in placing the ad, but believed the First Amendment protected it regardless of motive. "If Mr. Horowitz's goal was to raise his visibility on this issue, he has succeeded," Paulson wrote in a 2001 op-ed piece published in newspapers across the country. "If his goal was to demonstrate that college campuses are not exactly havens for free speech, he has succeeded many times over." [67]

Paulson cited his own experience as a daily newspaper editor to make his points. "I saw our advertising department reject many potentially controversial ads, including, most notably, anti-abortion ads containing graphic images of dead fetuses. What makes the current ad controversy particularly unsettling, however, is the number of student groups—particularly groups concerned about racism—that want to punish both Mr. Horowitz and campus newspapers for exercising their First Amendment rights. I don't question the passion of their beliefs or their sense of injury. I do wonder, however, how they've lost sight of the role free speech has played in righting wrongs." [68]

At many schools, student protestors claiming to represent African Americans and other minority students demanded that newspapers donate the revenue generated by the ad to organizations representing their interests.

Protestors knew that the newspapers had the First Amendment right to either accept or reject the ad and were miffed when their newspapers didn't choose the latter. Paulson pointed out the precedent set by daily newspapers that rejected anti-abortion ads they considered too offensive, but he nevertheless supported the student newspapers that found the Horowitz ad offensive but published it anyway. He pointed to the example set by the *New York Times*, which published the infamous "Heed Their Rising Voices" ad in 1960—a piece dealing with race relations in Alabama—that upset many readers and led to the most famous libel case in journalism history. "Those who would seek to punish student media for publishing a controversial ad have lost sight of the role of the First Amendment in transforming race relations in this country over the last fifty years," he wrote.[69]

Student journalists and faculty advisers at many college campuses reported that hundreds of copies of their publications had disappeared from their racks and were later found in garbage cans or recycling bins.

At Brown University in Rhode Island, offended students allegedly stole nearly 4,000 copies of *The Brown Daily Herald* in which the ad appeared.[70] A similar incident occurred at the University of California at Berkeley, prompting *Daily Californian* student editor Daniel Hernandez to apologize in print on the front page of a subsequent issue. A similar apology from Eleeza Agopian, student editor of *The Aggie* at the University of California at Davis, appeared on an inside page of that publication.

Horowitz also claimed that many papers ran the non-apology editorials to avoid losing out on journalism jobs after graduation. While denying that assertion, Hernandez claimed that many potential employers told him that with that incident in his background, he "would never get a job in journalism—ever."[71]

Instead of putting the controversy to rest, however, the apologies generated criticisms from off-campus newspapers and other First Amendment advocates. *The Boston Globe*, for example, chastised Hernandez, Agopian, and other student editors for caving in to pressure from offended students and faculty and expressed concerns about the status of the First Amendment on college campuses nationwide.

One publication refusing to apologize for the ad was *The Badger-Herald*, one of two student newspapers at the University of Wisconsin at Madison. Instead, the newspaper staff published a letter explaining the rationale behind its decision. The letter explained that the ad was consistent with the paper's advertising standards and could not be refused because it did not include material that was "libelous, in poor taste, or illegal." Critics disagreed with the paper's claim that the ad was "not in poor taste" and protested outside of the paper's offices. Student editor Julie Bosman later claimed that her staff had been treated to "an up-close and personal lesson in defending the First Amendment."[72]

Many papers that accepted the ad made sure it was accompanied by staff-written editorials (opposing the content of the message but defending their right to publish it) or paid advertisements (expressing an opposing viewpoints) placed by groups that had been tipped off about the content of the Horowitz ad. In at least one such case—in Princeton University's *Daily Princetonian*—Horowitz refused to pay his bill. No records exist to determine if the school ever collected, but its promise to donate the proceeds to the local chapter of the National Urban League probably didn't help. Offended by the language of the newspaper's editorial, Horowitz threatened to sue the paper for libel, but he dropped his case after realizing that his status as a public figure would render such a case unsuccessful.

Horowitz claimed on his website that slightly less than half of the seventy-one papers contacted agreed to run the ads, while the other half either rejected the ad or did not respond to his follow-up communication.[73]

On many campuses, student protestors demanded that the newspapers donate money collected from Horowitz to campus and community groups that promoted diversity and tolerance. At Brown University, student groups angry about the ad stole more than 4,000 copies of the paper, *The Brown Daily Herald*, and dumped them into campus recycling bins.[74]

In the late 1990s and early 2000s, fringe historian Bradley Smith attempted to place in college newspapers across the country a series of advertisements claiming that the Holocaust never happened. Smith's ads, which ran in approximately ninety papers, cost $150 to $450 for each insertion.

One newspaper accepting the ad was the *Spectator* at Valdosta State University in Georgia. The student editors of the paper claimed it accepted the ad not for economic reasons (as critics had accused), but instead because it was "morally bound to present divergent viewpoints, not matter how unpopular those ideas might be" and that it sought only to "protect the marketplace of ideas."[75]

Other editors claimed they accepted the ads based not on their First Amendment rights, but those of Smith and his organization. In interviews published in off-campus publications, some hinted that Smith had threatened to sue them for violating his free speech rights. Apparently not aware that the First Amendment gives editors the right to refuse advertising, one editor admitted that he had been "hoodwinked" by Smith. Smith's ad was based on what critics called "undocumented statistics and the claims of so-called authorities."[76]

The ad was also published by student newspapers at Duke, Cornell, Northwestern, the University of Georgia, and the University of Michigan. Refusing the ad were papers at Harvard, Yale, Brown, University of Wisconsin, and the University of California. In an editorial titled, "Unpopular Free Speech," the *Cornell Daily Sun* criticized its content but argued in favor of Smith's First Amendment right to publish it. Comparing the advertising pages to the letters page, the newspaper's staff argued that both were public forums and to limit access to either one would be a form of thought control.[77]

One critic of those papers' decision to run the Smith ad was Melvin Mencher, an emeritus professor of journalism at Columbia University and author of numerous books on media writing, law, and ethics. Mencher's 2002 opinion column in *College Media Review* called the VSU editors' rationale "lofty rhetoric," but then spent the bulk of his 3,000-word piece debunking their decision and that of other student papers.[78]

"The evidence of Nazi genocide is a solid as the video clips we watched in horror as the World Trade Center collapsed," Mencher wrote. "The perpetrators of the Holocaust are as forthright in describing their deeds as is Osama bin Laden's call for the destruction of the United States. . . . Not one historian grants Holocaust denial a wisp of validity."[79] Added Rutgers University historians: "If the Holocaust is not a fact, then nothing is a fact."[80]

Instead of using the advertising policy manuals of student journalism organizations or individual student publications, Mencher instead grounded much of his argument in the wording of the *New York Times'* Standards of Advertising Acceptability.

"The success of advertising depends on its credibility," the standards read. "No matter how technically brilliant or compelling an advertisement may be, unless readers believe it, it fails in its purpose."[81] A *Times* spokesperson, responding to an inquiry from Mencher, said according to his newspaper's standards, an ad would be considered "unacceptable" if it "ran into the wall of historical certainty as judged by reasonable people" and that the *Times* would not accept advertisements that "deny a recognized crime of substantial proportions or vividness, (such as) the Holocaust, the Irish famine, or slavery."[82]

Cardinal Points, the weekly student newspaper at Plattsburgh State University in New York, published the Holocaust denial ad on September 24, 1998—between the Jewish holidays of Rosh Hashanah and Yom Kippur. Many of the school's 5,500 students were Jewish, as were many faculty and staff. Anticipating the controversy, the ad was accompanied by a disclaimer that read, "This is a paid advertisement, and in no way reflects the opinion of *Cardinal Points*." It was the first time, university faculty and administrators claimed, that an advertisement in the student newspaper was accompanied by a disclaimer.[83]

Faculty adviser Shawn Murphy later explained that the ad appeared as a result of the paper not having a formal policy regarding what ads could and could not run in the paper, and that the controversy served as evidence that every college newspaper needed such a policy.

"Like many student newspapers across the country, *Cardinal Points* did not have a manual of policy and style because the students either did not have the time—nor would take the time—to draft one," Murphy wrote in *College Media Review.* "The way things were done was instead passed from one staff to the next by word of mouth."[84] Supporters of the students' right to publish the ad claimed that such ads fostered healthy debate on college campuses, even in cases that the material in question was based on historical inaccuracies and racist ideologies. They also claimed that the best way to address hateful speech was to get it out into the open where it could be discredited. "By driving racist expression underground, we make it harder to combat the attitudes it expresses," commented Nadine Strossen, a professor at the New York University Law School.[85]

Unlike the case of alcohol discussed in the following section, financial concerns were not a factor in the newspaper's decision.

Speaking out against the ads, critics claimed that publishing them might lead to more students embracing Smith's ideologies, and was evidence that the journalist faculty at PSU "had not taught the student journalists right from wrong," adding the disclaimer did not excuse the staff from moral responsibility.[86]

Further, they claimed, it was not necessary to publish a paid advertisement in order to prompt the discussion; alternatives such as publishing the same ideas as an opinion column, surrounding by one or more columns expressing the opposing viewpoint, would have introduced the topic without the negative result.[87]

One student paper that ran both the Horowitz and Smith ads was Duke University's *Chronicle*. Student editor Greg Pessin claimed the paper accepted both ads because "open debate and open discourse should never be sacrificed for comfort."[88]

The paper did reject a subsequent Smith ad that claimed much of the historical evidence supporting the Holocaust narrative had been fabricated. Pessin said he rejected that ad because the accusation of falsified evidence was an assertion of fact rather than opinion, and because the assertion was not supported by verifiable facts, the ad failed to meet the paper's advertising acceptance policy.

Ron Spielberger, executive director of the College Media Advisers, claimed that ads such as those placed by Horowitz and Smith were not as much about the First Amendment as they were about generating "free publicity" for their causes by being republished, either in their entirety or excerpted, in other media. "The purchasers of these ads are looking for publicity," he said in an interview with the Student Press Law Center's membership publication. "If these ads had been placed without controversy, then the placers of the ads would be highly disappointed."[89]

In addition to the anti-reparations and anti-Holocaust ads, other topics in paid advertising that caused controversy included those promoting alcohol or nightclubs, abortion services, attempting to recruit young women to work as exotic dancers or escorts, and offering female students thousands of dollars to donate their eggs to infertile couples.

In the 1990 case of *Lueth v. St Claire County Community College*, a Federal District Court ruled that the administration of a college could not prohibit controversial advertisements in the campus newspaper. The controversy began on November 1, 1988, when the staff of the *Erie Square Gazette*, the student newspaper at a community college in Port Huron, Michigan, published an ad for Cheri Champaigne's, an adult nightclub across the border in Point Edward, Canada.

The front-page ad noted that the drinking age in Canada was nineteen—compared to it being twenty-one in Minnesota—and that the club had dancers that were "totally nude," which was prohibited for nightclubs in Michigan. Frederick Hauenstein, dean of the college, told editor Elizabeth Lueth that she could not run the advertisement again, as it was "denigrating to women and promoted under-age drinking."[90] His ban was endorsed by a Student Government committee that controlled the newspaper, along with faculty adviser Jennifer Durham.

The following month, Lueth filed suit against the college, Hauenstein, and Durham, charging that the advertising ban violated the paper's First Amendment rights. A few weeks later, she resigned from her position, citing "personal and family reasons." That prompted the school to argue for dismissal of the case based on Lueth's lack of standing, but the court ruled that the case could proceed.

The court eventually ruled that because the paper was run based on the adviser model and not the laboratory model, it was a public forum and therefore all content decisions were the responsibility of the students and could not be limited by administrators.[91]

A similar controversy took place at the University of Hawaii at Manoa in 1999, when the student newspaper came under fire for publishing a series of advertisements for adult nightclubs. Administrators attempted to stop the ads, claiming the businesses put students at risk because of their reputation for being fronts for prostitution and illegal drug sales. When the management of the paper refused to cancel the ads and forfeit $60,000 a year in advertising revenue, the UHM administration attempted to cancel the paper's allotment of student activity fees, which would have exceeded the revenue generated by the ads.

After a controversy that ran most of the 1999-2000 academic year, the two sides reached a comprise that specified administrators would no longer exert pressure on the paper to influence advertising, while the paper would continue to accept the nightclub ads but reject more overt advertisements of a sexual nature, such as those for escort services.[92]

In 1996, Pennsylvania adopted a law simply known as Act 199, the purpose of which was to prohibit the paid placement of alcohol averaging in college newspapers and publications of college athletic departments.

The law was challenged by the *Pitt News*, the official student newspaper at the University of Pennsylvania, which claimed that is lost more than $17,000 in advertising revenue in the first full year after the law was passed. The legislators claimed that the law was aimed at dealing with the epidemic of binge and underage drinking on college campuses, but critics sarcastically said the rationale behind the law was the belief of state legislators that if students did not have access to the advertising of local bars, they would not drink as much.

A trial court accepted the "binge and underage drinking" rationale and ruled in favor of the university. But in 2004, the Third Circuit Court of Appeals reversed and ruled in favor of the students, based not only on the newspaper's First Amendment right to disseminate information but on the students' First Amendment right to receive it. The ruling was based in part on the Central Hudson Test, a legal standard that limited the regulation of truthful advertising to those cases in which (1) the government had a substantial interest in regulating the advertising (such as public health or safety), (2) the regulation advanced that interest, and (3) the regulation was sufficiently narrow.[93]

The appeals court determined that the university had failed to meet its burden of proof related to the connection between alcohol advertising and binge and underage drinking and was offering only "speculation and conjecture" to support its claim.

Related to the third clause, the court ruled that the law in question was actually *too narrow* because it dealt with such a specific form of advertising. The court also indicated that a more effective way for the university to address the problem of binge and underage drinking was to enforce laws related to the behavior rather than create new laws aimed at regulating speech already protected by the First Amendment.[94]

"Even if Pitt students do not see alcoholic beverage ads in *The Pitt News*, they will still be exposed to a torrent of beer ads on television and the radio, and they will still see alcoholic beverage ads in other publications, including the other free weekly Pittsburgh papers that are displayed on campus together with The Pitt News," the decision wrote.[95]

The ruling was expected to maintain the windfall for college newspapers across the country, including those that had lost their student-fee funding in recent years and had become more dependent on paid advertising. *The Pitt News*, for example, claimed it had lost $17,000 since the ban had gone into effect in 1999.[96]

Supporting the newspaper's case was the Pittsburgh chapter of the American Civil Liberties Union, the Student Press Law Center, the Pennsylvania Newspaper Association, and the Reporters Committee for Freedom of the Press.

A spokesperson for the Pennsylvania ACLU indicated the organization had assisted in challenging the law ten times previously and that this was the first time the student press had prevailed.

Brittany Litzinger, student business manager of *The Pitt News*, claimed the purpose of the law was well-intentioned but misguided. "We did understand the concerns of the legislators," she said. "They felt the ads promoted underage drinking. But seventy percent of our readers are over twenty-one."[97]

A closer examination of the law also found that the legislators had attempted to circumvent potential First Amendment concerns by carefully crafting the law. Instead of barring promotion of alcohol, the law simply prohibited newspapers from doing so with paid ads. "If the government were free to suppress disfavored speech by preventing potential speakers from being paid, there would not be much left of the First Amendment," the decision stated.[98]

The Office of the Pennsylvania Attorney General, the primary defendant in the case, pointed out that the law had been in effect for two years and had not resulted in the demise of any student papers. The AG's office also claimed that the law was aimed not at limiting the rights of journalists but decreasing alcohol consumption and underage drinking on and near campus.

Editor Hal Turner said the state was punishing the wrong people. "There are so many other things the government can do to fight alcohol abuse," he told local media. "They can educate and have stricter law enforcement, methods which have proven to work and don't violate the Constitution."[99]

District Court judge William Standish ruled that the newspaper lacked standing to challenge the Liquor Control Board's rule because the ban only prohibited businesses from placing the ads; it did not prohibit the newspapers from accepting them. The "so-what's-the-point?" question of how a newspaper could legally accept an advertisement that was illegal for the advertiser to place was never answered by the judge or state officials involved in the case.

Jason Gallinger, editor of the paper, estimated the rule cost the paper $17,000 in ad revenue—about 3 percent of its budget—for the 1998–1999 school year.[100]

Similar laws are on the books in New Hampshire and Utah, but those laws have not been challenged. Virginia's law allows alcohol advertising only if the ads include a "drink responsibly" message.

In New Hampshire, the staff of Keene College's *Equinox* announced its intention of to challenge the law, claiming it would lose more than $2,000 per week in advertising revenue if it could not accept alcohol advertising. No record of court cases could be found, but the staff did report that several local restaurants had revised their advertisements to avoid any references to alcohol.[101]

In Utah, the legislature passed a similar law in 1996 and put the state's Alcoholic Beverage Control Commission in charge of enforcement. The law was immediately challenged by a consortium of bar owners, who claimed that they had little interest in advertising in student papers, but were more concerned about the precedent. Student newspaper editors in Utah, citing the lack of alcohol-related advertising, expressed reluctance to challenge the law.[102]

Just as college newspapers create controversy and sometimes legal problems based on the ads they accept, they also create the same based on ads they reject—or attempt to reject.

In 1970 at Florida State University, for example, the staff of the *Flambeau* rejected an advertisement announcing a meeting of the Gay Liberation Front. The university's board of publications board overruled the newspaper staff, determining that because the GLF was an officially recognized student group funded by student activity fees, it could not be denied advertising space in a publication that was also funded by student fees. The board rejected the claims of the newspaper staff that a similar ad placed in the paper during the previous school year resulted in other advertisers canceling their contracts. The group's freedom of speech, the publications board said, took priority over the potential loss of advertising revenue.[103]

In the 1976 case of *Mississippi Gay Alliance v. Goudelock*, a Circuit Court of Appeals ruled that a university newspaper could not be compelled to accept advertising to which it objected. A gay rights group at Mississippi State University sued the student newspaper after it refused to accept an ad promoting its events, but both a Federal District Court and the Fifth Circuit Court of Appeals sided with the newspaper staff, determining that its First Amendment right of editorial control took priority over that of a student group claiming its First Amendment right to advertise in the student newspaper.[104]

CENSORSHIP BY THEFT

One disturbing trend of the 1990s and early 2000s was that of student newspapers being the target of individuals or groups who object to negative coverage in the student newspaper and retaliate by stealing copies, and in many cases, destroying them.

According to the Student Press Law Center, thousands of student newspapers disappear each year under suspicious circumstances. Campus police seldom consider it theft because the paper is free, but the SPLC claims otherwise. "Just because the paper doesn't have a sales price doesn't mean it doesn't have value," said Mark Goodman, then-executive director of the SPLC, in an interview with textbook author Rachel Kanigel. "That value can be measured in different ways—in the cost of printing and in the advertising revenue the copies of the publication represent."[105] The SPLC adds that newspaper theft is a form of censorship because taking newspapers out of circulation denies access to that information to students who may want it.[106]

Because student newspapers are distributed free, few administrators or campus police departments consider such incidents a law enforcement priority. Some observers even believe that administrators condone such activity. "On most college campuses, administrators are well aware that they cannot directly censor the student newspaper without risking a lawsuit and a lot of bad publicity," attorney and professor Wayne Overbeck wrote in his textbook, *Major Principles of Media Law*. "But with a wink and a nod, they can certainly encourage someone else to do the dirty work for them by rounding up all the copies of an offending newspaper."[107]

In order to make prosecutions more valid, Kanigel recommends assigning the paper a price. Even though many universities require papers to be free to students because they are partially funded by student activity fees, Kanigel suggests a statement clarifying that single copies are free but multiple copies can be purchased at the newspaper's business office. She also recommends that staffers conduct periodic "dumpster patrols" in which they search trash and recycling collection sites on or near campus, and when large quantities of the paper are found, staff photographers should record the find before contacting university police.[108]

One question that is often posed as part of the discussion of student newspaper theft: if there is no charge for the product, has a theft actually occurred?

In the last decade, three states—California, Colorado, and Maryland— have passed laws penalizing the theft of free newspapers. The laws apply to all free papers, not just those on college campuses. California's law provides a penalty of $250 for taking more than twenty-five copies of a free newspaper if it was done with the intent of depriving others access to the information.

In the fall of 1999, *The Viking News*, the student newspaper at Ocean County College in New Jersey, published a lighthearted story about student Allen Rubman's quest to get hugs from more than a thousand female students in order to win a bet with a friend. Many students were offended rather than amused by the sexist nature of the story, and they said so on the newspaper's editorial page in a subsequent issue.

Angered at the response, Rubman stole more than 1,200 copies of the paper and hid them in the trunk of his car. The theft was witnessed by other students, prompting his arrest. He was originally charged with possession of stolen property, but in exchange for his guilty plea, the charges were reduced to the lesser offense of "creating a disturbance." The newspaper staffers and faculty adviser were angered at the reduced sentence and minimal fine of $50. As a result, they promised to thoroughly publicize Rubman's crime on the pages of *The Viking News*—then watch carefully to make sure the papers would not be stolen.[109]

When two members of the wrestling team at the University of Tennessee at Chattanooga were arrested for allegedly assaulting another man in September 1999, the student newspaper put the resulting story on the front page. Two other wrestlers then retaliated by stealing more than 2,000 copies of the paper. The thefts were witnessed by *Echo* editor Jaime Lackey and news editor Nikki Middlebrooks.

Disciplinary action was taken against the students, but the results could not be published in the paper because of the private nature of the judicial proceedings.[110]

Also during fall semester of 1999, numerous incidents of theft were reported by the staffs of the *Yale Daily News* and its humor magazine, *Rumpa*. The number of copies in each incident ranged from 100 to more than 10,000, and each time the missing copies were later found in campus trash bins and recycling containers. The thefts were believed to be in retaliation for a story in the newspaper about members of the women's hockey team demanding the school hire a new coach and a story in the magazine that exposed members of the school's secret societies, including Skull and Bones.[111]

At Hofstra University, a student was seen by university police as he removed advertising inserts from 1,500 copies of *The Chronicle* early in 2000. The inserts carried a Holocaust revisionist essay that had caused controversy at other universities. The student's only punishment was to write a letter of apology to the newspaper staff.

The staff was angry at the minimal nature of the punishment, largely because it had been the victim of multiple newspaper thefts during the previous year, without anyone being held accountable. "This time we had somebody," editor Shawna Van Ness said. "This was the time to make a statement that this kind of thing would not be tolerated . . . having someone write a letter of apology is letting them get away with vandalism and infringement of everyone else's First Amendment rights."[112]

A rash of student newspaper thefts happened at numerous schools across the country during a three-month span in 2006. Some observers believe the thefts were carried out by students upset about negative news stories about them, their organizations, fellow students, or campus issues they were concerned about.

That was one theory posited at the Westminster College in New Wilmington, Pennsylvania. Around 7 a.m. on March 1, about 1,500 freshly printed copies of the student newspaper, *The Holcad*, were distributed across the campus. Within three hours, nearly all of them had disappeared. About 200 of the papers were later found in a recycling bin, but the other 1,300 copies were never found.

Some college administrators suspect that the theft resulted from the paper's coverage of an incident on campus in which the search of a student's room turned up a "hit list" that identified thirteen peers the student wanted to kill. Neither the front-page article, nor an editorial complaining that the administration was negligent in not taking the case more seriously, identified the student by name. Two unidentified students were later charged with "abridgement of freedom of speech" (but no criminal offenses). Later that year, a student facing drug charges was charged with the theft of more than 800 copies of the student newspaper that carried a story about her arrest.[113]

At Kansas State University, members of a campus fraternity allegedly stole more than 8,000 copies of the student newspaper that published a story critical of the group after university officials accused it of hazing and substance abuse.[114] At Pasadena City College in California, members of a Hispanic student group were more brazen. Not only did they steal 5,000 copies of the campus newspaper, *The Courier*, but bragged about it publicly and even sent to the newspaper offices garbage bags full of the torn-up copies of the newspaper, along with a note claiming responsibility for the theft. Members of the group said they looked at the incident not as a crime, but rather as a publicity stunt designed to draw attention to the newspaper's failure to cover the group's events.[115]

The same month, a student at Embry-Riddle Aeronautical University in Arizona admitted to stealing 800 copies of *Horizons*, the school's student newspaper, to protest a story about her arrest on charges of drunk driving and possession of marijuana. Brianna Hill, a member of the school's soccer team, admitted to stealing 600 copies of the paper's first run and then 200 of the second run published to replace those taken the first time. She claimed the dean's office authorized her to confiscate the paper, a charge that university administrators denied.[116]

The following month, more than 2,500 copies of *The Orion*, the student paper at the University of California at Chico, were stolen. A group of students claimed responsibility in an anonymous call to the newspaper office. The caller reportedly told sports editor Zuri Berry that the papers were being "held hostage" in retaliation for the paper's editorial opposing to referenda scheduled for a student vote later that week. None of the missing copies were ever found.[117]

The same month, two students at Kansas State University posed as members of the newspaper staff and confiscated about 8,000 copies of *The Kansas State Collegian*. The students were thought to be members of the Sigma Chi fraternity, which had been the subject of a newspaper story about substance abuse and hazing.[118]

Another case of student newspaper theft took place at Johns Hopkins University in Maryland, where more than 900 copies of *The Carrollton Record* disappeared shortly after being distributed on May 13. The theft was believed to have been in protest of a cover story titled, "How Your Tuition Goes to Fund the Gay Porn Industry."[119] The story explained how student activity fees were used to support a screening of the famous pornographic film *Deep Throat* and a speech by a prominent director in the gay porn industry. A student group supporting gay and lesbian students on campus complained that there were a number of inaccuracies in the story and that the paper had used photographs from its Facebook page without permission, but denied any knowledge of the thefts.[120]

In February 2013, almost 2,000 copies of the student newspaper at Tulane University, the *Tulane Hullabaloo*, were stolen by two students who confessed to university police. The students were members of the Kappa Sigma fraternity who were upset about a story concerning a police raid on their house.

The students were required to pay $1,896 in restitution; the figure was calculated based on the policy that each Tulane student were entitled to free copies of the paper and that additional copies were priced at $1 each.[121]

BEST OF THE REST

In the late 1970s and early 1980s, administrators at the University of South Florida demonstrated restraint in dealing with the controversies stemming from a series of articles published by the school's award-winning newspaper, *The Oracle*. Following up on nearly a decade of rumors, *Oracle* reporters investigated one of the most popular people on campus, John W. "Knocky" Parker, a tenured professor in the Department of English and one of USF's founding faculty members from the late 1950s. According to campus lore, Parker could be easily persuaded to change students' grades in exchange for gifts, and it was rumored that alcohol was the preferred offering. The stories resulted in considerable discussion in the community and the issue was later covered by the local daily, *The Tampa Tribune*. While not pleased with the articles in either *The Oracle* or *Tribune*, UWF administrators maintained their "hands off" policy and said they would take no action because there was nothing in the *Oracle* series that was either libelous or untrue. Ironically, the campus anger at the Parker stories came not from the administration or the English Department, but from the hundreds of students and alumni who had taken his classes.[122]

Local journalists noted the stark contrast between the commendable restraint shown by USF administrators and their counterparts at nearby Hillsborough Community College, where the *Tricamp*, a weekly that served the school's three campuses, was constantly under administrative attack. Following nearly a decade of campus turmoil, which included the firing of a popular African American basketball coach (and subsequent discrimination lawsuit) and what both on-campus and off-campus media called a "botched" presidential search, HCC administrators took out their displeasure on the softest target they could find—the *Tricamp*. Faculty advisers and student editors claimed that in private conversations, they were threatened with job termination and academic sanctions, respectively. Publicly, however, the administrators claimed they simply suggested that *Tricamp* publish "more good news" about the college and "fewer negative stories."[123]

As a student at Dartmouth University in 1983, Laura Ingraham wrote for the school newspaper, the *Dartmouth Review*, and while researching a story on controversial music Professor William Cole, audited his class. Cole was known for frequently sharing his Marxist-socialist views with his students, and when Ingraham's story reported those sentiments as well his lax grading policies, Cole reportedly confronted her in her residence hall. Cole demanded that she apologize to him, and when she refused, he launched into an obscenity-laden tirade in front of the class. Unknown to Cole, another *Dartmouth Review* reporter was present and wrote an article on the incident. Cole later sued both the newspaper and Ingraham for defamation and asked for $2.4 million in damages. The case was settled out of court, with the financial settlement not disclosed. Today, Ingraham is a nationally known conservative radio talk show host and continues to be a critic of higher education.[124]

In 1990, Ronald Rosenberger and other Christian students at the University of Virginia founded *Wide Awake*, a magazine to provide as alternative news source for conservative students. The student editors were successful in arranging for *Wide Awake* to be registered as an official student organization, and its inaugural issue, which included articles taking the Christian view of racism, unwed mothers, homosexuality, and eating disorders, was met with mixed reviews.

After that first issue was published, however, the students' request for $6,000 from the student activity fee pool was denied. The later denial was based on the administration's view of the paper as one that "promoted or manifested a particular belief in or about a deity or an ultimate reality."[125] The student editors took their appeal to every university administrator involved in the school's student-fee system, and each of them upheld the denial.

Rosenberger contacted the Center for Individual Rights, which helped him file suit against UVA. The Federal District Court for the Western District of Virginia ruled in favor of the university, as did the Fourth Circuit Court of Appeals. Rosenberger and CIR then appealed to the U.S. Supreme Court, which agreed to review the case during its 1994-1995 session. The Court reversed the decisions of the two lower courts and ruled that the university had violated the students' First Amendment rights of free press and free exercise of religion by not funding a student organization that the university had otherwise recognized as official. The Court further ruled that the university would not have violated the First Amendment's establishment clause by funding a student publication with a particular religious viewpoint.[126]

Today, *Wide Awake* is still popular at the university, but is published online rather than in print.

In 1996, student journalists at Virginia Polytechnic Institute learned about the danger of using placeholders on the pages of the student newspaper, the *Collegiate Times*. A story about the success of students participating in the Governor's Fellows Program included a quote box that featured a comment from administrator Sharon Yeagle. Unable to recall Yeagle's formal title, a placeholder line beneath her name identified Yeagle with the moniker, "Director of Butt Licking." Under deadline pressure, the paper went to press with the temporary line still in place.

The newspaper staff apologized, but that wasn't enough for Yeagle, whose actual title was vice president of student affairs. She filed a defamation suit based on Virginia's libel statute. The trial court dismissed the claim, ruling that the bogus title was "void of any literal meaning," was analogous to a satirical cartoon, and that "no reasonable person would conclude that the title conveyed factual information."

In her appeal to the Virginia Supreme Court, Yeagle claimed that a literal interpretation of the phrase connotes moral turpitude under a state statute outlawing sodomy and suggested that "she performs her job in an artificial, shallow, or other manner that generally lacks integrity." As a result, she claimed, the article harmed her career.

On February 27, 1998, the Court announced it agreed with the lower court's ruling and dismissed her claim.[127]

In October 2003, the student newspaper at St. Cloud State University in Minnesota published an article covering the lawsuit filed against the school by Richard Lewis, the former dean of the College of Social Sciences. Lewis had accused the university of age discrimination for removing him as dean.

The article in the *University Chronicle* made a simple lawsuit more complex. It accused Lewis of being anti-Semitic and treating the author of the article unfairly in one of his classes. Realizing too late that many of the charges in the article could not be substantiated, the *Chronicle* retracted the article on November 20. Unable to win his discrimination suit against the university, Lewis then focused his attention on the article and sued the university for defamation in March 2004. Lewis's attorney claimed that the article was published "with reckless disregard for the truth or with a high degree of knowledge of the statement's probable falsity."[128]

The county trial ruled against Lewis and in favor of the university, determining that the school could not be held liable for content in the paper because it did not attempt to exercise editorial control. A state appeals court confirmed that ruling.[129]

As a nineteen-year-old member of the student newspaper staff at Manatee Community College in Bradenton, Florida, David Kalwinski was thinking about student apathy—not the First Amendment—when he walked through a conference center where various student organizations had set up tables hoping to recruit new members. Kalwinski was puzzled as to why so few students had bothered to attend the event. That was midway through the fall semester of 2003, and the resulting story, titled "Dude, Where's My Student Activities?" caused a controversy that lasted the remainder of the school year.

Doug Osman, faculty adviser to *The Lance*, read the first draft of the story only because it was written as a class assignment in an introductory journalism class Osman taught. Osman called the called the first draft "kind of malicious," "potentially libelous," and "not well-researched." He also admonished Kalwinski for not disclosing that he was involved in student government—one of the organizations mentioned in the article—and had interviewed a number of his friends without disclosing their relationships. Osman accused Kalwinski of a conflict of interest and suggested that he either substantially rewrite the article or turn his notes over to someone else who could. When Kalwinski refused, Osman ordered the story killed.

That might have the end of the story if copies of the preliminary draft had not been leaked to administrators. When Kalwinski went to office of the college president for an interview on an unrelated topic, he saw a copy of the "Dude" story on the man's desk.

"Everybody had a copy of it," editor Jim Malec said. "Everybody had something to say about it."[130]

The more criticism the still-unpublished story generated, the more determined that Kalwinski and Malec were to see it published. After weeks of rewriting and trying to persuade Osman to agree that it should be published, the three were at a stalemate. Then Malec sought the advice of the Student Press Law Center, where lawyers told him that the final decision on what to publish lay with the student editor, not the adviser.

Kalwinski and Malec put more work into the story, clarifying quotes, adding new material, and removing potentially libelous details. When the paper was ready, Malec and Kalwinski drove the artwork directly to the printer without Osman knowing about it. In order to keep the papers out of Osman's hands as long as possible, they passed them out directly to students. Osman was outraged when he learned the students had defied his directive, even though the published article was far different from the version Osman had spiked. But Osman complained that certain parts of the story were still problematic. One of the quotes to which he objected was one from student government officer Jeff Snyder, who said that "students who came here to party should have gone instead to University of Florida, Central Florida, or Florida State."[131]

The story generated a lot of buzz across campus and even around the town of Bradenton, which was unusual in that MCC was a school where controversy and conflict were rare. It also came to the attention of the local daily newspaper, the *Bradenton Herald.* Reporters there decided to follow up, not only on the power struggle between the students and their adviser, but on the original issue of student apathy. *Herald* writers filed public records requests for documents related to student organization funding and even questioned Osman's credentials to serve as the paper's adviser.

After six months and twenty-four meetings involving Malec, Kalwinski, Osman, and numerous MCC administrators, the controversy eventually died. Both the student journalists and Osman kept their jobs, and the inquiries of the *Herald* into university funding procedures failed to uncover anything newsworthy. And the central question of the cause of student apathy was never fully answered.[132]

In 2004, Kansas State University removed journalism professor Ron Johnson as faculty adviser to the *Kansas State Collegian*. Journalism school director Todd Simon said Johnson was dismissed because of the "overall quality" of the paper as compared to those of newspapers at peer institutions. Johnson, however, claimed his dismissal was based on the paper's decision not to cover campus diversity issues, including a regional diversity leadership conference hosted by KSU.

Johnson and student editors Katie Lane and Sarah Rice filed suit against Simon and Stephen White, dean of the College of Arts and Sciences, claiming that Johnson's removal was a violation of the First Amendment. A Federal District Court ruled in favor of the university, determining that the personnel move was not a First Amendment issue because it was related to the "sub-par scope and overall content" rather than "specific content" of the paper. Lane and Rice appealed the case to the Tenth Circuit, but Johnson declined to participate. He accepted reassignment to a full-time teaching role in the school's journalism school, where he remained until 2008.

In an amicus curie brief filed on behalf of the students, the SPLC argued that if university administrators can "take punitive action against a student newspaper based on protected content decisions simply by justifying their action based on the 'overall content' of the publication, no editor can feel safe. . . . Today the complaint of the university is concern about a 'lack of diversity coverage,' tomorrow it could be concerns about insufficient coverage of an administrator's pet project or excessive coverage of campus crime." In 2007, a three-judge panel for the Tenth Circuit Court of Appeals ruled the case was moot because Lane and Rice were no longer enrolled at the school, and therefore they lacked standing to claim abridgment of their First Amendment rights.[133]

The previous year, at Vincennes University in Indiana, students had taken their support of an embattled faculty adviser a step further than students at KSU—by creating a competing underground newspaper. The paper, which was published only one time and at the students' expense, was called *The Intelligencer*. It was created to support the case of Michael Mullen, who was stripped of his duties as adviser to the *Trailblazer* and moved from the journalism program to the English Department. Much like the KSU case, administrators claim the move was based on the "overall quality" of the official paper, but Mullen and the students believed that administrators were firing a "warning shot" because of the articles critical of university leadership.

The case began in April 2003 when the copies of the paper's April Fool's Day edition disappeared from the racks. University officials claimed the issue was "vulgar and in bad taste," but nonetheless promised to investigate the apparent thefts. The paper had also published a controversial story about a recent drop in student enrollment and another that questioned the credentials of university President John R. Gregg, a former speaker of the Indiana House of Representatives.

Mullen claimed that the university violated his First and Fourteenth Amendment rights, basing the latter charge on a lack of due process. According to his lawyer, Ida Lamberti, the university's appeal process specified that employees with grievances could have them heard by persons not involved in the original decision. In Mullen's case, however, everyone he spoke to when appealing his case was party to the university's original action.

In February 2006, Mullen and the university reached an out-of-court settlement, with terms remaining unannounced.[134] As of early 2016, Mullen remains as a full professor in the English Department and recently celebrated his twenty-fifth anniversary at Vincennes.

––––––––––

During fall semester 2004, student journalists at Florida Atlantic University published a series of stories critical of student government officers for voting themselves a retroactive pay raise. The offended officers retaliated against the *University Press* by demanding the staff members surrender their keys to the newspaper's offices. The officers claimed their actions were not related to the negative stories, but were instead based on a paperwork issue, as the employment contracts for the newspaper staff had not been approved. The newspaper staffers disputed that claim, and closed-door meetings between the two student organizations averted a lockout.

The situation illustrated the danger of having one student organization hold so much power over the student newspaper. Ironically, the unusual relationship had been designed to curb the potential for administrative meddling seen thirty years earlier in the case of *Schiff v. Williams* (discussed earlier in this chapter).[135]

––––––––––

In 2004, the *State Press Magazine*, a weekly publication affiliated with Arizona State University's *State Press* newspaper, published a detailed story about the dangers of extreme body piercing. To draw attention to it, the magazine's cover showed photographer Andrew Benson's full-page image of a female nipple that had been pierced with a piece of jewelry.

ASU administrators threatened to cut off funding if the magazine published "offensive" material in the future. While student editors defended their decisions and refused to apologize, they did agree to work with administrators to develop internal guidelines to help future staffers deal with controversial material.

Meanwhile, one of the university's major donors was neither amused by the photo nor impressed by the compromise between the staff and administration. Ira Fulton, founder of Tempe-based Fulton Homes, had given $58 million to the university in the past two years and saw ASU's prestigious School of Engineering named after him. Offended by the nipple photo and accompanying article, Fulton called ASU President Michael Crow directly. Crow immediately admonished the paper over the photo and article, but he and Fulton denied rumors that he did so at Fulton's urging or that future Fulton donations were at risk.

The magazine won a Payne Award for Ethics in Journalism for its responsible handling of the controversy.[136]

In the fall of 2004, the chancellor at the University of Illinois believed the school's official newspaper had strayed so far from its purpose that he threatened to help students create a rival newspaper that would be more responsible. The controversy began with material in the *Daily Illini* that offended Jewish students. Examples included a cartoon that played on the stereotype of Jewish bankers being obsessed with profit and an opinion piece quoting Israeli Prime Minister Arial Sharon threatening to "burn every Palestinian child."[137] The quote had never been verified and government officials in Israel deny that Sharon ever said that. The writer apologized for the quote in a subsequent column, but it was repeated by another student in a letter to the editor.

Chancellor Richard Herman told *Daily Illini* the staff of his plans at the end of fall semester, and over the holiday break he met with the paper's adviser and several of its senior editors. Herman reportedly told the staff he believed the offensive material was published with the intention of stirring up the campus, but the editors claimed it resulted more from carelessness than malice. After the *Chicago Sun-Times* criticized Herman's plan to create a rival publication, the chancellor backed down from the plan. "In no way do I wish to censor the Daily Illini," he told the *Sun-Times*. "But it is also my responsibility to challenge student journalists to be deeply thoughtful about their work, which affects many thousands of people."[138]

Two years later at the same university, a student newspaper editor and opinion columnist were suspended and then fired after publishing cartoons critical of the Muslim prophet Muhammad—the same cartoons that caused deadly riots in Europe after being published in a Danish newspaper.

The *Daily Illini* had one of the more unusual leadership structures of any college newspaper in the country. While published by an off-campus, private company called Illini Media Co., the paper's day-to-day operations are entirely student run. Policy and oversight are provided by a board of directors consisting of four students and four faculty members. The board had previously set a policy barring the paper from publishing "inflammatory material." *Daily Illini* editor Acton Gorton and columnist Chuck Prochaska disputed the scope of the policy, claiming that it was designed to apply only to advertising. But the board of directors and interim editor Jason Koch disagreed, claiming that it applied to news and opinion content as well.

The call for Gorton's and Prochaska's suspension came not from the board itself, but from other students on the newspaper staff who complained the decision was made without their input. Gorton and Prochaska disputed that claim. The board of directors formed a committee to investigate how the decision to publish the cartoons was made, but it was unable to determine the level of input other staff members had.

Gorton and Prochaska were both unsuccessful in appealing their suspensions to the board of directors. The interim editors later offered to reinstate Prochaska, but he declined.

In its summary of the case, the Student Press Law Center determined that the firing of the two staffers would have been more defensible if the decision had been made by higher-ranking students on the editorial board. But since Gorton was the editor of the paper, there were no higher-ranking students to discipline him. The SPLC stopped short of supporting the editor and columnist's complaints, claiming that the unusual relationship between the paper and the private company meant the firings were problematic but not illegal.[139]

In 2011, *La Voz de Aztlan*, a radical left-wing supplement to Fresno State University's student newspaper, published a poem steeped in anti-American sentiment. It referred to America as "the land robbed by the white savage," the "land of the biggest genocide," the "place of greed and slavery," the "rapist of the earth," and the "land of the brute, the bully, the land of glorified killers, the eater of souls."[140]

The poem's publication sparked an immediate controversy, beginning with conservative students who questioned the propriety of the poem's selection. They claimed they were bullied by university officials in retaliation for the negative publicity the case brought to the FSU campus.

The controversy began when Neil O'Brien, a politically active Fresno State student who had founded the university's Young Americans for Liberty chapter and organized local Tea Party events, stumbled across the poem in *La Voz* and was outraged by its message. He confronted two faculty members in the Chicano and Latin American Studies Department, demanding to know whether the professors approved of the poem's content and publication.

Openly recording his interactions on video, O'Brien stood peacefully at the office doors of Victor Torres, faculty adviser to the publication, and his colleague, Maria Lopes. Both professors refused to respond, and instead reported O'Brien to campus police.

O'Brien provided his video recording to campus police, who examined it and determined that he had not demonstrated "threatening or intimidating" behavior that would have violated campus policy. Apparently unsatisfied with that finding, Torres and Lopes then petitioned the campus police to change their ruling to one less favorable for O'Brien.

Despite campus police absolving him of any wrongdoing, O'Brien received a letter from Carolyn Coon, assistant dean of student affairs, summoning him to a "judicial conference" on the basis of his actions. Torres and Lopes claimed they felt "threatened" and "endangered." O'Brien had to appear before Coon—without legal representation—or potentially have a disciplinary hold on his record.

Two months after that one-sided "conference," O'Brien received word from Dean Coon that charges had been filed against him for violating the Student Conduct Code, which prohibited behavior that "threatens or endangers the health or safety of any person . . . including physical abuse, threats, intimidation, harassment, or sexual misconduct."[141] O'Brien would have to appear at a judicial hearing, again without counsel, where he could contest the charges.

Several university leaders attended that hearing, including hearing officer Marcus Freeman, dean of social sciences Luz Gonzalez, Coon, Lopes, and Torres. Shockingly, even though he declined to watch the video recorded by O'Brien—the one reviewed by campus police showing O'Brien did not violate university rules—hearing officer Freeman found O'Brien in violation of the Student Conduct Code.

Freeman recommended prohibiting O'Brien from coming within 100 feet of CLS staff, faculty, offices, or classrooms, and also barring him from coming onto the second floor of the social sciences building unless he had a class or scheduled appointment. Coon applied the recommended sanctions and further placed O'Brien on disciplinary probation through the spring 2012 semester, well after he was scheduled to graduate. Such punishments, which could not be appealed, meant that O'Brien no longer could serve as an officer in any student organization.

Naming Coon, Torres, Lopes, and more than twenty-five other school faculty and staff as defendants, O'Brien filed suit for violation and conspiracy to violate his civil rights to free speech, due process, and equal protection. The suit also claimed that the California Code of Regulations, "which authorizes branches of California State University to discipline students for conduct that 'threatens or endangers the health or safety of any person . . . including . . . intimidation [or] harassment,'" was unconstitutionally vague.

In May 2013, nearly eighteen months after his panel hearing at Fresno State, the District Court for the Eastern District of California rejected the case, stating that O'Brien's actions were "nothing short of harassment and at least attempted intimidation."[142] The court also held that the California Code of Regulations was not "unconstitutionally overbroad or vague." On appeal, the Ninth Circuit upheld the lower court.[143]

At Bryan College in Tennessee, the student newspaper wanted to publish a story based on the August 2012 arrest of a biblical studies professor accused of attempted child molestation. David Morgan had already resigned after being arrested when he met two underage girls at a gas station in Ft. Oglethorpe, Georgia.

College president Stephen Livesay insisted the story planned for *The Triangle* be deleted, prompting editor Alex Green to instead post fliers publicizing the arrest around campus. "Bryan College is not Penn State," the fliers said, referring to the child molestation scandals that were uncovered at PSU the previous year.

Livesay claimed he ordered the story deleted from the paper because it was based on "facts that could not be confirmed," but the local media covering the story pointed out that the critical information came from Federal Bureau of Investigation sources and the Catoosa County Sheriff's Office. Livesay later said he was "disappointed" with the fliers but chose not to refer Green for disciplinary proceedings.[144]

At Fairmont State University in West Virginia, three student newspaper editors resigned in 2012 to protest the dismissal of their faculty adviser, Michael Kelly. Although administrators denied it, students claimed Kelly was dismissed because he encouraged them to pursue a series of investigative stories regarding the problem of toxic mold in the university's older buildings. Former editor Jacob Buckland told the media that the university preferred the newspaper function as a "PR front for the university rather than a watchdog."[145]

At the University of Memphis in 2012, reporter Chelsea Boozer claimed she was harassed by campus police after she wrote articles questioning the police department's slow response to a sexual assault and reporting that the school's football program was losing money. Administrators also cut the newspaper's operating budget.

After months of controversy, the funding was restored and Boozer received the Emerging Journalist Award from the UM Alumni Association and the SPLC's College Press Freedom Award.[146]

At Pensacola State College in Florida, faculty gave president Ed Meadows a "no confidence" vote in October 2014. The student newspaper, *The Corsair*, heard about the vote and published a front-page story about it on October 31. When staff members working on a follow-up story approached vice president of academic affairs Tom Gilliam about the ramifications of the vote, he informed them that it was part of ongoing negotiations between faculty and administrators and it would be illegal for them to discuss it in detail.

The newspaper staff then received a cease-and-desist letter from a Tallahassee-based law firm representing the college. It informed the students that the faculty members who provided them information for the original story violated a state law by involving students in the negotiating process. In his own response to the story, Meadows said, "It is my personal belief that bargaining should take place at the table and not be debated in the media."[147] United Faculty of Florida, the statewide union representing all of the state's college and university faculty members, accused Meadows of trying to "bully" the students out of their free speech rights and promised to intervene on behalf of the students if PSC administrators continued to harass the newspaper staff.

As of early 2016, Meadows was still president of PSC, and *The Corsair* was still publishing information about labor negotiations, over the objections of Meadows and other administrators.[148]

At Butler University, the student newspaper's four-year track record of winning journalism awards wasn't enough for Loni McKown to keep her job as its adviser.

During her tenure, the newspaper won an award from Investigative Reporters and Editors for its story documenting that a newly hired administrator had a criminal record in his home country of South Africa.

In hindsight, McKown believes the paper may have been *too* successful. As late as April 2015, she received glowing evaluations from her superiors, but after she accidentally forwarded an email regarding the university's budget to newspaper staffers without noticing it was marked "confidential," her superiors used it as an excuse to remove her as adviser while allowing her to remain on the faculty of the journalism department.

The real reason for her reassignment, McKown believed, was her "hands-on" approach to advising the paper. She received a written notice that she was no longer allowed to advise the newspaper, *The Butler Collegian*, either "directly or indirectly."

What infuriated newspaper staffers and journalism alumni the most was that her temporary replacement as adviser was a member of the university's public relations staff. That reinforced the criticism that university officials preferred the paper to function as a "PR tool" for the university.

"It's a clear conflict of interest for a university public relations professional to advise a college newspaper," wrote Rachele Kanigel, president of the College Media Association, in an official statement opposing the personnel move. "How could students feel free to seek this person's advice when his primary job is to protect the university's image and reputation?"[149]

After weeks of negative publicity, administrators replaced the public relations staffer with another faculty member who would advise the paper until a permanent replacement could be hired.[150]

While university administrators may have little control over student newspapers, that is not the case with student-run television and radio stations because of the Federal Communications Commission licensing procedure. In 1982, for example, the president of Indian River Community College in Florida instructed the staff of campus radio station WQCS to cease broadcasting stories that were critical of area real estate developers, many of whom were also major donors to the college. President Herman Heise claimed the stories, many of them provided by National Public Radio, were "slanted" and might cause contributors to withdraw their support of the college. Heise also attempted to prohibit Brian Schneider, manager of the station, from interviewing state legislator Dale Patchett.

When Schneider refused to go along with the president's admonitions, Heise sent him a letter of termination, prompting Schneider to sue the college in Federal District Court.

After seven years of litigation, both the Federal District Court and Court of Appeals for the Eleventh Circuit ruled that the college's board of trustees held the power to regulate content on the station because the FCC license was issued to them—not to the students or their adviser—and they had the right to delegate control of the station to the university president. While the Court ruled that administrators had the right to control content, it could not exercise any authority over personnel, meaning the firing of the station manager had been unconstitutional. [151]

Student journalists at Syracuse University met a similar fate in the fall of 2005—not only because of nature of broadcast regulation, but because of the Syracuse's status as a private institution. The controversy began when the students produced a news-parody program in the style of *The Daily Show with Jon Stewart*. Titled *Over the Hill*, the program was broadcast on the student-run television station, HillTV, and included stories about "smelly Indian kids," jokes about disabled students, and sexual entendres directed at Chancellor Nancy Cantor.

Cantor reacted by attempting to permanently disband the station. Journalism Professor Charlotte Grimes said Cantor's move created a "bitter, emotional, and very divided debate on campus," while Associate Dean Joel Kaplan described it as a "paternalistic, improper role for the chancellor of a university. . . . It was a raw display of power. . . . why not just let the students work it out?" [152]

An appeals panel consisting of faculty members inside and outside of the journalism school overturned Cantor's directive but attempted to find a middle ground by requiring the staff of the station to form a "Cultural Competence Committee" to evaluate content that might potential offend minority groups on campus. [153]

NOTES

1. "Why Our Story Named Names." *The Parthenon*, September 22, 1992, p. 7.
2. Tom D. Miller, "Rape Case Divides Marshall Campus." *Herald-Dispatch*, October 15, 1992.
3. Janet L. Johnson, "Reporting Rape a Major Decision." *The Parthenon*, October 9, 1992.
4. Pat Young, "Mother Appalled by Assault Story." *The Parthenon*, September 29, 1992.
5. Ralph J. Turner, "Editors Thoughtful in Making Decision." *The Parthenon,* September 29, 1992.
6. Harold C. Shaver, "Naming Names Not a Gender Issue." *The Parthenon*, October 7, 1992.
7. David Rogers, "MU Officials Open Fire on The Parthenon." *Herald-Dispatch*, September 30, 1992, p. A-2.
8. Tim Massey, "Gilley Says Problem Goes Beyond Parthenon." *Herald-Dispatch*, October 8, 1992.
9. Gary Smith and Andrea Runion, "Panel Says U.S. Constitution Doesn't Apply to Student Paper." *The Parthenon*, October 16, 1992.
10. Smith and Runion.
11. Smith and Runion.
12. Chris Miller, "Board Controls Marshall Paper." *Charleston Gazette*, October 17, 1992.
13. Tom D. Miller, "Gilley Sets up Board to Oversee Marshall's Student Publications." *Herald-Dispatch*, October 17, 1992.

14. Tom D. Miller, "Gilley Sets up Board to Oversee Marshall's Student Publications."

15. Wallace E. Knight, "Gilley's Order Will Harm MU Journalism for Years." *Herald-Dispatch*, October 22, 1992.

16. Knight

17. Knight.

18. "Marshall Mess." *Charleston Gazette*, October 18, 1992.

19. Dave Payton, "Gilley's Broad-Based Committee Flies in the Face of Court Rulings." *Herald-Dispatch*, October 21, 1992.

20. David Rogers, "Gilley Denies He Threatened Job." *Herald-Dispatch*, October 23, 1992.

21. Smith and Runion.

22. Massey, "Gilley, Journalism Faculty to Discuss Compromise Board." *Herald-Dispatch*, November 13, 1992. See also: Massey, "MU Media Control Battle Halted." *Herald-Dispatch*, November 17, 1992.

23. Randy Bobbitt, "Lou Grant in Sweat Socks." *The Tampa Tribune*, September 1, 1981, p. D-1.

24. Leo Reisberg, "Student Press at Black Colleges Face a New Wave of Censorship." *Chronicle of Higher Education*, March 3, 2000, p. 37-A.

25. *Dickey v. Alabama State Board of Education*, 273 F. Supp 613 (1967). See also: *Law of the Student Press*. Arlington, VA: Student Press Law Center, 1993, p. 104.

26. *Antonelli v. Hammond*, 308 F. Supp 1329 (1970).

27. *Trujillo v. Love,* 322 F. Supp 1266 (1971).

28. *Bazaar v. Fortune*, 489 F.2d 225 (1973).

29. *Joyner v. Whiting*, 477 F. 2d 456 (1973).

30. *Schiff v. Williams*, 519 F.2d 257 (1975).

31. *Stanley v. McGrath,* 719 F. 2d 279 283 (1983).

32. *Kincaid v. Gibson*, 191 F.3d 719 (1999).

33. *Kincaid v. Gibson.*

34. Billy O'Keefe, "Court Rules in Favor of Free Speech." *The Seahawk* (University of North Carolina Wilmington), January 11, 2001, p. 3.

35. Joe Strupp, "Censored, Censored, Censored." *Editor & Publisher*, September 18, 1999. p. 12.

36. O'Keefe.

37. O'Keefe.

38. *Hosty v. Carter,* 412 F.3d 731 (2005).

39. *Hosty v. Carter.*

40. Geoffrey C. Campbell, "Trials, Tribulations, and Ongoing Litigation." *Fort Worth Star-Telegram*, October 2, 2005.

41. *Hosty v. Carter.*

42. College Media Advisors news release, February 21, 2006.

43. *Blahut v. Oden* (Case 05C 4989 N.D. Ill.), 2001.

44. *Channing Club v. Texas Tech University*, 317 F.Supp. 688 (1970).

45. *Papish v. Board of Curators of the University of Missouri*, 410 U.S. 677 (1973). See also: Charles A. Kors and Harvey A. Silverglate, *The Shadow University: The Betrayal of Liberty on America's Campuses*. New York: Simon and Shuster, 1998, pp. 46-47.

46. *New Hampshire v. Seil*, 8 Med.L. Rep. 1625 (1982). See also: Wayne Overbeck, *Major Principles of Media Law*. Fort Worth, TX: Harcourt Brace, 1999, p. 522.

47. *Zurcher v. Stanford Daily* (1978). See also: *Branzburg v. Hayes*, 408 U.S. 665 (1972).

48. Bobbitt, *Exploring Communication Law*, p. 193.

49. Allan Wolper, "Student Journalists Forced to Give Police Unpublished Photos." *Editor & Publisher,* January 28, 1995, pp. 16-19.

50. Wolper.

51. Wolper.

52. Wolper.

53. Peter Baniak, "Videotapes Subpoenaed Over Fan Violence." *Lexington Herald-Leader*, April 6, 1996, p. 1-C.

54. SPLC Alert, March 21, 2001.

55. "What Every Student Journalist Should Know." *Quill*, September 1997, pp. 44-49. See also: Debra Gersh Hernandez, "House Demands Enforcement." *Editor & Publisher*, November 2, 1996, pp. 10-12

56. Kim Strosnider, "Ohio's Top Court Orders Miami U. to Give Disciplinary Records to Student Paper." *Chronicle of Higher Education*, July 10, 1997.

57. Bobbitt, *Exploring Communication Law*, p. 93.

58. Open Records and Meetings Opinion, No. 2008-07, office of the North Dakota Attorney General).

59. Don R. Pember and Clay Calvert, *Mass Media Law*. New York: McGraw Hill, 2015, p. 101.

60. *Shuck v. Daily Herald*, 215 Iowa 1276 (1933).

61. *Lee v. Board of Regents*, 306 F.Supp. 1096 (1969).

62. *Lee v. Board of Regents*. See also: George E. Stevens and John B. Webster, *Law of the Student Press*. Ames, IA: University of Iowa Press, 1973, pp. 66-7.

63. *Sinn v. Daily Nebraskan*, 829 F.2d 662 (Eighth Circuit, 1987). See also: "Students and ACLU Fight for the Right to Advertise Alcohol Advertising in Newspapers." *SPLC Report*, Spring 1999, p. 36.

64. Bobbitt, *Exploring Communication Law*, p. 253.

65. Kenneth S. Devol, *Major Areas of Conflict in the Control of College and University Student Daily Newspapers in the United States*. Ph.D. dissertation, University of Southern California, 1965, p. 200. See also: George E. Stephens, and John B. Webster, *Law and the Student Press*. Ames, IA: The Iowa State University Press, 1973, p. 63.

66. Ken Paulson, "How Free is Campus Speech?" Syndicated newspaper column, April 24, 2001.

67. Paulson, "How Free is Campus Speech?"

68. Paulson, "How Free is Campus Speech?"

69. *New York Times v. Sullivan*, 376 U.S. 254 (1964). See also: Paulson, "How Free is Campus Speech?" "Battle Brews Over Alcohol Ads in College Media," *SPLC Report*, Fall 1999.

70. Paulson, "How Free is Campus Speech?"

71. "The Price of Paid Speech." *SPLC Report*, Spring 2001, pp. 14-17.

72. "The Price of Paid Speech."

73. "The Price of Paid Speech."

74. Mencher, "Put it to Rest: Holocaust Denial Ads Should be Refused." *College Media Review*, Winter 2002, pp. 24-27).

75. Mencher, "Put it to Rest: Holocaust Denial Ads Should be Refused."

76. Alison Alexander and Jarice Hanson, *Taking Sides: Clashing Views on Controversial Issues in Mass Media and Society*. Guilford, CT: Dushkin Publishing, 2013, p. 190.

77. Alexander and Hanson.

78. Alexander and Hanson.

79. Mencher, "Put it to Rest: Holocaust Denial Ads Should be Refused."

80. Mencher, "Put it to Rest: Holocaust Denial Ads Should be Refused."

81. Mencher, "Put it to Rest: Holocaust Denial Ads Should be Refused."

82. Mencher, "Put it to Rest: Holocaust Denial Ads Should be Refused."

83. Shawn W. Murphy, "Furor Over Holocaust Denial Ad Publication Raises Pros, Cons." *College Media Review*, Fall 1999, pp. 9-11.

84. Murphy.

85. Murphy.

86. Murphy.

87. Murphy.

88. "The Price of Paid Speech."

89. "The Price of Paid Speech."

90. *Lueth v. St Claire County Community College*, 732 F. Supp. 1410 (E.D. Michigan 1990); see also *Law of the Student Press*, Arlington, VA: Student Press Law Center, 1994, p. 55.

91. *Lueth v. St Claire County Community College*.

92. "Students and ACLU Fight for the Right to Advertise Alcohol Advertising in Newspapers." *SPLC Report*, Spring 1999, p. 36.

93. *Central Hudson v. Public Service Commission*, 447 U.S. 557 (1980). See also: Bobbitt, *Exploring Communication Law*, p. 249.

94. *Pitt News v. Pappert*, 379 F. 3d 96 (3d Cir. 2004). See also: "Private Universities, Newspapers Clash Over Ads." *SPLC Report*, Spring 2004, p. 38. "Students and ACLU Fight for the Right to Advertise Alcohol Advertising in Newspapers." *SPLC Report*, Spring 1999, p. 36. "Battle Brews Over Alcohol Ads in College Media," *SPLC Report*, Fall 1999.

95. "Private Universities, Newspapers Clash Over Ads."

96. "Court: Ban on Alcohol Ads in College Newspapers Unconstitutional." CNN.oom, July 30, 2004.

97. "Court: Ban on Alcohol Ads in College Newspapers Unconstitutional."

98. "ACLU Fights for the Right to Advertise Alcohol Advertising in Newspapers." See also: "Battle Brews Over Alcohol Ads in College Media."

99. "ACLU Fights for the Right to Advertise Alcohol Advertising in Newspapers."

100. "ACLU Fights for the Right to Advertise Alcohol Advertising in Newspapers."

101. "ACLU Fights for the Right to Advertise Alcohol Advertising in Newspapers."

102. "ACLU Fights for the Right to Advertise Alcohol Advertising in Newspapers."

103. George E. Stevens and John B. Webster, *Law of the Student Press*. Ames, IA: University of Iowa Press, 1973, pp. 67-8.

104. *Mississippi Gay Alliance v. Goudelock,* 536 F.2d 1073 (1976).

105. Rachele Kanigel, *The Student Newspaper Survival Guide*. Malden, MA: Wiley-Blackwell, 2012, p. 169-170.

106. "Newspaper Thieves Face Punishment." *SPLC Report*, Spring 2000, p. 7.

107. Wayne Overbeck, *Major Principles of Media Law*. Boston: Wadsworth, 2009, p. 594.

108. Kanigel, p. 169-170.

109. "Newspaper Thieves Face Punishment."

110. "Newspaper Thieves Face Punishment."

111. "Thieves Filch Newspapers at Six Colleges." *SPLC Report*, Spring 2000, p. 8.

112. "Thieves Filch Newspapers at Six Colleges."

113. "Hit List Story Prompts Theft of 1,300 Newspapers." *SPLC Report*, March 2006.

114. "Stolen Papers Cost $6,500, Editor Says." *SPLC Report*, March 31, 2006.

115. "Student Journalists Still Waiting for Answers." *SPLC Report*, March 2006.

116. "Student Admits to Taking 800 Copies of Student Paper." *SPLC Report*, March 2006.

117. "Anonymous Caller Warns Student Editor of Newspaper Theft." *SPLC Report*, March 2006.

118. "Around 8,000 Papers Stolen at KSU." *SPLC Report*, March 2006.

119. "Student Editor Says University Doesn't Care About Theft." *SPLC Report*, March 2006.

120. "Student Editor Says University Doesn't Care About Theft."

121. Pember and Calvert, p. 104.

122. Bobbitt, "Lou Grant in Sweat Socks."

123. Bobbitt, "Lou Grant in Sweat Socks."

124. Bobbitt, *Us Against Them: The Political Culture of Talk Radio*. Lanham, MD: Lexington Books, p. 113.

125. *Rosenberger v. Rector and Visitors of the University of Virginia*, 515 U.S. 819 (1995).

126. Ibid.

127. *Yeagle v. Collegiate Times*, Virginia Public Record No. 971304; see also: Libby Fraas, "Censorship of Student Press Violates a Fundamental Freedom." *Lexington Herald-Leader*, April 3, 2009.

128. "Court Dismisses Libel Suit." *SPLC LegalAlert*, September 2004.

129. Kelley Benham, "First Amendment 101." *St. Petersburg Times*, July 22, 2004.

130. Benham.

131. Benham.

132. Benham.

133. *Lane v. Simon*, 495 F. 3d 1182 (2005); see also: "Federal Court Dismisses Suit," *SPLC LegalAlert*, September 2005 and December 2005.

134. "Students at Indiana College Go Underground," *SPLC LegalAlert*, September 2004. See also: "Former Advisor Settles Lawsuit Against University." *SPLC LegalAlert*, March 2006.

135. "Florida Student Newspaper Avoids Newsroom Lockout." *SPLC LegalAlert*, January 2005.

136. Joe Watson, "Quid Pro Crow." *Phoenix New Times*, November 18, 2004.

137. "Tempers Cool at University of Illinois." *SPLC LegalAlert*, January 2004.

138. "Tempers Cool at University of Illinois."

139. "University of Illinois Student Editor Fired After Publishing Muhammad Cartoons." *SPLC LegalAlert*, April 2006.

140. Clark Connor, "Vague Campus Rules Undermine Students' Due Process and Free Speech Rights." PopeCenter.org, May 27, 2016.

141. Connor.

142. Connor.

143. Connor.

144. "College Censors News Story of Professor's Arrest." Associated Press Report, September 27, 2012.

145. David R. Wheeler, "The Plot Against Student Newspapers?" *The Atlantic*, September 30, 2015.

146. Wheeler.

147. Steve Poulin, "Free Speech and Faculty Morale at Pensacola State College." *Independent News*, December 11, 2014, p. 6.

148. Poulin.

149. Wheeler.

150. Wheeler. See also: "Butler Reverses Decision to Have Spokesperson Advise Student Paper." *Indianapolis Business Journal*, September 12, 2015.

151. *Schneider v. Indian River Community College*, 875 F. 2d 839 (1982).

152. "Syracuse University's Commitment to Free Speech Questioned Following Campus TV Controversy." *SPLC LegalAlert*, January 2006.

153. "Syracuse University's Commitment to Free Speech Questioned Following Campus TV."

Chapter Four

Religious Issues

GOBITIS AND BARNETTE

On November 6, 1935, the school board in Minersville, Pennsylvania—a town mired in the Depression—decided that at the beginning of every school day, students should demonstrate their respect for the country and its government by standing and reciting the Pledge of Allegiance. It enacted a rule to that effect.

By the time the rule met its first court challenge, the country was in the early stages of World War II. In defending the rule, school officials argued that during wartime, allegiance to the flag, and to the country it represented, was a value so important that it should be backed up by the force of law.

Three children—siblings William and Lillian Gobitis and classmate Edmund Wasiewski—were Jehovah's Witnesses, and they told their teachers and the school principal that their faith prohibited them from worshiping inanimate objects, including the flag. The administrators did not accept that explanation, nor did the Minersville School District Board, which voted to expel all three children. Their parents sued in Federal District Court, and when the case went to trial, both sets of parents cited a Bible passage (Exodus, chapter 20, verses 4 and 5), that says, "Thou shall not make unto thee any graven image, or any likeness of anything that is in heaven above, or that is in the earth beneath, or that is in the water under the earth, though shalt not bow down thyself to them nor serve them."[1]

Both the District Court and Third Circuit Court of Appeals sided with the families. While recognizing the motive of encouraging patriotism was an admirable one—especially during wartime—the Court stated that forcing children to disobey their parents and disavow their legitimate religious beliefs was not within the purview of school authorities.

The school district appealed to the U.S. Supreme Court, which reversed the lower court rulings in 1940. The 8–1 decision shocked free speech advocates across the country, as even First Amendment advocates such as William O. Douglas, Felix Frankfurter, Hugo Black, and Chief Justice Charles E. Hughes were among the justices voting in favor of the school district. In his majority opinion, Frankfurter wrote that it was not appropriate for the Court to second-guess the authority of school officials in disciplinary matters, even when free speech was the primary issue.[2]

The lone dissent came from Justice Harlan F. Stone, who acknowledged that teaching patriotism and love of country were important goals for public schools, but also believed that schools should not be in the business of compelling students to declare a belief. He added that his interpretation of the First Amendment to the Constitution was that "government should allow for freedom of speech but cannot require someone to participate in speech."[3]

Partly in reaction to the *Gobitis* ruling, the West Virginia Legislature enacted a law much broader than the school board rule in Minersville. The West Virginia law specified that all public schools in the state would be required to conduct courses of instruction in history, civics, and the Constitution of the United States, "for the purpose of teaching, fostering, and perpetuating the ideals, principles, and spirit of Americanism, and increasing the knowledge of the organization and the mechanism of government."[4]

The legislature left it up to the state's Board of Education to handle the details of that mandate, and one of the details it chose was to require school students and teachers to recite the Pledge of Allegiance at the beginning of every school day. "Refusal to salute the flag shall be regarded as an act of insubordination, and shall be dealt with accordingly," the board's new rule stated.[5] The law specified that students who did not salute the flag could be suspended and their parents fined.

Like the Gobitis and Wasiewski families, the Barnettes were Jehovah's Witnesses and argued their cases using the same Bible passages. Even though the war was still going on at the time of the *Barnette* case, the Court reversed course from the *Gobitis* ruling, determining that individual beliefs took priority over coerced patriotism. The Court added that the flag salute was "a form of utterance which is a primitive but effective way of communicating ideas" but that the school could not mandate that students went along with it.[6]

"If there is any fixed star in our constitutional constellation, it is that no official, high or petty, can prescribe what shall be orthodox in politics, nationalism, religion, or other matters of opinion or force citizens to confess by word or act their faith therein," wrote Justice Robert Jackson in his majority opinion. "If there are any circumstances which permit an exception, they do not occur to us."[7]

The Court distinguished the *Barnette* case from one of a decade earlier in which it ruled that the display of a red flag (depicting communism) was a permissible commentary used by labor groups to complain about working conditions. It that case, the party was participating in consensual speech, while in *Barnette*, the speech was compelled. [8]

"The right of West Virginia to utilize the flag salute as part of its educational process is denied because, so it is argued, it cannot be justified as a means of meeting a "clear and present danger" to national unity," the court ruled. [9]

Seventy years after the Barnette ruling, a nearly identical case took place in Spring Hill, Florida, where a fourth-grade teacher required a student, who was a Jehovah's Witness, to recite the Pledge of Allegiance.

According to investigative reports, Anne Daigle-McDonald was leading students in the pledge when she noticed the eleven-year-old boy was standing but not reciting the pledge nor placing his hand over his heart. She twice placed the boy's hand over his heart, but he resisted, explaining that he stood beside his classmates to show respect for the country but that his religion forbade him from placing his hand over his heart. The teacher then reportedly walked to the front of the class and said, "If you don't want to say the pledge, you still have to put your hand on your heart, and if you don't want to do that, you should move out of the country." [10]

School district officials confirmed that Daigle-McDonald violated numerous school district and state rules and principles of professional conduct, as well as the student's right of freedom of speech and freedom of religion. The teacher was suspended for five days without pay and required to take a diversity training course.

In New Town, North Dakota in 2014, a six-year-old boy refused to stand for the Pledge of Allegiance. After weeks of controversy, the parties decided that the child would not be allowed to remain seated but would be allowed to come to school late or remain outside of the classroom during the pledge.

"Allowing students to exercise their rights to sit out the pledge is a matter of free speech and freedom of conscience," said David Niose, an attorney for the American Humanist Association, which assisted the child's family. [11]

The child's older brother stood during the pledge but did not recite it, a decision that the parents also supported. "We're trying to raise free thinkers," the boy's father told local media. [12]

USING SCHOOL FACILITIES

In 1980 and 1981, the U.S. Supreme Court and the Second Circuit Court of Appeals made differing rules in cases involving Christian student groups that were not allowed to use school facilities for voluntary prayer group meetings when those spaces were not being used for instructional purposes.

In the 1980 case of *Widmar v. Vincent*, the Court ruled in favor of students who sued the University of Missouri at Kansas City after administrators denied them the right to use campus facilities for prayer meetings. The Court determined that the university had violated their rights under the First Amendment's Free Exercise clause.[13]

The case of *Brandon v. Guilderland Central School District* began the previous year when students at a high school in upstate New York asked for permission to use an otherwise-empty classroom for a prayer group meeting before the start of the school day. The principal, school superintendent, and school board denied the request. The students sued the school district based on the Free Exercise clause. A Federal District Court, as well as the Second Circuit Court of Appeals, ruled in favor of the school district, determining that it had not violated the students' rights because it was not required to provide meeting space to a group that was not an official student organization and had no faculty adviser.[14]

Although the two rulings appear contradictory, there is a simple explanation. Unlike many other free speech cases—in which the Court decided in favor of the students in college campus and in favor of the administration in K-12 cases—the difference in these cases was based more on equal treatment of student groups. In the *Widmar* case, other student groups were allowed to use school facilities and the Christian group was asking only for equal treatment. In *Brandon*, the students were asking for a variance in an existing rule, which the Court ruled the school was not obligated to grant.[15]

SCHOOL PRAYER AND BIBLE READING

The landmark decision on the issue of school prayer resulted from the case of *Engel v. Vitale* (1962), in which lawyers from the American Civil Liberties Union, representing the parents of students who objected to prayer being a formal part of the school day, argued that such prayer violates the Establishment Clause of the First Amendment.

The controversy began at a public school in New Hyde Park, New York. Steven Engel, a follower of Judaism, was upset that his children were being forced to recite protestant prayers. His position was supported by followers of other non-protestant faiths, as well as atheists. The Court ruled 6-1 in favor of the plaintiffs, determining that government-written prayers served to promote a particular religious viewpoint violated the First Amendment. Despite the defendant's claims to the contrary, telling students it was "voluntary" was insufficient because of the potential for coercion.[16]

The *Engel* case set the precedent for a plethora of similar decisions over the next four decades, including *Lee v. Weisman* (1992)[17] and *Santa Fe Independent School District v. Doe* (2000).[18]

In the 1963 case of *Abington School District v. Schempp*, the Supreme Court ruled 8–1 that school-sponsored Bible reading was unconstitutional. The case began when Edward Schempp, a resident of Abington Township, Pennsylvania, and a Unitarian Universalist, was upset when his children were required to hear, and sometimes read, passages from the Bible as part of their education. The readings were required by a Pennsylvania statute, in effect since 1928, which required that "at least ten verses from the Holy Bible shall be read, without comment, at the opening of each public school on each school day" and provided that "any child shall be excused from such Bible reading, or attending such Bible reading, upon the written request of a parent or guardian."[19]

Schempp testified in the Federal District Court proceeding that he considered simply asking that his children be excused, but decided against it because he did not want his children's relationships with their teachers to be adversely affected. But by pursuing the court challenge, he was in effect asking for all students to be excused. The District Court concurred and declared the law unconstitutional. The school district appealed the ruling, and while waiting for the appeal, it reemphasized to parents that individual students could be excused from the practice with written permission.

By the time the case reached the Supreme Court, it had been consolidated with a similar case filed by Madalyn Murray O'Hair, founder of American Atheists. She had sued a school district on behalf of her son, William J. Murray III, who was required to participate in Bible readings at his school in Baltimore, Maryland.

The Supreme Court ruled in favor of Schempp and O'Hair and ruled that even voluntary participation would still violate the Establishment Clause. The only dissent came from Justice Potter Stewart, who argued that schools should not be treated differently from other government agencies, many of which employed long-standing practices that seemed inconsistent with the court's ruling, including "In God We Trust" appearing on U.S. currency, Congress beginning each session with a prayer, and even the Supreme Court's tradition of opening each session with the declaration, "may God save the United States and this honorable court."[20]

Five years after the decision, in an interview with the *New York Times*, Justice William Brennan was asked to describe the hardest decision he had to make as a justice. "The school-prayer cases," said Brennan, who wrote a concurring opinion. "The position took a long time to come around to. In the face of my whole lifelong experience as a Roman Catholic, to say that prayer was not an appropriate thing in public schools, that gave me quite a hard time. I struggled."[21]

At Pace High School in Santa Rosa County, Florida, a three-year battle over school prayer cost the school system almost $600,000 in legal fees. The controversy began in 2008 when two students, assisted by the American Civil Liberties Union, sued the administration of the school over faculty- and staff-led prayer during school hours.

Liberty Counsel, a conservative Christian group, supported the position of the administrators, who contended that no students were required to participate in the prayer.

After more than a year of preliminary hearings, the Santa Rosa County School Board agreed to eliminate all religious activity at the school in exchange for the ACLU dropping the suit. Twenty-four school officials, teachers, and students, backed by Liberty Counsel, then counter-sued the ACLU.

The plaintiffs in the second case insisted on a written agreement clarifying that the definition of "religious activity" would not include comments such as "thank heavens" or "God bless you" or a student expressing religious beliefs in a written or oral class assignment.[22]

In 2011, both cases were settled out of court, the consent degree was endorsed by both sides, and the school board reimbursed Liberty Counsel about $257,000 for its legal costs. A public records request by local media revealed the school board had already incurred $340,000 in legal fees before Liberty Counsel came to its aid. The public records also indicated that nearly all of the legal costs would be covered by the school board's liability insurance policy.[23]

"Public schools exist to educate, not indoctrinate," wrote columnist Reginald T. Dogan in the *Pensacola News Journal*. "Making prayer an official part of the school day is coercive and divisive. The Supreme Court on June 25, 1962, declared prayer in public schools to be unconstitutional. Santa

Rosa schools spent three years and thousands of dollars in legal fees to reach essentially the same conclusion."[24]

School superintendent Tim Wyrosdock told the media that if both cases had gone to trial, the costs might have exceeded $1 million—win or lose. "To spend only $257,000 is a deal," he said. ACLU regional director Susan Watson called the counter-suit a "non-issue" and accused Liberty Counsel of getting involved solely for the publicity that would help in its national fund-raising programs. "School teachers and administrators can now refocus on teaching and running the schools," Watson told the *Pensacola News Journal.* "And we should all be happy the unnecessary fighting is over."[25]

THE ELEVENTH COMMANDMENT: THOU SHALL NOT TAKE DOWN THE FIRST TEN

In the 1980 case of *Stone v. Graham*, the U.S. Supreme Court ruled that schools posting the Ten Commandments in classrooms, offices, hallways, or lobbies violated the Establishment Clause of the First Amendment because such action would suggest the school's endorsement of a religious doctrine. The case involved a Kentucky law that required—not just allowed—the Ten Commandments to be posted in every public school classroom in the state. The Court hinted in its published ruling that such a display might be allowed in cases in which there was a secular and pedagogical purpose (such as a in a bulletin board display surrounded by other historical documents). But the school officials in the *Stone* case could make no such argument, and their argument that the display was paid for by a private nonprofit organization did not change the Court's position.[26]

Three decades after *Stone*, school districts around the country were still grappling with similar cases.

One such case began in 2010 in Giles County, Virginia, when the Wisconsin-based Freedom From Religion Foundation received complaints from parents and other parties about the posting of the Ten Commandments in classrooms and hallways at Narrows High School. Over the next six months, the Commandments were removed, reposted, removed, and eventually relocated to become part of a display of historical documents that also included the Constitution, Declaration of Independence, and the National Anthem. In September 2011, FFRF and the ACLU of Virginia filed a suit on behalf of two families who claimed the posting of the Ten Commandments violated the Establishment Clause.

After months of preliminary hearings that at times became contentious, U.S. District Court Judge Michael Urbanski ordered the two sides in the conflict to seek mediation in order to avoid the legal costs, negative publicity, and emotional drain that might result from a trial. The parties eventually agreed to a resolution under which the Ten Commandments would be removed from locations within the school and could not be reposted unless another case settled before the Fourth Circuit Court of Appeals or the U.S. Supreme Court resulted in a contrary ruling. Urbanski approved the agreement.[27]

A controversy closely related to the Ten Commandments issue took place at Parkersburg South High School in Parkersburg, West Virginia, in 2014. The first issue involved the T-shirts worn by the wrestling team, which carried the Bible verse from Philippians 4:13, "I can do all things through Christ who strengthens me."[28] The passage had been the team's motto for more than a decade. The Freedom From Religion Foundation complained about the shirt in a letter to school officials, claiming the phrase violated the First Amendment's establishment clause.

Because the shirts were paid for by the wrestlers' parents, the school district resisted the effort to have the motto removed, but the school did agree to remove the same passage from a wall in the school's gymnasium and from its website.[29]

COMMENCEMENT

Between 1992 and 2000, three Supreme Court cases dealt with public schools accused of violating the Establishment Clause of the Constitution by offering prayer in various forms, and in all three cases the Court ruled against schools.

In the 1992 case of *Lee v. Weisman*, the Supreme Court ruled that a public school in Rhode Island violated the First Amendment when it invited clergy from local churches to give invocations and benedictions at graduate ceremonies because those clergy "carried the imprint of approval from the school."[30] In short, the Court ruled that such activities subjected unwilling audience members to religious influence. Despite the ruling, schools across the country, mostly those located in rural communities, practice what they call "civil disobedience" in flouting the rule.[31]

Four years later, the Court ruled in *Moore v. Ingebretsen* that a Mississippi law allowing students to give voluntary prayers at assemblies and over the school intercom was also unconstitutional.[32] In 2000, the Court ruled in *Santa Fe Independent School District v. Doe* that organized prayer at ceremonial events such as commencement exercises and sporting events also violated the First Amendment.[33]

In 2006, at Foothill High School in Carson City, Nevada, the commencement address of valedictorian Brittany McComb was cut off in mid-sentence when she began speaking about her Christian faith. McComb was one of three co-valedictorians scheduled to speak, and all three were required to submit their texts for approval by the school's assistant principal. According to news reports, the students were told they could include statements attesting to their religious faith, but not any that could be considered "sectarian" or "proselytizing."[34] In McCombs's case, the assistant principal allowed her to speak about how her religious faith affected her performance as a competitive swimmer, but would not allow her to cite Bible passages nor speak about the virtues of the Christian lifestyle. McCombs was warned that if she varied from the approved text, her microphone would be cut off.

Aided by the Rutherford Institute, a conservative Christian group, McComb sued the Clark County School District, claiming officials had violated her rights of free speech, religious expression, and equal protection. A Federal District Court ruled in favor of the school district, as did the Ninth Circuit Court of Appeals. She continued her appeal to the U.S. Supreme Court, which declined to hear the case.

In the decade that has followed the original incident, her abbreviated commencement address has been viewed more than 170,000 times on You-Tube.[35]

At the 2013 commencement ceremony for Liberty High School in Liberty, South Carolina, valedictorian Roy Costner IV wanted to protest the school's decision to eliminate the long-standing tradition of opening the ceremonies with a prayer. As he approached the podium, he tore up his pre-approved speech and instead recited the Lord's Prayer in its entirety. Some in the crowd cheered and some booed, but most were simply stunned. John Eby, spokesperson for the Pickens County School District, told local media that while administrators were disappointed in Costner's decision to shred his approved text, "the bottom line is that we don't punish students for expressing their religious faiths."[36]

Within weeks of the speech, Costner's speech had been viewed on You-Tube more than 250,000 times.[37]

In 2013, school officials in Lake City, Arkansas, were threatened by a law-suit if that year's commencement ceremonies at two elementary schools opened with prayers. The Freedom From Religion Foundation had written a letter to the Lake City School Board complaining about the practice and promising a lawsuit if the prayers were not deleted. Board members came up with a novel solution: instead of canceling the prayers, they voted to cancel the entire ceremonies.

Many Christian parents arranged for smaller ceremonies at local churches, where the principle of "no school prayer" would not apply.[38]

In other communities, school officials know better than to open a ceremony with a prayer, but based on case law, student speakers are allowed to mention religious themes in their remarks as long as they are not mandated to do so and the comments were not sanctioned by the school. Civil liberties attorney Charles C. Haynes recommends that schools avoid controversy by including in the printed program a disclaimer that student comments represent the views of the students, not the schools.[39]

For most students, the designation of having a "feather in their cap" is the recognition of a specific accomplishment. But for seventeen-year-old Chelsey Ramer, a graduating senior at Escambia Academy in southern Alabama in 2013, the feather in her cap nearly cost her $1,000.

Ramer was a member of the Poarch Band of Creek Indians and chose to wear the feather to honor her religious and family upbringing. School head-master Betty Warren told her the school's dress code prohibited "extraneous items during graduation exercises unless approved by the administration."[40] When she wore the feather in spite of Warren's admonition, she was told she would not receive her diploma or transcript until she paid a fine of $1,000.

"It will be worth every penny of it," Ramer told the local media as she prepared to pay the fine. "This is what I've been waiting on, and I feel like I had the right to wear it."[41]

After weeks of negative publicity, school administrators informed the family that Ramer could receive her diploma and transcripts without paying the fine. An online fundraising campaign aimed at covering the cost of the fine generated about $1,100, which after the cancellation of the fine went into Ramer's college scholarship fund.[42]

Two years later in Nebraska, a nearly identical controversy took place at Omaha South High School. A graduating senior who was a member of the Sicangu Lakota tribe was told by school officials she could not display a feather on her graduation cap because it would have violated its rule banning "bling." After weeks of controversy and passionate pleas on behalf of the student made by her parents, friends, and representatives of several local Native American tribes, the school district reversed its position and allowed the girl to display the feather. [43]

THE COLLEGE CAMPUS

In 2016, a group calling itself Grace Christian Life sued four administrators at North Carolina State University after they denied its members the right to distribute fliers and talk to other students about their religious beliefs. NCSU officials told group members must apply for a permit and then be restricted to a table in the student union. Administrators claimed they were merely enforcing a rule that had been in place for more than two decades, but the students claimed that the rule was not enforced against other groups seen wandering around campus, handing out political literature, and gathering signatures on petitions.

The lawsuit was filed by Alliance Defending Freedom, a conservative Christian organization based in Arizona that had been involved in similar conflicts at other campuses. "Public universities are supposed to be the marketplace of ideas, not places where students need a permit to exercise constitutionally protected freedoms," said ADR attorney Tyson Langhofer in a prepared statement. "The only permit needed to engage in free speech is the First Amendment." [44]

University officials cited a policy, in effect since 1993, which required permits for distributing materials on campus "subject to constitutionally appropriate and reasonable time, place, or manner limits, without regard to the content or the viewpoint of the information being distributed." [45] Regarding the GCL issue, the university claimed the policy was "constitutional, did not infringe on First Amendment rights, and was in compliance with applicable state and federal law." [46]

The school also denied that the group's claim that it "selectively enforced" the policy. [47] As of summer 2016, the court case had still not been decided.

In 2004, the Christian Student Fellowship at Indian River Community College in Florida was told that it could not show the award-winning film *The Passion of the Christ* on campus because the administration considered it "too controversial." After FIRE intervened and generated months of negative publicity, the ban was lifted the following spring. [48]

The issue of faith-based student organizations on college campuses generated numerous controversies across the country between 2012 and 2015.

In 2012 alone, fourteen student organizations at private Vanderbilt University lost their official status at the school because they refused to go along with its non-discriminatory policies. A Christian group was allowed to keep its charter after it agreed to delete the words "personal commitment to Jesus Christ" from its list of membership requirements.[49]

A similar controversy took place within the California university system during the 2013-2014 school year when the system stripped twenty-three chapters of the InterVarsity Christian Fellowship (IVCF) of their official standing. The decision stemmed from a 2011 order from the chancellor of the system stating that, "No campus shall recognize any student organization unless its membership and leadership are open to all currently enrolled students." The problem with the IVCF chapters, administrators said, was that their requirements that officers affirm belief in "evangelical Christian values" violated the school's anti-discrimination policies.

As a result of losing their status as official organizations, chapters could no longer use campus facilities, request student organization funding, or claim affiliation with the university.

"The policy guts the free association right that was enshrined in the First Amendment precisely to protect minority or unpopular views," wrote civil libertarian Harvey A. Silverglate in an op-ed in *The Wall Street Journal*. "Limiting the First Amendment rights for Christians undercuts rights for everyone else."[50]

Four years earlier, the U.S. Supreme Court had set the legal precedent in this area with its ruling in *Christian Legal Society v. Martinez* (2010). In that 5-4 decision, the Court determined that a state university (in this case, Hastings Law School in California) did not violate the First Amendment "freedom of association" rights of student groups when it required them to accept all interested students—regardless of their religious affiliation or lack of it— who met other membership requirements.

Justice Ruth Bader Ginsburg, writing the majority, offered a hypothetical of a "Male Supremacy Club" that stated in its guidelines that it would accept women as members but not as officers unless they "adhered to the doctrine of male supremacy."[51]

The actual issue was related to the CLS policy of accepting gay students while not allowing them to hold leadership positions, but Ginsburg wrote that her premise behind her hypothetical and the premise behind the actual case were nearly identical.

In a concurring opinion, Justice John Paul Stevens wrote that the group's policy of denying leadership positions based on sexual orientation was analogous to "mistreating Jews, blacks, and women"—an exclusion that would obviously be illegal.[52]

The ruling in favor of the school generated a new legal term for college campuses: the "all comers policy." If student organizations were to seek official university status and request student activity funds, they would need to abide by non-discrimination policies. In the four-year gap between the *Martinez* ruling and the California cases, there were few well-publicized cases in this area, and none since 2014.[53]

BEST OF THE REST

In 2011, a fifth grader at a Pocono County elementary school in Pennsylvania was not allowed to hand out invitations to a Christmas party at her church, while her classmates were allowed to distribute messages of all kinds—from birthday party invitations to Valentine's cards. When the girls' parents sued the school district, administrators defended their actions by claiming the issue was based not on religious content, but rather the sponsorship of the event by an outside party, which was prohibited by school district policy. A Federal District Court ruled in favor of the girl, who was identified in court documents by her initials, K. A., saying she (and other students) had the right to distribute information (even that of a religious nature) during non-instructional time, as long as it did not disrupt the educational process. The school district appealed the case to the Third Circuit, but two years later, a three-judge panel upheld the lower court's ruling, citing the *Tinker* standard and determining that administrators failed to prove that the girl's invitations created a substantial disruption.

John E. Freund, the attorney for the school district, had used the "slippery slope" argument in defending the school's position. "Suppose the next thing that a student brings in are right-to-life materials, or the Aryan Nation wants to have a rally," Freund told the court. "The courts make it ever more difficult to maintain an environment focused on learning."[54]

At the close of the school year in 2015, a sixth grader at Somerset Academy, a private charter school in North Las Vegas, Nevada, was barred from using a Bible verse as part of a class assignment. For an assignment in which students were asked to make a PowerPoint presentation that included a quote they found inspirational, Mackenzie Frasier chose John 3:16.

After the Liberty Institute, a Plano, Texas-based religious freedom organization, threatened to sue the school on Frasier's behalf, the school issued an apology and the chairman of the school's board of directors said the teacher and assistant principal made an inadvertent error in interpreting federal guidelines regarding religious expression.[55]

In Dyersburg, Tennessee, in 2014, a high school student was sent to the principal's office after saying "bless you" to another student who sneezed. Seventeen-year-old Kendra Turner told local media that the phrase was on a list of things students were not allowed to say, including "my bad," "hang out," "dumb," "stupid," "retarded," and "stuff."[56]

Assistant Principal Lynn Garner declined to discuss specifics of the case in media interviews, but said teachers were allowed to set their own rules of classroom behavior and expression as long as they were reasonable. "If a teacher asks his or her students to do something reasonable to avoid a distraction in the classroom, then we expect students to follow the rules," Garner said. "If it's not a reasonable request, then we'll sit down and talk about it and get it right."[57]

Turner told the assistant principal that after she said "bless you," the teacher stood up and asked who had spoken. "She asked me why I said it, and I told her I was being courteous, and then she asked me who told me it was a courtesy," Turner told local media. "I told her my pastor and my parents taught me to say it."[58]

Turner was then sent to the principal's office, where she was placed on in-school suspension for the remainder of the class period. The following week, Turner held a news conference at Dyersburg First Assembly of God to talk about the incident. "I wanted to be able to talk about God in school," she said. "I want them to realize that God is in control, and they're not."[59]

Garner responded that the issue had been exaggerated on social media and was more about a classroom distraction than a religious issue.[60]

In 2014, the Tennessee Legislature passed a law that would protect students in public schools who mentioned religious beliefs in homework, artwork, essays, or other school assignments. The legislation was introduced by republican Representative Courtney Rogers of Goodlettsville, a Nashville suburb, after a student in her district was not allowed to select God for an assignment in which students were told to write an essay about someone they admired.[61]

NOTES

1. *Minersville School District v. Gobitis*, 310 U.S. 586 (1940).
2. Ibid.
3. Ibid. See also: William W. Van Alstyne, *The First Amendment: Cases and Materials*. Westbury, NY: The Foundation Press, 1995, pp. 615-16. Nat Hentoff, *Free Speech for Me, But Not for Thee*. New York: Harper Perennial, 1993, pp. 240-242.

4. *West Virginia Board of Education v. Barnette* 319 U.S. 624 (1943).

5. Ibid.

6. Ibid.

7. Ibid.

8. *Stromberg v. California*, 283 U.S. 359 (1931). See also: Van Alstyne, The First Amendment, p. 616.

9. *West Virginia Board of Education v. Barnette*. See also: Van Alstyne, The First Amendment, p. 622.

10. "School Board Suspends Teacher Over Pledge." Associated Press report, November 7, 2013.

11. "Pledge of Allegiance Central to North Dakota School Dispute." Associated Press report, September 16, 2014.

12. Ibid.

13. *Widmar v. Vincent*, 454 U.S. 263 (1981).

14. *Brandon v. Guilderland Central School*, 487 F.Supp. 1219 (1980). See also: Craig R. Smith and David M. Hunsaker, *The Four Freedoms of the First Amendment*, Long Grove, IL: Waveland Press, 2004, p. 55.

15. Ibid.

16. *Engel v. Vitale*, 370 U.S. 421 (1962).

17. *Lee v. Weisman*, 120 L.Ed. 480 (1992).

18. *Santa Fe Independent School District v. Doe*, 120 S.Ct. 226 (2000).

19. *Abington School District v. Schempp*, 374 U.S. 203 (1963).

20. Ibid. See also Bruce J. Dierenfield, "The Most Hated Woman in America: Madalyn Murray O'Hair and the Crusade Against School Prayer." *Journal of Supreme Court History*, vol. 32, no. 1 (2007), pp. 62-84.

21. Nat Hentoff, *Living the Bill of Rights: How to be an Authentic American*. Berkeley, CA: University of California Press, 1999, p. 51.

22. Erin Kourkounis, "Three-Year Prayer Battle is Over." *Pensacola News Journal*, July 6, 2011, p. 1-A.

23. Reginald T. Dogan, "Prayer Issue Was a Waste of Money." *Pensacola News Journal*, July 7, 2011, p. 1-B.

24. Kourkounis.

25. Ibid.

26. *Stone v. Graham*, 449 U.S. 39 (1980).

27. Charles C. Haynes, "The State Shall Not Endorse Religion." Syndicated newspaper column, May 22, 2012.

28. "Wrestling Team Vows to Keep T-Shirts." Associated Press report, April 24, 2014.

29. Ibid.

30. *Lee v. Weisman.*

31. Haynes, "A Novel Solution to Graduation Prayer." Syndicated newspaper column, May 25, 2013.

32. *Moore v. Ingebretsen*, 519 U.S. 965 (1996).

33. *Santa Fe Independent School District v. Doe*, 120 S. Ct. 226 (2000).

34. *McComb v. Crehan*, Ninth Circuit (Case 07-16194). See also: Wilson Huhn, "McComb v. Crehan Won't Make it Onto Supreme Court Docket." *Akron Beacon-Journal*, November 25, 2009. Sean Whaley, "Student Speech Rights Bill Debated in Legislature." *Las Vegas Review Journal*, February 15, 2015.

35. Ibid.

36. "Student Won't be Punished for Lord's Prayer." Associated Press Report, June 10, 2013.

37. Ibid.

38. Haynes, "A Novel Solution to Graduation Prayer."

39. Ibid.

40. Beth Greenfield, "Native American Feather Sparks Graduation Debate: Schools' Tough Rules for Grads." Yahoo News, June 7, 2013.

41. Greenfield.

42. Ibid.

43. Erin Duffy, "South High Reverses Position." *Omaha World-Herald*, May 29, 2015. See also: David Edwards, "Nebraska School Calls Native American Girl's Religious Feather 'Bling' and Bans it at Graduation." Rawstory.com, May 19, 2015.

44. Stradling, Richard. "Christian Group Sues N.C. State University Over Speech Policy." *Raleigh News and Observer*, April 27, 2016.

45. Ibid.

46. Ibid.

47. Ibid.

48. Greg Lukianoff, *Unlearning Liberty: Campus Censorship and the End of American Debate*. New York: Encounter Books, 2014, p. 163.

49. Kirsten Powers, *The Silencing: How the Left is Killing Free Speech*. Washington, DC: Regnery Press, 2012, p. 101.

50. Harvey A. Silverglate, "A Campus Crusade Against the Constitution." *Wall Street Journal*, September 19, 2014, p. 11-A.

51. *Christian Legal Society v. Martinez*, 558 U.S. 661 (2011). See also: Silverglate, "A Campus Crusade Against the Constitution."

52. Ibid.

53. Ibid.

54. *K. A. v. Pocono Mountain School District* (2011). See also: Haynes, "Students Also Have the Right to Free Speech." Syndicated newspaper column, March 29, 2013.

55. "Student Barred From Using Bible Verse." Associated Press report, May 30, 2015.

56. "DCHS Responds to Incident Involving Student." *Dyersburg State Gazette*, August 20, 2014.

57. Ibid.

58. Ibid.

59. Ibid.

60. Ibid.

61. "Bill Gives Students Freedom of Religious Expression." Associated Press report, March 15, 2014.

Chapter Five

Speech Codes, Speech Zones, and Political Incorrectness

FREE SPEECH AT THE UNIVERSITY OF PENNSYLVANIA, OR MAYBE NOT

In 1987, over the strenuous objections of faculty members, University of Pennsylvania president Sheldon Hackney introduced an executive order establishing a "Code of Conduct and Racial Harassment Policy"—in essence, the school's first speech code. The policy prohibited "any behavior, verbal or physical, that stigmatizes or victimizes individuals on the basis of race, ethnic, or national origin, and that has the purpose or effect of interfering with an individual's academic or work performance and/or creates an intimidating or offensive academic, living, or work environment."[1]

What concerned some Penn faculty members the most about the new code was how it was selectively enforced. In 1988, when Nation of Islam founder Louis Farrakhan spoke at Penn, he made comments that even Hackney admitted were "racist and anti-Semitic," yet no one outside of the Jewish organizations on campus and in the surrounding community seemed to be concerned. When asked about it, Hackney responded that "in an academic community, open expression is the most important value . . . we can't have free speech only some of the time for only some of the people. Either we have it, or we don't. At Penn, we have it."[2]

Yet the following year, when incoming freshmen were oriented on the rule, administrators provided the following hypothetical examples of speech that would be punished:

- Students create a poster to advertise a "South of the Border" party which shows a Mexican student taking a siesta.

- A professor refers to modern-day blacks as "ex-slaves" when he/she meant to say "descendents of slaves."
- On Gay Jeans Day, when students are asked to wear jeans to show support for gay and lesbian students on campus, one student creates a satirical poster advertising "Heterosexual Footwear Day."[3]

The first legal test for the policy came in 1993. On the night of January 13, freshman Eden Jacobowitz was working on a paper for an English class, but was having difficulty concentrating because about fifteen members of the Delta Sigma Theta sorority were partying in the common area below his residence hall window. At one point, Jacobowitz went to the window and shouted, "Please keep quiet." Twenty minutes later, the noise had only gotten louder, so he returned to the window and shouted, "Shut up, you water buffalo. If you want to party, there's a zoo about a mile from here." The latter comment referred to the Philadelphia Zoo, which was about a mile north of the campus.

The women complained to university police, who scoured the building, knocked on doors, and asked residents to admit to what they had shouted. In between Jacobowitz's first plea for the women to "please be quiet" and "shut up, you water buffalo," several other residents had also requested that the noise stop, but reportedly used more offensive terms, including "black asses" and "black bitches." Jacobowitz was one of the few to answer his door in response to the police inquiries, and the only resident to admit what he had said.

Jacobowitz soon found himself the target of a student judicial investigation at which he would be accused of violating the anti-harassment policy. His punishment was swift and certain: it required him to (1) write a letter of apology to the women who claimed they were offended, (2) present to fellow members of his residence hall an "educational program" on campus diversity, (3) remain on probation for the remainder of his time at Penn, with a second offense being grounds for expulsion; and (4) have a notation of the offense indicated on his transcript with the stipulation that it would be removed at the beginning of his junior year.

Jacobowitz was given a choice—accept the penalties, withdraw from the university, or have his case heard by the university's judiciary office. He chose the third option, claiming that he could not have violated a policy against racial harassment because his comments were not related to the women's race. He was willing to go along with the first condition—the apology—but only if he could include the clarification that his "water buffalo" comment had nothing to do with race.

Administrators denied the counteroffer, leaving Jacobowitz no other choice but to proceed with the hearing. In order to prepare, he consulted with Charles A. Kors, a Penn history professor and expert on civil liberties and free speech. According to the school's judicial charter, accused students could be represented by another member of the Penn community but not by outside lawyers.

The first objective for Kors and Jacobowitz was to prove to the satisfaction of the hearing panel that the term "water buffalo" had no racial connotation. University administrators claimed that the term was "racist" because it described water buffalo as "large black animals living in Africa," unaware that water buffalo are actually native to Asia. Some viewed the geographic gaffe as incidental, but civil libertarian Rodney A. Smolla offered it as evidence that there was "wide dispute on which words might arouse anger based on race."[4]

Kors and Jacobowitz enlisted the testimony of a professor of African history, who confirmed there was nothing racial or racist about it. Numerous other scholars in the fields of African American studies and linguistics submitted letters denying the connection. Kors and Jacobowitz and also identified dozens of references to the term "water buffalo" being used as a criticism in literature and popular culture, with not one of them having racial overtones. At worst, they found, the term was used as a synonym for "clumsy," "fool," or "overeater."

In addition to arguing the semantics of his words, Kors and Jacobowitz presented character witnesses who testified to the latter's character. A freshman who had spent much of his childhood in Israel, Jacobowitz was described as a bright, kind, and serious student who never lost his temper and always treated both friends and strangers with respect. The words he used that night were chosen out of frustration with being unable to work, not out of any racial bias.[5]

Civil rights activist Vernon Jordan was one of the few national figures siding with the university, although he didn't do so until many years later. In the foreword to Hackney's political memoirs, he wrote that "the participant in the white mob became a hero for the right wing, while the four black women remained faceless and the objects of national ridicule."[6]

By mid-April, the Jacobowitz case had become a national story, with much of public opinion siding with him and against the climate of political correctness on college campuses in general. Hackney was rumored to be a candidate for the position of chairman of the National Endowment for the Humanities, which would have required a presidential appointment from Bill Clinton and approval by the U.S. Senate. Penn journalism alumni working at newspapers across the country wrote editorials questioning how someone with a inconsistent record on free speech issues (there were other incidents of a racial nature before and after the water buffalo affair) could be considered for a position running an arts organization. International media took note as well, as newspaper editorials in Canada and Europe all supported Jacobowitz. Editorial cartoonists, including *Doonesbury* creator Garry Trudeau, ridiculed Penn and its "language police."[7]

On the *NBC Nightly News*, commentator John Chancellor commented that while Jacobowitz was capable of defending his case, "the rest of us are all in trouble . . . the language police are at work on the campuses of our better schools. The word cops are marching under the banner of political correctness. The culture of victimization is hunting for quarry. American English is in danger of losing its muscle and energy. That's what these bozos are doing to us."[8]

Amid the negative publicity that began with the campus newspaper and spread across the state and nation and then around the world, the university postponed the hearing indefinitely. Administrators claimed it was a "cooling off period" that was necessary in order to preserve the fairness of the proceedings, but critics charged that it was intended to help Hackney's candidacy for the NEH job.

On May 24, university officials held a news conference at which they announced that the women filing the original complaint did not believe the process had been fair to them and were no longer pursuing the case. The university dropped the charges against Jacobowitz, and two years later abolished its "racial harassment code."

Hackney was confirmed for the NEH job that fall. In his political memoir, he claimed the case "had been hijacked for ideological purposes" and that dismissing the phrase as harmless "ignores the long history of animalistic representations of African Americans as part of white supremacy's mind game [and] ignores the question of what the women thought they heard and why they got so angry."[9]

In 1997, Jacobowitz sued the university for inflicting emotional distress by dragging out the proceedings and using him as a "test case" for its harassment policy even after determining his innocence. He asked for only $50,000—a modest sum considering the national publicity sparked by the case—but instead got only attorney's fees with no admission of responsibility.[10] The university's final report also concluded that Jacobowitz had not been treated fairly, but the women had been treated even worse and had suffered more harm.

The ACLU applauded the resolution of the case, saying that the university should "spend more time educating students and less time limiting their freedom of expression." Even after the charges were dropped, the "water buffalo" case created a public relations nightmare for the university, as newspaper editorials and radio talk shows kept the story alive for more than a year.[11]

In 2002, when a student posted an offensive political message on a university-sponsored website, administrators encouraged students to debate the issue from multiple points of view, following the stance of many speech code opponents that "the best response to offensive speech is more and better speech."[12]

LEGISLATING POLITENESS

Today, policies regulating hate speech exist at nearly every public college and university in the country, but the extent to which they are enforced varies. An outgrowth of diversity programs and other efforts to support multiculturalism on campus, the codes are designed to protect women, gays, African Americans, the disabled, and other minorities. Critics of speech codes, however, claim they constitute prior restraint and are examples of political correctness out of control.

Speech codes became popular in the late 1980s, as colleges across the country grappled with finding a balance between the competing ideals of free speech and the need to provide a "comfortable learning environment" to minority students. Some universities, according to civil libertarians, developed solutions that were too close to the "comfortable" end of the scale. At the University of Wisconsin, for example, the Board of Regents in 1989 enacted a "speech code" that would expel from the school any student caught "hurling racial epithets in a threatening manner."[13]

The regents were responding to a rash of obnoxious behavior by white students.

In one incident, white male students were heard calling out to passing black women, "I've never tried a nigger before."[14] The previous fall, the Zeta Beta Tau fraternity had staged a mock "slave auction," complete with some members in blackface. No students were ever accused of doing so under the new policy, and within a few years it was softened to "discourage" rather than "punish" racially offensive speech.[15]

"Speech code" is a generic term that is seldom, if ever, described as such. In fact, there are few university policies that make even the slightest reference to a restriction on speech. Instead, they are more likely to be labeled by some less onerous term and tucked neatly inside other policies that incoming students may or may not read, such as anti-harassment policies, policies governing on-campus living, policies regarding computer use, and policies prohibiting disorderly conduct.

"Students who don't want to risk punishment might censor themselves from engaging in these types of discussions and debates, which should form the heart of university life," stated a 2006 policy report from the Pope Center for Higher Education Policy and the Foundation for Individual Rights in Education.[16]

Opponents of speech codes criticize them as examples of "political correctness taken to an extreme" and the universities' efforts to punish students not only for what they say, but also for what they think. Among the opponents is the Foundation for Individual Rights in Education, which defines a speech code as a policy that would "prohibit expression that would otherwise be protected in society at large."[17]

Nearly all university speech codes are loosely based on the legal delineation between *hate speech* and *fighting words*. Hate speech, according to court cases, is "hostile (but non-violent) speech that is addressed at groups of people (not specific individuals), and is based on race, religion, ethnicity, sex, or sexual orientation." Fighting words are "direct personal insults made against a specific person or persons in their presence, those words which by their very utterance inflict injury or tend to incite an immediate breach of the peace."[18]

The problem, however, is that the codes take great liberties in using the definitions abstractly, and when administrators attempt to apply the codes to specific situations, they tend to err on the side of restricting offensive speech rather than tolerating it.

PUSHBACK

Long before speech codes became popular, Yale University decided to take preemptive measures to prevent political correctness from gaining a foothold. In 1975, history professor C. Vann Woodward headed a commission to develop a long-term strategy for dealing with free speech issues on campus, and it determined that speech codes would be inconsistent with the school's values of free inquiry and expression. The report stated that the university "cannot make its primary and dominant value the fostering of friendship, solidarity, harmony, civility, and mutual respect . . . if (free) expression may be prevented, censored, or punished because of its content or because of the motives attributed to those who promote it. It will be subordinate to other values that we believe to be of lower priority in a university."[19]

Benno Schmidt, president of Yale University in the 1980s, opposed speech codes because he viewed them as "well-intentioned but misguided efforts to give values of community harmony a higher place than freedom . . . when the goals of harmony collide with freedom of expression, freedom must be the paramount obligation of an academic community."[20]

In 1991, Representative Larry Craig, a Republican from Idaho, introduced the Freedom of Speech on Campus Act, which would have permitted the Department of Education to withhold federal funding from colleges and universities that prohibit speech that is otherwise protected by the U.S. Constitution. A member of Craig's staff later said the bill never made it to the floor of the House of Representatives for a full hearing because "it was difficult to convince Congress there was a constituency concerned with this issue."[21]

During the same session, Representative Henry Hyde, a Republican from Illinois, introduced a more narrowly tailored bill—called the Collegiate Speech Protection Act—that dealt strictly with private colleges. The proposal, which would have been an amendment to the Civil Rights Act of 1964, would have provided students at private universities the same level of First Amendment protection as enjoyed by their counterparts at public schools. It was supported by the American Civil Liberties Union but opposed by enough members of the House to kill it.

Many Democrats were against it because they were aware of some of the more outrageous incidents of hate speech on campuses, while many Republicans were simply opposed to government interference with the operations of private institutions.[22]

In 1992, California Governor Pete Wilson signed a piece of legislation called Leonard Law. The law gave students at the state's private universities the same First Amendment rights that previously were enjoyed only by their public university counterparts. "It is the intent of the legislature that a student should have the same right to exercise his or her right to free speech as he or she enjoys when off campus," said Bill Leonard, the state legislator who introduced the bill and became its namesake.[23]

In February 1995, the first challenge to the Leonard Law reached a California trial court, which ruled against Stanford University in its attempt to enforce a campus speech code. The private school had claimed it was not subject to the First Amendment, but the court ruled that the Leonard Law was content-neutral and was therefore valid. The court also rejected the school's claim that allowing campus speech to be unregulated might lead the public to assume it endorsed any controversial expression that might result.[24]

"For many Americans, the term 'speech code' sends shivers up the spine," wrote political commentator Kirsten Powers in her 2012 book, *The Silencing: How the Left is Killing Free Speech.* "Yet these noxious and un-American codes have become commonplace on college campuses across the United States. They are typically so broad that they could include literally anything and are subject to the interpretation of school administrators, who frequently fail to operate as honest brokers. Speech codes are used as weapons to silence anyone—professors, students, visiting speakers—who express a view that deviates from the left's worldview or ideology."[25]

Civil libertarian Greg Lukianoff agrees. "Campus administrators have been successful in convincing students that the primary goal of the university is to make students feel comfortable," Lukianoff wrote in his 2014 book,

Unlearning Liberty: Campus Censorship and the End of American Debate.
"Unfortunately, comfortable minds are not thinking ones. Students should,
however, be able to feel comfortable with engaging in devil's advocacy and
thought experimentation, and, perhaps more importantly, the possibility of
being wrong. Making it safe for people to be wrong is one of the first steps in
creating an atmosphere that is intellectually vibrant enough to produce good
ideas and meaningful discussion."[26]

A 1990 report from the Carnegie Foundation for the Advancement of
Teaching added that, "Speech codes may be expedient, even grounded in
conviction," but the university cannot submit the two cherished ideals of
freedom and equality to the legal system and expect both to be returned
intact."[27]

According to FIRE, most private schools go "above and beyond" in
promising free speech rights to prospective students and faculty, believing
that such policies would be effective in luring the most talented students and
faculty, who presumably would want to study and teach where they could
speak and write freely.[28] FIRE believes that the move toward speech codes is
in part due to some administrators misreading or misinterpreting federal
laws, enforced by the Department of Education's Office of Civil Rights,
which call for punishment for institutions that don't protect students from
harassment and discrimination.[29]

In a 2014 report, FIRE issued a report that more than half of all universities it surveyed still employ some form of speech code, and the organization labeled many of those codes as "severely restrictive" and "prohibiting
clearly protected speech."[30]

Lukianoff, co-founder and president of FIRE, warned universities in a
2014 address to the National Press Club that universities needed to start
practicing the free speech principles they claim to support in their publications and on their websites. "Colleges need to do the right thing and dump
their speech codes," Lukianoff told the group. "If not, we might see them in
court."[31]

In a July 5, 2014, briefing on sexual harassment on college campuses,
Michael Yaki, head of the U.S. Commission on Civil Rights, explained that
speech restrictions on college campuses were "necessary infringements on
free speech because adolescent and young adult brains process information
differently from adult brains."[32]

THE CASE FOR SPEECH CODES

*Hate speech, like libel and child pornography, can be limited because it can
be proven to have no social value.* The court system, including the U.S.
Supreme Court, has a demonstrated history of finding little First Amendment

support for libel and child pornography based on its perceived lack of contribution to useful discourse.

Universities are obligated to provide all their students with a comfortable learning environment. In defending their school's speech code, University of Michigan administrators cited the Supreme Court's 1919 decision that the principle of free speech does not allow a man to "shout 'fire' in a crowded theater" and said that the institution should not allow "discriminatory remarks which seriously offend many individuals beyond the immediate victim, and which therefore detract from the necessary educational climate of a campus."[33] Harmful expression that goes unpunished may lead students to believe that their schools are taking sides by doing nothing and will feel alone and powerless in dealing with hurtful expression.

Dr. Amitai Etzioni, professor of sociology at George Washington University, says that hate speech should receive no protection, especially on a college campus where it may influence the audience to harm innocent persons. "When words take action, then we need to be concerned," Etzioni says. "Expressions of hate speech on campus should be seen as an indication that we haven't done our jobs as educators."[34]

Speech codes represent a reasonable balance of competing interests. In this case, administrators enforcing speech codes to protect minority students are placing their Fourteenth Amendment rights above the First Amendment rights of the speakers.

THE CASE AGAINST SPEECH CODES

Speech codes tend to be vague and overbroad and are often found unconstitutional when challenged. A 1993 editorial in *Quill* criticized speech codes for "blurring the lines between fighting words and speech that intellectual and moral guardians don't like." The editorial criticized universities for using the term "hostile learning environment" and claimed that borrowing such a term from the legal area of employment discrimination means that the "intellectual mission of the university is fundamentally the same as that of an insurance company or an undertaker's office."[35]

Ken Paulson, executive director of the First Amendment Center, adds that universities have historically been places where people could express their views openly in hopes of building a better society. "Sometimes these viewpoints come in the form of speeches or articles; sometimes they come in the form of ads," Paulson wrote in a 2001 op-ed piece. "Sometimes these views refresh; sometimes they repel. Unless we embrace free expression on America's campuses, our universities risk becoming doctrinaire boot camps teaching intolerance rather than free-speech forums preparing young people for citizenship in the world's oldest democracy."[36]

Like many civil libertarians, Alan C. Kors and Harvey A. Silverglate find campus speech codes problematic due largely to their fuzzy and non-specific language. Such codes, Kors and Silverglate claim, "create a world in which speakers must walk in a fog on the edge of a cliff."[37]

Rodney Smolla, writing about speech codes in his 1995 book, *A Year in the Life of the Supreme Court,* attempted to compile a comprehensive list of words that would be prohibited by speech codes on college campuses. He wrote that administrators he interviewed could agree only on "nigger," "bitch," and "fag," but beyond that, there was no consensus, leading Smolla to be concerned about the inconsistency among codes.[38]

The college campus is a unique setting where controversial ideas are supposed to be debated and evaluated. University administrators should therefore encourage free speech rather than attempt to stifle it. In his 1993 book, *Speech Acts and the First Amendment,* author Franklyn Haiman opposes speech codes and instead recommends that universities respond to hate speech by challenging its accuracy and value rather than attempting to eliminate it. "The answer to offensive speech is more speech, not less speech," Haiman wrote.[39]

Constitutional law scholar Gerald Gunther adds that, "Clearly, there is ample room and need for vigorous university action to combat racial and other discrimination . . . the proper answer to bad speech is usually more and better speech—not new laws, litigation, and repression."[40]

In his 1993 book on political correctness in government, *Leaving Town Alive,* civil liberties attorney John Frohnmayer added that, "speech codes on college campuses eliminate the most effective means of moderating antisocial behavior—the disapproval of classmates and colleagues."[41]

Nadine Strossen, a professor at New York University Law School and general counsel for the ACLU, claims to speak for all civil libertarians when she acknowledges the pain that harmful speech causes but nonetheless prefers that it be countered with opposing speech instead of government restriction. She points to the 1978 decisions by the Seventh Circuit Court of Appeals and the Illinois Supreme Court—which resulted in decisions in favor of neo-Nazis creating speech offensive to the town of Skokie's Jewish citizens—that allowing hate speech is the price we pay for preserving free speech rights for society at large.[42]

Another analogy came from the 1989 Supreme Court case of *Texas v. Johnson,* which dealt with individuals burning the American flag as a form of political protest. "The way to preserve the flag's special role is not to punish those who feel differently about these matters," Justice William Brennan wrote in his majority opinion. "It is to persuade them that they are wrong."[43]

Speech codes take away an important safety valve for dissent. Like most forms of hate speech, expressions of dissatisfaction that take place on a college campus provides students and others the opportunity to "blow off steam."

The most extreme codes, critics say, might preclude pro-life students from wearing T-shirts with the phrase "Abortion stops a beating heart" or abortion-rights advocates from wearing T-shirts with the phrase "Keep your rosaries off my ovaries."[44]

Paulson adds that, "The First Amendment has served us extraordinarily well. Is it possible that we're now seeing a generation so committed to inoffensive speech that it's willing to chip away at these fundamental freedoms? Speech that offends no one is generally speech without substance."[45]

Speech codes are unnecessary. Critics of speech codes point are fond of saying either that such policies "address problems that don't exist" or are "solutions in search of a problem."[46]

They support their belief that such proposals are overreactions by pointing out many such codes are enacted without evidence that the problems they are designed to address occur no more frequency than they do at other institutions. Many, the critics contend, are knee-jerk reactions to trivial incidents or preemptive responses to negative media coverage of more serious incidents at other schools.[47]

Political columnist A. Barton Hinkle wrote in a 2015 article in *Reason* that the "slippery slope" argument that "hate speech leads to violence" is not supported by the facts. "Racial epithets might lead to lynching is cited as one example," Hinkle wrote. "But there is simply no empirical evidence to support that claim. Indeed, on today's campus any violence is more likely to be directed at the offending speaker, rather than at his intended target." Hinkle also argued that the job of protecting students' feelings from all possible harm should be beyond the purview of school administrators. "The effort is self-defeating," Hinkle wrote. "Even if it were possible to measure emotional pain, and to decide at what point such pain should trigger the censor's veto, it is not possible to protect everyone's feelings the way we can protect everyone's rights."[48]

Kors claims that speech codes result in the "infantilizing of students" and that the irony of speech codes is that they were created by administrators who themselves celebrated free speech as students in the 1960s.[49]

Some critics of speech codes say that at best, they are unnecessary; at worst, they are violations of the First Amendment's free speech clause. Others say they are evidence of the "political correctness" climate pervasive on many college campuses. Alison Alexander and Jarice Hanson, authors of the 2013 textbook titled *Taking Sides: Clashing Views on Controversial Issues in Media and Society*, included an entire chapter on campus speech codes and prefaced it by claiming that the speech code/political correctness movement "centers around the alleged tendency of university communities to stifle discussion that is not appropriately liberal."[50]

Civil libertarian Nat Hentoff, also an opponent of speech codes, claims they are superficial efforts at best. "Because a campus may have seen racist, sexist, or homophonic taunts, the administration believes it must *do something*, so it cheapest and quickest way it can demonstrate that it cares is to *appear* to suppress racist, sexist, and homophobic speech."[51]

Speech codes serve to "infantilize" students and are viewed by some as condescending. Hentoff cites examples from conversations with his own students to illustrate his belief that many minority students are offended by speech codes because they see them as unnecessary and condescending. One student told him in the late 1980s that he "had been familiar with hateful speech his entire life; he learned how to deal with it in the past and could continue to do so in the future." Hentoff said he witnessed the same student once tell a white classmate that it was "condescending to say that black students needed to be protected from racist speech . . . it was more racist and insulting to say that to me than to call me a nigger."[52]

Many minority students claim they are fully capable of processing hateful speech and are offended by the university's insistence on trying to protect them.[53]

Speech codes are ineffective. There is little evidence to support the belief that speech codes, or any other form of speech limitation, has the power to change deeply held racist, sexist, or homophobic beliefs.

Such codes may achieve the short-term goal of providing a "comfortable learning environment," but in the long term serve only to generate resentment among those whose speech is limited and make that speech more appealing to audiences who might otherwise be uninterested.[54] Hentoff adds that "Eliminating hate speech will not eliminate hate . . . it will instead force it underground, where it is most comfortable."[55]

The slippery slope. Gwen Thomas, a black administrator at a university in Colorado, says that universities need to protect free speech in all of its forms, now matter how objectionable, because "if we infringe on the rights of any person, we may be next." Thomas adds that "Young people have to learn to grow up on college campuses. We have to teach them how to deal with adversarial situations. They have to learn how to survive offensive speech they find wounding and hurtful."[56]

Lukianoff warns that, "Whatever reason is given for establishing a speech code, such as the prevention of bullying or harassment, time and time again the school administration ends up using the code to insulate itself against mockery. . . . People in power bamboozle the public into supporting rules that ultimately are used to protect the sensibilities (and sensitivities) of those in power."[57]

FROM THE SUBLIME TO THE RIDICULOUS, BUT MOSTLY THE RIDICULOUS

The Stanford University speech code, as well as many of the more reasonable and legally defensible speech codes in the country, uses the *Chaplinsky* definition of fighting words as "those that by their very utterance inflict injury or tend to incite an immediate breach of the peace."[58]

Unfortunately, other codes don't provide any definitions at all, or if they do, the definitions are so vague as to be meaningless. As Alan C. Kors (of "water buffalo" fame) and Harvey A. Silverglate, authors of *The Shadow University: The Betrayal of Liberty America's Campuses,* wrote, "Speech codes have the potential to trap the innocent by making it impossible to know what was and was not prohibited."[59]

Examples:

- The University of Maryland has a sexual harassment policy that bans "idle chatter of a sexual nature, sexual innuendoes, comments about a person's clothing, body, and/or sexual activities, comments of a sexual nature about weight, body shape, size, or figure, and comments or questions about the sensuality of a person."[60]
- The University of Connecticut has outlawed "inappropriately directed laughter," and numerous schools now employ sexual harassment policies that prohibit "suggestive looks" and "unwelcome flirtations," but none provide meaningful definitions.[61]
- At Syracuse University, a speech code prohibits "offensive remarks" and provides examples such as "sexually suggestive staring, leering, sounds, or gestures."[62]
- At the State University of New York, a speech code says that "All members of the college community should respect the rights and dignity of other individuals and avoid display of bias in public actions or utterances."[63]
- At the City University of New York, a speech codes puts the responsibility for determining guilt or innocence solely on the offended party. The code, which was originally developed to deal with accusations of sexual harassment but has since been applied to other forms of speech, defines offensive speech as that which is "defined not by intentions, but by impact on the subject."[64] Herbert London, professor of humanities at rival New York University, notes that by basing accusations on "impact rather than intention," the accused party is "automatically guilty if the accuser believes he is guilty."[65]
- At the University of Puget Sound in Washington, a campus speech code may fit the description of "vague and overboard" better than any other

code in the nation. UPS's code does not require a complaining party or that anyone offer evidence of being offended; it merely requires that the speech be "unwelcome"—without specifying a yardstick by which one could measure the speech's "unwelcomeness."[66]

- At Shippensburg University in Pennsylvania, a clause in the Student Code of Conduct prohibits expression that is "inflammatory, demeaning, or harmful toward others."[67]
- The University of Connecticut speech code bans "inappropriate laughter."[68]
- Colby College in Maine bans speech that could "lead to a loss of self-esteem."[69]
- At the California Institute of Technology, a policy prohibits any speech that "demeans another because of his personal characteristics or beliefs."[70]
- At Macalester College in Minnesota, a policy prohibits "speech that makes use of inappropriate words or non-verbals."[71] FIRE points out that the policy does not attempt to define an "inappropriate word," leaving it up to the speaker to guess at what might be prohibited.[72]
- Princeton University states that sexual harassment includes "comments or behavior that may be intentional or accidental, subtle or obvious." FIRE points out that this conflicts with federal guidelines used in sexual harassment cases, which require that comments or behavior can be considered harassment only if they are "repeated and unwanted."[73]
- West Chester University in Pennsylvania prohibits "any actions which demonstrate a lack of respect for the human rights and personal dignity of any individual."[74]
- Saint Cloud State University in Minnesota bans "any derogatory remarks about a person's race, class, age, gender, or physical limitations."[75]
- Rutgers University in New Jersey prohibits "joking comments (including those between friends, roommates, of floormates) which may be racist, sexist, heterosexist, or homophobic, even when it is believed or discovered that the perpetrator(s) has no specific or general intent to harm an individual or group."[76]
- New York University prohibits "insulting, teasing, mocking, degrading, or ridiculing another person or group."[77]
- The College of Holy Cross prohibits speech "causing emotional injury through careless or reckless behavior."[78]
- The University of Connecticut bans "actions that intimidate, humiliate, or demean persons or groups, or that undermine their security or self-esteem."[79]
- Virginia State University bars students from "offending any member of the university community."[80]

- The University of Wisconsin-Stout technology policy prohibits the distribution of any messages that include comments about a variety of attributes, including hair color.[81]

FREE SPEECH AT THE UNIVERSITY OF MICHIGAN, OR MAYBE NOT

The most significant conflict involving campus speech codes is the 1989 case of *Doe v. University of Michigan*. The genesis of the case began in early 1987, when the university was plagued by multiple incidents of sexual and racial harassment among students, including sexist and racist graffiti (flyers distributed anonymously on campus declared "open season" on black students), the display of swastikas and other offensive symbols in dormitory windows, and racist and sexist jokes on the campus radio station. At the height of the controversy, one student anonymously wrote on a blackboard: "A mind is a terrible thing to waste—especially on a nigger" and an announcer on the radio station posed the question, "Who are the most famous black women in history? Aunt Jemima and Mother Fucker."[82]

On December 14, 1987, the university's acting president circulated a confidential memorandum to other university administrators outlining a new "speech code" that prohibited speech that "stigmatized or victimized" women, minorities, or gays. Comments on the early drafts were mixed, and the university's legal counsel expressed doubts as to its constitutionality, but the president insisted on pushing it forward.

When the speech code, formally titled "Policy on Discrimination and Discriminatory Harassment," became public, it appeared at first to serve the university's legitimate interest in providing what it called a "comfortable learning environment" for minority students. In defending the policy, the university president cited the Supreme Court's 1919 decision that the principle of free speech does not allow a man to "falsely shout 'fire' in a crowded theater"[83] and said that the institution should not allow "discriminatory remarks which seriously offend many individuals beyond the immediate victim, and which, therefore detract from the necessary educational climate of a campus."[84]

Ironically, during the eighteen months of controversy generated by the new rules, the frequency of racist and sexist incidents either remained the same or increased slightly, depending on whose statistics were being cited. One of the first students to be disciplined was an African American student who jokingly used the term "white trash" in a conversation with a white student.[85]

Critics of the code objected when a follow-up document, issued by the Office of Affirmative Action, attempted to clarify the policy by providing examples such as, "A male student makes a remark in class such as, 'Women just aren't as good in this field as men,' thus creating a hostile learning atmosphere for female classmates." Other examples of offensive behavior listed in the document included "racist graffiti written on the door of an Asian student's study carrel," and "students in a residence hall have a floor party and invited everyone except one student because they think she might be a lesbian."[86] A lawsuit challenging the case was filed by a graduate teaching assistant using the pseudonym John Doe. Assisted by the ACLU, he claimed that the code would limit speech in a psychology class he taught because the subject matter called for the discussion of differences between the races and sexes and that he could not effectively teach the class because of his fear that offended students could file complaints against him or other students in his classes based on the policy.

In his affidavit filed with the Court, the plaintiff claimed that "the policy is an official statement that at the University of Michigan, some arguments will no longer be tolerated."[87]

"Rather than encourage maturing students to question each other's beliefs on such diverse and controversial ideas as the proper role of women in society, the merits of particular religions, or the moral propriety of homosexuality, the university has decided that it must protect its students from what it considers to be 'unenlightened' ideas," Doe wrote. "In so doing, the university has established a secular orthodoxy by implying, among other things, that homosexuality is morally acceptable and that feminism is superior to the traditional view of women."[88]

A federal court judged in the student's favor, ruling that the code was vague and overbroad, based on its use of terms such as "victimize" and "stigmatize" that were too difficult to define. Further, the court ruled that the code was so broad that it "swept within its scope a significant amount of verbal conduct which is unquestionably protected under the First Amendment." The court also determined that while the university's motive of providing a "comfortable learning environment" was admirable, it feared that the code could also be misused in order to limit speech on other topics, such as comments critical of the university.[89]

Despite the court ruling, many observers claim the climate of "political correctness" still prevails at the University of Michigan. Just a few years after the *Doe* case, a UM student was threatened with sexual harassment charges after a female graduate teaching assistant claimed to be offended by an essay he wrote that included a character he named "Dave Stud." The question he was responding to dealt with problems in opinion polling conducted by telephone because of poor sampling techniques. "Let's say Dave Stud is entertaining three beautiful ladies in his penthouse when the phone rings," his essay began. "A pollster on the other end wants to know if we should eliminate the capital gains tax. Now Dave is a knowledgeable business person who cares a lot about this issue. But since Dave is 'tied up' at the moment, he tells the pollster to 'go bother someone else.' Now this is perhaps a ludicrous example, but if this segment of the population is never actually polled, then the results of the poll could be skewed." The student dropped the class and the teaching assistant withdrew her complaint. [90]

In 1992, administrators at the University of California at Berkeley suspended students for wearing T-shirts showing a Hispanic man sitting on a beach and the caption, "It doesn't matter where you came from, as long as you know where you are going." The action was prompted by complaints by Mexican American students, but after the students threatened to sue the university for violating their free speech rights, the suspensions were lifted. [91]

SLAVE AUCTION

In the 1991 case of *UWM Post v. the University of Wisconsin System*, a Federal District Court ruled that speech codes on college campuses constituted a violation of the students' First Amendment rights. Three years earlier, the University of Wisconsin System had adopted "A Design for Diversity," a comprehensive plan to increase minority representation among the faculties and student bodies at the state's twenty-six campuses. The plan included a speech code, which was included in response to a number of racially insensitive incidents in the previous two years. The most outrageous example was a fraternity fund-raiser, called a "Slave Auction," in which white pledges wearing blackface were auctioned off to do menial work for other students.

Eleven students worked as a group to challenge the speech code on constitutional grounds. The students claimed that not only was the policy an obvious violation of their First Amendment rights, but also their rights of due process and equal protection, as it was structured in a "guilty until proven innocent" manner that offered no indication that accused parties would have the opportunity to offer a defense.

Attorneys for the UW Board of Regents argued that the rule applied only to speech not protected by the First Amendment, citing the "fighting words" definition from the 1942 Supreme Court Case of *Chaplinsky v. New Hampshire* as one example. But attorneys for the plaintiffs countered that no such limitation could be found in the policy, and while administrators in office at the time might have the proper intentions, the text of the policy was so vague that future administrators might easily abuse it to limit the most benign speech, such as simple criticism of university policy.

After the court agreed with the students' "overbreadth and vagueness" claim and decided the case in their favor, the University of Wisconsin System declined to appeal the case. Because the case was decided at such a low level of the court system, the decision is not binding on universities in other states, but it is often cited by plaintiffs in similar cases.[92]

At the University of Wisconsin, the speech code in place at the time of the *UWM Post* case identified harassing speech as that which "has little value because of five reasons— 1) it is not intended to inform or convince the listener, 2) it not part of any dialogue or exchange of views, 3) does not provide an opportunity to reply, 4) constitutes a kind of verbal assault on the person to whom it is directed, and 5) is likely to incite a reaction."[93]

FREE SPEECH AT SHIPPENSBURG UNIVERSITY, OR MAYBE NOT

In 2003, a U.S. District Court in Pennsylvania struck down a Shippensburg University rule that limited student speech of a "controversial nature" to two designated areas on campus. The location of the free speech zones did not bother students as much as the requirement that they were required to reserve the locations in advance and disclose the purpose of their gatherings or demonstrations before being allowed to do so. University President Anthony P. Ceddia contended that free speech zones represented nothing more than a "reasonable and content-neutral time, place, and manner restriction" and were not designed to discourage or prohibit speech to which the administration objected.

FIRE filed suit in Federal District Court against Shippensburg, calling its speech code unconstitutional. Co-founder Alan Kors claimed that the Shippensburg code was so "vague and sweeping" that it created a "chilling effect on students' rights to freely and openly engage in appropriate discussions of their theories, ideas, and political and/or religious beliefs." In court documents, FIRE listed examples from the code it found problematic, including prohibitions on speech that "demeans, annoys, or alarms others." In defending the code, Shippensburg administrators claimed that the institution "strongly and vigorously defends the right of free speech" but that the school "has expectations that our students conduct themselves in a civil manner that allows them to express their opinions without interfering with the rights of others."[94]

A federal judge ruled in favor of the students and enjoined Shippensburg from enforcing key provisions of the code after finding that the university failed to show that the code was needed to protect students' rights or to avoid disruption of the educational process. Attorneys for the students urged the court to "restore the marketplace of ideas and remind the university that it is a laboratory of democracy—not an incubator of indoctrination."[95]

Lawyers for the university argued that the speech code was "merely aspirational" and therefore was not subject to First Amendment scrutiny. But in his thirty-two-page opinion, U.S. District Judge John E. Jones III of the

Middle District of Pennsylvania found that while the speech code was "obviously well-intentioned," it went too far in attempting to regulate the speech of adult students. Jones found that "the university speech code, even narrowly construed, prohibits a considerable amount of speech that is neither vulgar nor obscene."[96]

OUR NEXT PROTEST WILL BE ABOUT IRONY

At New Mexico State University in 2001, student Sean Randolph wanted to hand out fliers critical of the administration, but he was arrested for doing so outside of the designated free speech zone. What campus policy was he most upset about? The administrations' insistence on having a free speech zone in the first place. The irony was lost on school administrators, but not on Randolph.[97]

A free speech zone is an area of campus, typically a common area such as a plaza or other gathering place, where students are allowed to hold rallies, distribute literature, or make extemporaneous speeches on controversial topics. Such a gathering place generally fits the description of a "traditional public forum."[98] Students engaging in controversial speech outside of the free speech zone would be subject to the institution's disciplinary policies.

Institutions often defend their free speech zones as content-neutral and reasonable "time, place, and manner" restrictions that are necessary to minimize disruption of academic activities elsewhere on campus. Some claim a free speech zone is a "traditional public forum" while the remainder of the campus is a "limited public forum." Opponents, however, claim that such zones are unnecessary forms of prior restraint and because university campuses are designed to be locations where controversial ideas are debated, the entire campus should be a free speech zone.

There are no Supreme Court cases involving free speech zones on college campuses, but lower courts typically rule that such policies violate the First Amendment. Before such conflicts can reach the courtroom, however, most policies regarding free speech zones are abandoned after student and faculty protests or under the threat of legal action. Other universities still have free speech zones but are reluctant to enforce those policies.[99]

Free speech zones are an artifact of the 1960s-era protests against the Vietnam War, when conservative university administrators believed both faculty and students should not draw negative attention to the university. It created the zones, which were sometimes logically chosen common areas such as those outside of student unions or administration buildings. But other schools, opting for the "out of sight, out of mind" approach, chose to put their zones in remote and low-traffic areas of the campus.

In the postwar era of the 1970s and 1980s, free speech zones lost their appeal, and the few students who chose to protest were allowed to do so anywhere on campus as long as they did not produce noise that would disrupt classes. But in the late 1980s and early 1990s, as the United States assumed a broader role in military conflicts around the world, administrators reintroduced the concept.

The first post-Vietnam War era free speech zone is believed to have been created at Tufts University in Massachusetts, where administrators attempted to restrict not only anti-military speech but also "any speech that might offend." One example of the latter was the case of a student who wanted to sell T-shirts listing "Reasons why beer is better than women." In response, administrators required that all potentially "sexist and racist speech" would be limited to the free speech zone.[100]

In response, students used chalk and yellow tape to delineate the parts of campus on where free speech was and was not allowed. After the local media published photographs and broadcast video of the satirical response, President Jean Mayer was embarrassed enough to do away with the restrictions.[101]

At many universities, the designation of free speech zones is made worse by the provision requiring that groups request permission to use the zone in advance—sometimes as much as two weeks—and also disclose the topics of the information or opinions they intend to disseminate. "They want to know what you plan to say before they give you permission to say it," commented Tammy Bruce, a long-time critic of free speech zones and other forms of infringement on campus speech.[102]

Certain parts of a college campus present problems in determining an appropriate level of speech protection because they share characteristics of both private homes and public forums. Administrators can (and do) argue that within residential buildings, hallways, dining areas, and other common areas constitute extensions of individual student rooms. But free speech advocates could argue that such areas also constitute gathering places and therefore should be regarded as public forums, open to expressive activities at least by residents of that building if not by the larger community. Supreme Court decisions in cases involving anti-littering ordinances and abortion protests would support the latter view, as the Court has determined that "a resident's right to stop the free flow of information into his household does not allow him to impede the flow of the same information to his neighbors."[103]

Lukianoff compares campus speech zones to whack-a-mole games at the county fair. "For every free speech area the courts strike down, another one pops up," he wrote.[104]

Opponents of free speech zones believe firm parameters are not necessary, and that rules related to behavior rather than speech, such as prohibiting blocking traffic or disrupting classes, could be enacted without violating the First Amendment.[105]

In 2014, the Virginia Legislature enacted a law barring "free speech zones" after a series of well-publicized cases in which even non-controversial groups were forced to hand out literature in free speech zones located in remote corners of campus.[106]

AN UNCIVIL WAR

When Randolph Community College administrator Rhonda Winters approved a proposal for a noncredit "community outreach" course on the role played by North Carolinians in the Civil War, she could not have predicted the course nearly setting off an uncivil war—one involving southern heritage, political correctness, sloppy journalism, and a reporter and his newspaper stubbornly refusing to admit a series of mistakes.

It was fall semester 1998, and Jack Perdue, a sixty-year-old community volunteer and historian, worked with members of the Sons of Confederate Veterans to develop the course that would be offered at the college's branch campus in Archdale, a town of about 9,000 located twenty miles south of Greensboro, North Carolina. Consisting of stimulating readings, costumes, artifacts, and presentations by guest speakers, the ten-week course was offered for a mere $40 and attracted a small but enthusiastic class roster of eleven students.

In his introductory comments, Perdue said "it was time for a balanced view of the history of this era to be presented . . . it should no longer be acceptable to make young North Carolinians feel ashamed of their ancestors—white, black, Hispanic, and Native American—who fought for North Carolina and the Confederacy."[107]

The controversy began when Ethan Feinsilver, a reporter for the *Greensboro News & Record*, showed up late for the first class meeting and approached Perdue during the break to explain his idea to write a story about the class. Perdue said the tone of the reporter's questions foreshadowed trouble.

Feinsilver was not seen again for six weeks, but a *News & Record* photographer did take pictures at a class field trip to an outdoor replica of a Civil War encampment. After not hearing from Feinsilver for so long, Perdue assumed the reporter had lost interest in the story. But he did learn that Feinsilver had called one of the class's guest speakers, Reverend Herman White, and demanded a copy of his lecture notes. When White refused, Feinsilver confronted him and Perdue at the November 5 class meeting. The reporter asked the two men a number of loaded questions about how slaves were treated on southern plantations and the role of black soldiers fighting for the Confederacy. Feinsilver then inquired about Perdue's credentials to teach the class, asked if he approached teaching the class with "an agenda," and questioned whether the "taxpayers of North Carolina should be footing the bill for such a controversial course."[108]

During the break, Feinsilver interviewed two students about their interest in the class, and after it adjourned, he asked three other students to remain behind for a brief conversation. Two were public school teachers who had overheard his conversation with Perdue and White and were suspicious of his intentions. In later conversations with Perdue, all five students interviewed said that while slavery was only a small part of the class discussion, it seemed to be the only topic Feinsilver was interested in.

Word of Feinsilver's behavior reached Winters the next morning. She called Feinsilver's editor and told him that the reporter should not have been attending the class without paying the fee and that his confrontational interviewing technique had upset several students. The editor had more sympathy for his reporter than for Winters and asked her the same questions the reporter had asked Perdue and White: why was the college offering such a class, and what was its "agenda"?[109]

The following Thursday night, scheduled to be the next-to-last class meeting, Feinsilver again confronted Perdue before the class began. Perdue told him he could not remain in the class without permission from Winters, and the reporter quickly left the building. About that same time another nonstudent showed up: Richie Everette, president of the local chapter of the National Association for the Advancement of Colored People. He had come to check out the "controversy," but left satisfied with the content of the class and told Perdue he would like to register himself the next time it was offered.

On Sunday, November 15—after the class had met nine times—the *News & Record* published its first story on the matter. Photographs showed Perdue in his Confederate uniform and displaying the Confederate battle flag and other artifacts, but it was the accompanying text that Perdue found the most problematic.

Unable to stay for the previous week's class, Feinsilver had missed the comments offered by White, making his second appearance as a guest speaker. Feinsilver claims he got photocopied notes taken by one of the students, and based on those notes, quoted White as saying that "slaves in North Carolina were happy." A videotape of the class proved that White made no such comments, but he did make references to the fact that many slaves had access to better food and health care than they might have had if they had not been slaves. In addition to misquoting White, Feinsilver's story was also marred by numerous spelling errors and other factual discrepancies.

The story became national news within days. National newspapers and television networks called Feinsilver to interview him for more information about his story and contacted the college to demand an explanation for the explosive comments. The NAACP promised to investigate, as did the U.S. Commission on Civil Rights. Despite the fact the course was self-supporting and no taxpayer dollars were spent to offer it, both local and national media stories portrayed the story as one involving "state-sponsored racism."[110] Early the following week, RCC administrators canceled the remaining class and issued refunds to the students.

On December 1, the Sons of Confederate Veterans ran a half-page ad in the *News & Record* that attacked Feinsilver and accused him of race-baiting.

The controversy came to the attention of Jerry Bledsoe, a former *News & Record* reporter and columnist who left the paper after twenty years to begin a second career in writing true crime books. Although not a crime story per se, Bledsoe saw the controversy as a story that needed to be written—and that he was the person to write it. He spent more than two years interviewing members of Perdue's family, members of the SCV, students who took the class, and staff members of the *News & Record* who insisted on anonymity. His requests to interview Feinsilver, as well as senior editors and the publisher of the newspaper, were declined.

The major player in the controversy could not be interviewed either. Before the controversy waned, Perdue had died of a heart attack in February 1999—a death his family and friend blamed on the stress of the controversy. Perdue's death gave Bledsoe the title for book: *Death by Journalism*.

One journalist who reviewed Bledsoe's book claimed that Perdue and the school were partially to blame for the controversy lasting as long as it did. Perdue held only one news conference and granted only one solo media interview, and the school took the advice of its external public relations consultant, who told administrators to "say as little as possible and let the whole thing blow over." The school issued only one news release related to the controversy.

Even though no one at the *News & Record* would admit the shortcomings of the story, the paper did suspend Feinsilver for six months—then accepted his resignation. The management of the paper claimed that both personnel moves were unrelated to the controversy.[111]

POLITICALLY CORRECT, OR MAYBE NOT

Beginning in the early 1990s, many faculty members became so concerned about the potential for student complaints based on innocent yet misunderstood comments that they began taping their classes. Alan Dershowitz, a professor at Harvard Law School, for example, began recording his lectures on sensitive topics such as rape after a student accused him of sexual harassment—simply for suggesting that some men accused of rape might be innocent.[112]

"There are very strong reasons for protecting even racist speech," wrote Stanford Law School Professor Charles R. Lawrence in a 1990 article in *Duke Law Journal*. "Perhaps the most important reasons are that it reinforces our society's commitment to the value of tolerance, and that, by shielding racist speech from government regulation, we will be forced to combat it as a community."[113]

But Lawrence stopped short of allowing for racist speech to be completely unregulated. He recognized the distinction customarily drawn by the Supreme Court between conduct and speech—allowing for the regulation of the former but not the latter. Claiming that racism is simultaneously 100 percent conduct and 100 percent speech, Lawrence suggests that racist conduct often communicates the message of white supremacy and suggests that non-whites are deserving of less status and privilege. Instead of attempting to eliminate all racist speech, which is a popular sentiment on college campuses, Lawrence endorsed a model that had been proposed at Stanford, which placed an emphasis on the difference between captive and noncaptive audiences and obtrusive and nonobtrusive speech. On a continuum where obtrusive speech to captive audiences is at one extreme and nonobtrusive speech to noncaptive audience is at the other, Stanford's proposed code would allow administrators to regulate the former but not the latter.[114]

Cornell University Law School Professor Steven H. Shiffrin is a leading First Amendment scholar and co-author of a widely used free speech casebook. While free speech advocates point to examples of how political correctness infringes upon the First Amendment, Shiffrin argues the reverse—that too much freedom of speech is sometimes a bad thing and the First Amendment sometimes gets in the way of civility.

In a 2014 journal article titled, "The Dark Side of the First Amendment," Shiffrin proclaimed, "The First Amendment is at odds with human dignity" and "protecting racist speech is undermining racial equality."[115]

Eric Posner, Shiffrin's counterpart at the University of Chicago Law School, adds that, "For the left, the First Amendment today is like a dear old uncle who enacted heroic deeds in his youth but on occasion says embarrassing things about taboo subjects in his decline."[116]

Many modern-day civil libertarians are fond of using ideas of the past to support their positions that college campuses should concentrate on expanding free speech rights rather than limiting them and that students are better served when contrary ideas are not only welcome but also encouraged. One of those philosophers often quoted about the value of having all ideas out in the open, instead of suppressing those that appear unpopular on the surface, was Plato. Speaking more than 2,000 years ago, the Greek philosopher commented that "we can easily forgive a child who is afraid of the dark; the real tragedy of life is when men are afraid of the light."[117] More recently, English Prime Minister Winston Churchill expressed similar sentiments when he said that "men occasionally stumble over the truth, but most of them pick themselves up and hurry on as if nothing happened."[118]

In a 2010 study of 24,000 students and faculty conducted by the Association of American Colleges and Universities, only 30 percent of students and 17 percent of faculty responded that "it was safe to have unpopular views" on their campuses. Lukianoff, a critic of speech codes, free speech zones, and the general climate of "political correctness" on campus, explained in a 2014 book that students and faculty who are frowned upon for having the "wrong opinions" respond by "talking only with people they agree with, keep their mouths shut in mixed company, and often don't even bother arguing with the angriest or loudest person in the room."[119]

PROFESSORS BEHAVING BADLY

In his 2000 novel *The Human Stain*, Pulitzer Prize-winning author Philip Roth told the story of Coleman Silk, a professor of classics at a fictional private university in New England, who ran afoul of the administration after inadvertently referring to two students missing from class as "spooks." Sisk was simply joking about their frequent absenteeism and was unaware that they were black, but that wasn't enough for his superiors, who responded to student oversensitivity and their own "white guilt" by terminating the tenured professor who was already close to retirement.

In media interviews, Roth disclosed that he based the novel and its protagonist on the real-life story of Melvin Tumin, a professor of sociology at Princeton University, who faced a similar ordeal that nearly ended his thirty-year career.[120]

The fictional Silk (who, much like Tumin, ironically was later exposed as a light-skinned black man who passed for white for much of his life) was an obvious victim of "campus correctness" who did not deserve his fate. Other professors who many critics believe were far more deserving of termination eventually met that fate, but it took much longer—and required a series of incidents rather than a single one—to justify their firings.

At Florida Atlantic University in Boca Raton, professor of media history James Tracy made national headlines by claiming the December 2012 murders of twenty students and six employees at Sandy Hook Elementary School in Connecticut was a hoax—that killed no one—carried out by hired actors and staged by the federal government to generate support for gun-control legislation.

The following April, Tracy floated his theory that the bombing at the Boston Marathon that killed three spectators and injured hundreds of others was actually a "mass casualty drill" and that no one really died. The university distanced itself from Tracy's conspiracy theories, which were posted on his personal blog and not the FAU website. "Florida Atlantic University does not agree with Mr. Tracy's views or opinions," the university clarified on its website. "His editorialized postings do not reflect the positions of the university or its leaders. The university stands with the rest of the country in our support of the victims of these two tragedies."[121]

More recently, Tracy has suggested the government staged news stories such as murders in San Bernardino, California; Charleston, South Carolina; and the Navy Yard in Washington, DC.

In early 2016, FAU fired Tracy, claiming his behavior was outrageous enough for his tenure to be revoked. The university claimed the dismissal was not related to his outrageous theories, but was based instead on him contacting parents of Sandy Hook children killed in the tragedy and accusing them of taking part in the conspiracy. After the parents of Noah Pozner, a six-year-old killed at Sandy Hook, asked Tracy to remove their son's photograph from his blog, Tracy responded with a demand that the parents provide proof that Noah ever lived and that they were his biological parents.[122]

In 2014, a political science professor was offered a position at the University of Illinois, but saw the offer withdrawn after he posted on Twitter his anti-Semitic comments about the bombing of settlements in Gaza. Steven Salaita, who gave up a tenured positioned at Virginia Polytechnic University, claimed his comments were "taken out of context" and that he has strongly opposed to all forms of racism. But that wasn't enough for Illinois president Robert Easter, who told a reporter for the *New York Times* that, "Professor Salaita's approach indicates he would be incapable of fostering a classroom environment where conflicting opinions would be given equal consideration." The president later clarified that the withdrawal of the offer was based not on the content of his statements, but rather the tone with which they were made.

Senior Joshua Cooper had collected 1,300 student signatures on a petition opposing Salaita's hiring, and numerous alumni had threatened to stop their annual donations to the university if Salaita's hiring went forward.

Following his loss of the job at Illinois, Salaita was hired to teach at the American University in Beirut, Lebanon.[123]

———————

At the University of Michigan in 2014 and 2015, a sociology doctoral student caused controversy by posting on Twitter a number of comments considered racist by her colleagues and students, including "white college males are the 'problem population' in America," "every year during MLK week I commit myself to not spending a dime in white-owned businesses," and "can we just call St. Patrick's Day the white people's Kwanzaa that it is?"

But the controversy surrounding Saida Grundy was not enough to discourage Boston University from hiring her for her first full-time teaching job in 2015. Virginia Sapiro, the dean of the BU College of Arts and Sciences, defended the hire. "Universities are not opposed to controversy," Sapiro told a reporter for *The Boston Globe*. "Education requires that people be able to communicate with each other and listen and tolerate people communicating."[124]

At the University of Missouri in the fall of 2015, a communications professor interfered with the free speech rights of student journalists covering student protests on campus. The mostly peaceful gatherings resulted from weeks of unrest over charges of racial discrimination on the campus that protestors said had been festering for more than a decade. Students demanded the firings of university administrators who failed to respond to incidents of racial discrimination and harassment, and the university's football team threatened not to compete or practice until changes were made.

The students eventually got their way, as several high-ranking administrators were either fired or reassigned, and the state legislature ordered an investigation into a decade of race-related events leading up to the protests.

One highlight of the controversy came on November 9, when Melissa Click, a veteran professor with the ironic teaching assignment of courses in free speech, attempted to block student journalists and photographers from covering the event. At one point, she asked for university police to provide "some muscle" in order to stop the journalists from doing their job.

"I can't defend the way I handled that encounter," Click told *USA Today* in a February 2016 interview. "I was very flustered. But it was one moment in my twelve years at Missouri. It was one moment in a full day in a historic moment on our campus."

Despite hiring a public relations firm to help improve her image and save her job, Click was fired early in 2016.[125]

TO KILL A DRAMA CLUB PRODUCTION

At Fort Walton Beach High School in northwest Florida in 2007, a drama club production of *To Kill a Mockingbird*, a play based on the Pulitzer Prize-winning Harper Lee novel about racial tensions in the rural south in the 1930s, almost didn't make it to the stage because the Okaloosa County School Board feared controversy over repeated use of the term "nigger." The drama club asked the New York-based publisher of the play for permission to delete the word, but was told it would violate copyright law as well as the licensing agreement—which the drama club had agreed to—that required the production of the play follow the original text verbatim.

At first, school superintendent Alexis Tibbetts insisted that the play be canceled, but students, parents, and community leaders urged her to allow the play to go forward as it was written.

One local pastor, Larry Boldin, told the media that the debate was not about censorship but rather sensitivity. Other religious leaders, as well as educators, said that to cancel the play would be to miss a "teaching opportunity" during which students and their teachers could debate not only the use of the word, but also racial issues in general.

Boldin and Arden Farley, equity officer for the Okaloosa County School District, participated in a public forum in the school auditorium held three weeks before the scheduled opening night of the production. The following week, the two men continued the debate in the editorial boardroom of a local daily newspaper.

A local chapter of the NAACP raised the first objections to the production, but after the issue was debated for several weeks, the civil rights group dropped its objections and the play was presented without further controversy.[126]

In 2003, the drama club at Columbus East High School in Indiana faced a similar controversy involving the same play, but after being told by the publisher that they could not alter the content, school administrators canceled the production.[127]

WHAT'S IN A NAME?

In the spring of 2016, student activists on college campuses across the country found a new target for their angst—statuary and buildings they believed honored historical figures undeserving of being honored. Inspired partly by the trend of removing the Confederate battle flag from the grounds of public buildings across the Southeast, students demanded that statues of Civil War generals be removed and buildings bearing their names—or the names of other individuals with questionable pasts—be renamed.

The movement affected Stanford, Amherst, Georgetown, Harvard, Princeton, Yale, the University of Alabama, and the University of California-Berkeley.

At Stanford, students demanded (unsuccessfully) the name of Junipero Serra, an eighteenth-century priest who founded numerous missions along the California coast but was also known to be cruel to Native Americans in the region, be removed from a campus building.

At Princeton University, students demanded (unsuccessfully) the school distance itself from the legacy of Woodrow Wilson, president of the university from 1902 to 1910 and president of the United States a decade later. Their main demand was that the school remove Wilson's name from the School of Public Policy. Wilson, in their view, was slow to react to racial issues facing the university during his tenure there, and as U.S. president did not do enough to integrate society.

At Berkeley, students demanded (unsuccessfully) the school remove the name of Supreme Court Justice Earl Warren from an administrative building. Protestors pointed to the fact that as attorney general of California during World War II, Warren oversaw the detention of thousands Japanese-Americans in internment camps. Protestors overlooked the fact that as chief justice a decade later, Warren would write the majority opinion in *Brown v. Board of Education*—believed to be the most important civil rights case ever decided by the Supreme Court.

At the University of Alabama, a newly formed coalition of students and faculty supporting faculty diversity demanded (unsuccessfully) that the school remove from its buildings the names of "white supremacists, Klansmen, Confederate generals, and eugenicists." One of their targets was Morgan Hall, dedicated in 1911 and named after Alabama senator and Ku Klux Klan leader John Tyler Morgan. Protestors wanted the building renamed for Harper Lee, a UA alumnus and author of *To Kill a Mockingbird*.

In 2016, students at the University of Tulsa urged (unsuccessfully) the administration to remove the name of John Rogers from the building that houses its College of Law. Rogers was a key figure in the development of the university in the 1940s, but, it turned out, was also a key figure in the early days of the Ku Klux Klan.

Harvard University may have been the only major university to give in to student demands. The Harvard Law School dropped its seal, based partially on the coat of arms of the Isaac Royal family, because the family owned slaves in the 1700s. Isaac Royal Jr., who died in 1781, donated his estate to the university, which provided much of the funding used to establish the law school.[128]

UNINVITING THE SPEAKER

In 2013, college campuses began experiencing a unexpected challenge to free speech—the trend of schools withdrawing the invitations of commencement speakers and other campus visitors because of faculty and student protests.

The idea of uninviting speakers—or not inviting them in the first place—happened as far back as the 1960s, but it was based on the opposition of political leaders more so than student and faculty angst. In 1963, the North Carolina General Assembly passed a law that prohibited "known communists" as well as anyone known to have invoked the Fifth Amendment in defending themselves against accusations of involvement with communists, from speaking on the state's college campuses. As the Vietnam War escalated, the emphasis of the speaker ban shifted from alleged communists to anyone opposed to the war. Some of the speaker ban's more noteworthy victims were geneticist J. B. Haldane and playwright Arthur Miller, both of whom were "uninvited" when their dubious connections to the Communist Party became known.

Students challenged the law in 1968 and persuaded a federal court to declare it unconstitutional based on the First and Fifth Amendments.

In 2005, a film professor at the University of North Carolina at Chapel Hill produced a documentary film titled *Beyond the Wall*, which compared the anticommunist obsession of the Cold War era to the zeal with which today's politicians equate criticism of U.S. foreign policy with being nonpatriotic. Gorham Kindem's film, as well as William Billingsley 1999 book *Communists on Campus*, explain that the speaker ban was aimed not only at communists, but also African Americans. [129]

Shortly after the terrorist attacks of September 11, 2001, a Washington-based political group calling itself the American Council of Trustees and Alumni began assembling a list of statements by professors and guest speakers it considered "unpatriotic." The group was founded by Lynn Cheney, wife of vice president Dick Cheney, and Joe Lieberman, a Democratic senator from Connecticut and unsuccessful vice-presidential candidate in 2000. Both refuted criticism of the group's tactics as "McCarthy-like," while critics pointed out the similarities between its work and that of Joseph McCarthy, the Wisconsin senator best-known for his campaign against alleged communists employed by the federal government in the 1950s. At one time there were more than one hundred names on the ACTA list, but most for statements as benign as "the U.S. needs to break the cycle of violence in the Middle East" and "we need to end global violence." [130]

Between 2000 and 2014, FIRE has noted 257 incidents in which students and faculty have pushed for commencement speakers or other visiting dignitaries to be un-invited because of their controversial viewpoints. Almost half of those were successful, according to FIRE co-founder Greg Lukianoff, meaning either that the invitations were rescinded or the speakers withdrew voluntarily. Of the cases in which speeches went on as scheduled, most speakers were heckled by the audience. [131]

Potential speakers who were "uninvited" included a pastor scheduled to speak at historically black Morehouse University (because he was openly critical of President Obama), a former player for the Cincinnati Bengals scheduled to speak at Xavier University (because of his opposition to gay marriage), and former Secretary of State Condoleezza Rice, scheduled to speak at Rutgers (because of her association with President George W. Bush).

In other cases, schools stood by their controversial invitees, but the speakers nonetheless canceled their appearances after negative publicity and fears of violence. Among the cancellations were noted neurosurgeon Ben Carson, who withdrew from his commitment to speak at the commencement ceremony at Johns Hopkins University after students protested his traditional views of marriage; former World Bank President Robert Zoellick, who backed out of his scheduled commencement speech at Swarthmore College because students complained about his support of the Iraq War; and former United Nations Ambassador Jeanne Kirkpatrick, who withdrew following a vote of opposition at Lafayette College.

"An education isn't supposed to be about reinforcing ideas in which you already believe, but also competing ideas," wrote political pundit Cal Thomas in a 2013 commentary in *USA Today*. "What about the rights of conservative students to hear these speakers? Don't they get a vote?" In that same column, Thomas and co-author Bob Beckel mused that the last "non-controversial" commencement speaker on an American campus may have been Kermit the Frog, the Muppets character who addressed the graduates of Southampton College in 1996, where he received a "doctorate in amphibian letters."[132]

According to the conservative student group Young America's Foundation, liberal commencement speakers typically outnumber conservative speakers by a ratio of seven to one. However, when liberals are invited to speak at commencement ceremonies, conservative students are just as vocal in their opposition. One such case took place at Goddard College in Plainfield, Vermont, in 2014. Mumia Abu-Jamal, convicted of killing a Philadelphia police officer in 1989, was invited to be the commencement speaker based on his claim that he was wrongly convicted by a racist jury, even though the evidence that convicted him was overwhelming. One of the strongest voices opposing the invitation was that of Pennsylvania Senator Pat Toomey. "This is not a question of free speech," Toomey wrote in an online essay. "It is a question of judgment and the college's basic sense of right and wrong."[133]

Even speakers at events other than commencement ceremonies can be problematic. In 2014, Brandeis University invited, then uninvited, an internationally known advocate for women's rights who was scheduled to receive an award for her work. Ayaan Hirsi Ali was uninvited in 2014 after faculty and students protested because of her public criticisms of Islam. In a statement released about the decision, Brandeis called Ali "a compelling public figure and advocate for women's rights." "We respect and appreciate her work to protect and defend the rights of women and girls throughout the world," the statement added. "That said, we cannot overlook certain of her past statements that are inconsistent with Brandeis' core values. For all concerned, we regret that we were not aware of these statements earlier." The irony of that case was that the university was named in honor of Supreme Court Justice Louis Brandeis, who for decades championed the principles of free speech.[134]

At Harvard, students wanted the university to rescind an invitation to 2014 commencement speaker Mike Johnston, a democratic state senator from Colorado, because they disagreed with his policies on school reform. The university refused.[135]

At Haverford College in Pennsylvania, a former chancellor of the University of California at Berkeley was scheduled to be the commencement speaker in May 2014. But students and faculty objected to the invitation given to Robert J. Birgeneau because of how UC police used excessive force against campus protestors. The Haverford students and faculty sent Birgeneau a letter indicating they would go along with the invitation provided he met nine conditions, including "issuing a public apology, providing reparations for the victims, and explaining in writing his position on the events at UCB and 'what he learned from them.'" Birgeneau understandably withdrew from the engagement.[136]

At Scripps College in California, a scheduled appearance by Pulitzer Prize-winning columnist George F. Will was canceled in October 2014 after his controversial column that questioned the government's statistics on campus sexual assault. The controversy followed Will to Miami University in Ohio, where more than a thousand students, faculty members, and alumni signed an open letter urging the university to uninvite him. The faculty of the school's Department of Women's, Gender, and Sexuality Studies asserted that Will's column was "hate speech as opposed to free speech" and accused him of "bullying rather than seeking dialogue." The Miami administration refused to fold, and despite protests, the speech went forward without incident.[137] Two months later, Will was scheduled to speak at the commencement ceremonies at Michigan State University and briefly considered canceling because of student protests. But instead he kept the commitment, and while his speech was not interrupted, eighteen graduating students stood and turned their backs during his speech.[138]

STUDENT FEES AND COMPELLED SPEECH

Mandatory student activity fees are sometimes the basis of student claims of "compelled speech," but the courts typically reject those claims. In the 1983 case of *Stanley v. McGrath*, for example, a federal appeals court ruled that students at the University of Minnesota could not refuse to pay a portion of their student fees allocated to the student newspaper simply because they objected to content of the publication.[139] (This case is discussed in more detail in chapter 3.)

At the University of North Carolina in 1983, students objected to their activity fees going to fund the student newspaper because they were offended by its editorial positions. Both a Federal District Court and Fourth Circuit Court of Appeals ruled against the students. The Circuit Court determined that the students' First Amendment rights had been infringed "only minimally and indirectly" and the funding process for the student newspaper helped to "expand the exchange of information, ideas, and opinions" on campus. It added that university would be in violation of the First Amendment if it compelled that newspaper to provide equal access to those disagreeing with its editorial positions.[140]

In a more recent case, *Board of Regents of the University of Wisconsin System v. Southworth,* students were unsuccessful in challenging their university's fee system.

The conflict began when Scott Southworth, a law school student at the University of Wisconsin who identified himself as a political conservative, refused to pay his $331 student activity fee for the 1995-96 academic year. Jordan Lorence, Southworth's attorney, believed the university should restructure its fee system to allow students to "opt out" of funding—albeit indirectly—any student groups whose activities or messages they found objectionable.

Southworth claimed that the student fee system was a form of compelled speech because he and other UW students were being forced, through payment of the fees, to participate in speech to which they objected.

A Federal District Court and Circuit Court of Appeals ruled in favor of Southworth. But the Supreme Court overturned that ruling early in 2000, rejecting the "compelled speech" argument and ruling in favor of the university, which claimed that its mandatory fee system was "appropriate to further its educational mission." Writing the majority decision, Justice Anthony Kennedy stated, "The First Amendment permits a public university to charge its students an activity fee used to fund a program to facilitate extracurricular student speech if the program is viewpoint-neutral."[141]

The Court also ruled that universities had the option of providing students an "opt out" but were not legally obligated to do so. But Kennedy added a caution that allowing students to "opt-out" of the fee system because it indirectly subsidizes speech with which they disagree would be "so disruptive and expensive that the program to support extracurricular speech would be ineffective."[142]

Part of the Court's rationale in deciding in favor of the university is that it would create more opportunity for speech instead of creating opportunities for limiting speech.[143]

University administrators across the country celebrated the ruling, saying afterward that if the Court had found in favor of Southworth, they would have had to dismantle or abolish their fee systems, which would have been to the detriment of all student organizations, especially those representing minority groups or espousing political or religious ideologies. Media advisers were also relieved, as any alternations to the fee system would have a devastating effect on campus newspapers, magazines, and broadcasting outlets.[144]

According to the National Association for Campus Activities, approximately 70 percent of the nation's universities employ some type of mandatory fee system. If the Court had ruled in favor of the students, the SPLC feared, it would have caused those schools to eliminate or substantially redesign their fee programs, meaning the loss of many smaller, esoteric groups, especially those involved in potentially controversial issues. The SPLC also expressed concern over the potential for administrators using the ruling as an excuse to defund campus media.[145]

NOW WEDNESDAY IS JUST WEDNESDAY

At Vernon Center Middle School in Hartford, Connecticut, several teachers banned the use of the term "hump day" by students parroting a popular television commercial aired by the Geico Insurance Company. In the thirty-second ad, which aired for about a year on major television networks, a camel walks around a business office asking "What day is it?" Annoyed at the repetitive nature of the expression and worried about a potential sexual connotation, several teachers, with permission of the school's principal, prohibited it in their classrooms.[146]

The following year, at the University of St. Thomas in Minnesota, student leaders in scheduled an event called "Hump Day." The event was to offer students the opportunity to pet a camel and raise money for charity. After students created a Facebook page to protest the event—concerned for the welfare of the animal and possible offense taken by students from the Middle East—organizers canceled the event.[147]

K-12 CASES

The idea of speech codes is not limited to college campuses. As early as elementary school, students and their parents are being advised by school administrators to avoid using slang terms that may offend classmates.

Many such rules are the result of anti-bullying efforts, and while commendable, are often seen by civil libertarians as unnecessary and harmful in that they confuse students about the dividing line between impoliteness and harassment.

The most common examples include use of the word "gay." Students making comments such as "that's so gay" are either given warnings (and parental notification) or disciplined by detention. One such case took place at Gibson Elementary School in Fresno, California, where a fourth-grader was suspended for a day in 2007 for using the phrase "that's so gay" during a playground soccer game.

The boy's mother, Lena Fisher, said she didn't condone the use of phrase in that manner, but she accepted the punishment even though she believed it was excessive. After Fisher complained that other students used the same term and were given lighter punishments, Principal Helen Cabe removed the suspension from the child's records and sent a new letter to parents that changed the language of the policy to indicate that use of the word was "discouraged" rather than "prohibited." While Fisher and other parents complained that the rule was silly and a possible violation of free speech, no lawsuits have yet resulted from the rule.[148]

At St. Albans High School in West Virginia in 2015, an annual tradition that encouraged students to dress in costumes to celebrate homecoming resulted in a local controversy when the theme chosen was "Hobo Day."

In photos that showed up on social media, students were seen pushing shopping carts full of their possessions up and down school hallways, while two were seen dressed as homeless women holding signs that said, "will teach for food."

Administrators claimed the idea was to teach students about the plight of the homeless, but local advocates for the homeless took offense. Not only did the school fail to understand the difference between true homeless persons and the stereotype of train-hitchhiking "hobos," social workers said, but the administrators and students trivialized a problem that plagued the town of St. Albans and much of the state.

Critics of the event also pointed out a double standard in how schools were treating the homeless, as opposed to how they treated other groups. "There seems to be an acceptance that it's OK to make fun of people and to talk in inappropriate ways (about the homeless) in ways we no longer talk about people of other ethnicities and LGBT people. There's a political correctness that doesn't exist with people of poverty."[149]

In the spring of 2016, the Wisconsin Interscholastic Athletic Association enacted a policy directing schools to prohibit "unsportsmanlike" chants at basketball games. Included on the list of forbidden chants was "scoreboard," "airball," and "Na Na Na Na—Hey Hey Hey—Goodbye." The policy also discouraged "booing of any kind," which it referred to as "taunting and disrespectful." After days of criticism, the WIAA clarified that its directive was a "suggestion" and not a "requirement." Critics of the policy called it the "wussification of Wisconsin," and evidence that "someone has way too much time on their hands."[150]

In May 2015, TNT Academy (Georgia) principal Nancy Gordeuk was fired after a racially insensitive remark at the school's graduation ceremony. Gordeuk was presiding over the event when she inadvertently failed to introduce the valedictorian and instead dismissed the crowd. As parents started to file out of the room, Gordeuk realized her mistake and then attempted to call the parents back in. "You people are rude to not listen to his speech," Gordeuk said. "It was my fault that it was left out of the program. Look who's leaving— all the black people."

The board of directors of the private school voted the following week to dismiss the principal. The move was praised by Francys Johnson, president of the Georgia NAACP. "This is not just about her comments," Johnson told local media. "As a private citizen she has the right to free speech. However, those entrusted with responsibility for our children must set a higher standard marked by civility. That is obviously a test the former principal failed."[151]

BEST OF THE REST

At Harvard University in 1987, Professor Stephan Thernstrom was accused of racism for simply using the term "Indians" instead of the preferred "Native Americans" and assigning a book that mentioned that some people regard affirmative action as preferential treatment. "It's like being called a Commie in the fifties," Thernstrom told a reporter for *New York* magazine. "Whatever explanation you offer, once accused, you're always a suspect." Thernstrom stopped teaching the class in race relations in order to avoid being misquoted or misunderstood.[152]

In the late 1980s, Stanford University was the site of a two-year debate over a proposed speech code intended to protect the school's female, gay, African American, Jewish, and other minority students from "words that wound." The president of the university was one of the last holdouts among administrators, saying in media interviews that "if you begin by telling people what they can't say, you will end up telling them what they can't think."

In a letter to the *Stanford Daily,* the leader of an influential African American student association wrote that "we don't put as many restrictions on free speech as we should."

The pro-code students and faculty members won the debate, and for the last two decades Stanford has had one of the most restrictive speech codes in the country.[153]

On the eve of Yom Kippur in 1990, readers of the *Dartmouth Review,* the school's underground newspaper, were shocked to see that the newspaper's regular masthead had been replaced by a passage from Adolf Hitler's manifesto, *Mein Kampf.* At first the newspaper's critics assumed it was an intentional act of religious insensitivity, but it was later determined that the paper was the victim of a prank by a disgruntled staff member.[154]

Despite the editor's apology to the school's Jewish population and the student body in general, university president James O. Freedman accused the paper of creating the climate that allowed the act to happen. He organized a "Rally Against Hate" the following week, continuing to blame the newspaper staff for the incident and deflecting responsibility from the university as a whole. Meanwhile, the university's admissions office organized a "Take Dartmouth Home" campaign, urging students to visit their hometown high schools and take copies of *The Dartmouth,* the school's "official" student newspaper.

Despite the administration's efforts, records show the number of black applicants declined after the incident, and the Rockefeller Foundation rejected the school's application for a grant that would have helped it recruit more minority faculty members.[155]

At Arizona State University in 1991, a form appeared on the door of an on-campus apartment. Titled, "Work Application—Simplified Form for Minority Applicants," the satirical job application form played on a number of stereotypes about blacks and Mexicans. One clause that read, "Black applicants—it is not necessary to attach a photo since you all look alike." The form also asked for information such as, "Number of children claimed for welfare," "Number of legitimate children (if any)," and, "List approximate income and source—theft, welfare, or unemployment."

Four black female residents saw the form, persuaded a roommate to remove it, and submitted it to campus officials. Administrators told the women they could not punish the responsible person or persons even if it could be determined who posted the flier. Instead, the university apologized to the students and helped them organize a forum that would be attended by residents of the apartments as well as other students, faculty, and administrators.[156]

In 1991, Brigit Kerrigan was a twenty-one-year-old pre-law senior at Harvard University when she decided to hang a Confederate flag from her fourth-floor residence hall window. She said she did so to show her "pride in her southern heritage" and also to "stick it to Harvard's northeastern liberal establishment." The student body reacted immediately, organizing protest marches outside of the building, publishing angry letters in student publications, and attracting local and national media attention.

The official student newspaper, the *Harvard Crimson*, published a profile of her which revealed that while a senior in high school, Kerrigan was the driver of a car involved in an accident that killed a passenger, her best friend. Kerrigan said she was hurt by the disclosure, which she believed was irrelevant to the flag issue, and for a while considered taking down the flag. But she eventually decided that do so would be "giving in to terrorists."

Jacida Townsend, a black, nineteen-year-old junior from Kentucky, was outraged by the flag. "Even though I know that no one is waiting for me with a rope, the sight of the flag is very frightening to me," Townsend told a reporter for the *Boston Globe*. "It's a violent flag. I don't see it so much as part of free speech, but as a threat of violence."

In order to test how far her own free speech could go, Townsend used black spray paint to create a swastika on a white bed sheet and hung it from her own residence hall window. The reaction to her speech was similar to that of Kerrigan: protest marches and angry letters to student publications, and local and national media attention. University President Derek Bok declared both displays "insensitive and unwise" but maintained Harvard's commitment to free speech.

Townsend eventually took the swastika down, while Kerrigan kept up the Confederate flag until the week of her graduation. Both women announced their plans to pursue law school after graduating from Harvard. [157]

In 1992, a tenured English professor at the University of New Hampshire was reprimanded for sexual harassment when after he compared belly dancing to a "plate of Jello with a vibrator underneath it." He intended it as an example as a simile in his writing class, but one student called it sexual harassment, which was enough for the administration to take notice. The professor was suspended and ordered to undergo psychiatric evaluation.

At the same school, another professor using the term "more bang for the buck" during a lecture heard a female student gasp and feared he might be accused of sexual harassment, but after he explained that the metaphor was military rather than sexual, the student did not complain to administrators. In defending his case, he factiously worried that he might offend students from the Netherlands by saying "let's go Dutch," students from Asia by using the term "Chinese fire drill," or animal rights activists by using the term "wild goose chase." [158]

In 1993, the Sigma Chi fraternity at George Mason University in Virginia staged an event called the "Ugly Woman Contest" which featured members dressed as caricatures of various types of women, including one "welfare mother" that was merely a white man wearing blackface and stuffing his shirt with a pillow to simulate pregnancy.

More than two hundred students signed a petition protesting the event, leading the university to suspend the fraternity for two years and require it to plan an a diversity education program for its members. The fraternity apologized for the incident, admitting that it was "sophomoric and offensive," but nevertheless complained that the penalty was excessive and filed suit to have the suspension overturned.

In its defense, the university claimed the event "created a threatening environment for students." The Federal District Court agreed with the students and nullified the suspension, a decision that was later upheld by the Fourth Circuit Court of Appeals. The appeals court agreed with the university's position that the theme of the event was an embarrassment to the university and inconsistent with its values, but ruled that the university "could have reached its goals in some fashion other than silencing speech on the basis of its viewpoint."[159]

In 1993, graduate teaching assistant Toni Blake was lecturing to her human sexuality class at the University of Nebraska-Lincoln. She used a banana to represent the penis in a demonstration in which her point was that even in the case of premature ejaculation, pregnancy might still result. "Many men, like basketball players, tend to dribble before they shoot," she told the class. A male student objected to the demonstration and basketball analogy and told university administrators that it was "sexual harassment" and it "objectified him as a man."

Blake received a letter of reprimand in her permanent file and was cautioned not to make such comments "at least while the case was being investigated." She decided to take it a step further, and simply asked not to be assigned the human sexuality course again. "Not in Nebraska," she told Nat Hentoff, who included the anecdote in a 1994 *Village Voice* column. "I won't go through that again."[160]

In 1993, University of California Santa Cruz student Scott Smith, known to his classmates as "Smitty," was a frequent contributor to the school's alternative newspaper. His column, "Smitty on a Hill," often poked fun at political correctness and university administrators in general. For one column, he invented a fictional campus event called the "Miss Nude UCSB Pageant" that required all potential contestants send their photographs to him. Instead of his mailbox being filled with provocative photographs, in it he found only a letter from university administrators indicating seven female students had charged him with sexual harassment as a result of the column. Instead of asking for help from the ACLU, he turned to the National Writers Union, which represents freelance writers in their quest for greater financial compensation and fairer treatment. Robert Chatelle, political issues chair for the NWU, wrote a letter to UCSC administrators defending Smith's work as "definitely not sexual harassment" and pointing out that the NWU membership was more than half women, and the union's position was that cases such as Smith's were "making something out of nothing" and only served to "detract from the more serious cases of harassment that should be the university's focus."[161]

During Rush Week at the University of California Riverside in 1993, members of the Phi Kappa Sigma fraternity threw a "South of the Border Fiesta" that included publicity materials and T-shirts that were viewed as offensive by the school's Latino and Native American students. One of the images included a caricature of a sombrero-wearing Mexican carrying a bottle and a bare-chested Indian carrying a six-pack of beer.

Student groups claiming to represent the interests of Latino and Native American students complained to school administrators, who referred the matter to the school's Interfraternity Council. That body imposed an array of sanctions that included requiring each member of the fraternity to perform sixteen hours of community service in a Chicano or Latino community and attend two multicultural awareness seminars. Fraternity officers were required to write letters of apology to campus groups that were offended. That plan was endorsed by the fraternity's national headquarters, which said "the chapter was stupid for not realizing people could be offended."

Not satisfied with those sanctions, members of Mecha, a campus group representing Latino students, took their complaint to administrators and demanded the Phi Kappa Sigma chapter be disbanded. Assistant vice chancellor Vincent Del Pizzo stopped short of that measure, but he did suspend the chapter for three years, calling the T-shirt incident "the last straw" in a series of other disciplinary issues involving the fraternity.

In defending their chapter, student leaders pointed out that one of the T-shirts bearing the slogan "It doesn't matter where you come from as long as you know where you are going" was anti-racist and was taken from a popular Bob Marley song. Further, the student leaders claimed, the shirt was designed by two Latino members of the fraternity. The students also pointed out their fraternity was one of the most diverse on campus, with more than a third of its members being minority students. Mecha, on the other hand, did not have a single non-Latino member.

Civil rights attorney John Howard, representing the fraternity on a pro-bono basis, took the case to Riverside County Superior Court. Howard told the court that campus administrators had stereotyped the fraternity members as "beer-swilling vulgarians who represented centers of white, male, and heterosexual privilege."

The response of school administrators was that university policy required student groups to attempt to resolve issues through the institution's own grievance procedure before resorting to legal recourses. That policy was not supported by state law, however, and the court ruled in a preliminary hearing that the case could move forward.

When they realized that public opinion was in favor of the students, administrators decided to settle the case outside the courtroom. They were also aware of a clause in the Leonard Law that would have required the university to pay the students' legal fees if the case was decided in the fraternity's favor. Howard said he would waive his fee if university administrators agreed to attend a First Amendment seminar.[162]

At George Washington University in Washington, DC, in 1998, students protested outside the offices of *Project This*, a student-run humor magazine that satirized domestic violence and rape and lampooned events such as a school shooting in Jonesboro, Arkansas. Another edition of the same publication ran parody ads for a "Masta-Card" credit card designed to "help Whitey keep us down" and the Asian Student Alliance that featured five photographs of the same young Asian man, each with a different name. Text accompanying the photographs read, "We all look the same."[163]

In 1999, a conservative student group at Pennsylvania State University calling itself Young Americans for Freedom invited Star Parker, a black conservative and former recipient of welfare payments, to speak on campus. Her speech, titled "From Entitlement to Empowerment," which called for the rethinking the welfare system in order to help low-income individuals escape poverty and become less dependent on government assistance, but it was perceived by other students as racist. Protestors interrupted her speech by blowing whistles, marching to the stage in military clothing, and performing a skit. Parker felt so threatened by the incident that she left the building through a back door.[164]

When Dorothy Caruso and her friends showed up for fall semester 1999 at Irvine Valley College in California, they immediately noticed something unusual about campus bulletin boards. Over the summer, the administration installed Plexiglas covers, secured by locks. It was part of new President Raghu Mathur's two-fold plan to crack down on campus speech. Both individuals and groups would have to obtain permission to use the bulletin boards, and a fourteen-day time limit for all material not posted by the administration would be enforced. It was a plan by Mathur and the administration to "strategically suppress students and faculty and reduce us to second-class citizens," Caruso told the local media.

The second unusual rule was that in-person displays of free speech, including extemporaneous speeches and the distribution of literature, would no longer be allowed in front of the Student Services Center, one of the busiest parts of campus and the obvious place for a free speech zone.

Other schools in California had been successful in declaring the outside of classroom buildings off-limits because of the potential for disrupting the academic activities inside. But in the IVC case, the administrators had no valid claim of the potential for disruption, as there were no classroom buildings in the vicinity of the SSC. Caruso joined with classmates Diep Burbridge and Scott Stephansky to sue IVC over both issues. A federal judge issued an injunction barring the university from enforcing both rules, after which the school announced plans to develop a new, less restrictive policy.[165]

At Pasadena City College in California in 2000, sophomore Philip Gibson wanted to illustrate the discrepancy between the salaries of top administrators and lower-level staff members by posting a list of employee salaries on a public bulletin board. At first, he attempted to comply with the college's policy that required all bulletin board postings be approved by the student affairs office. Administrators denied his request, claiming that the accuracy of the information could not be verified, even though they came from the college's own public records. Administrators further claimed the bulletin board was not a public forum, and it was simply applying the concept of "time, place, and manner." Gibson posted the information without permission, which resulted in a written reprimand, but not the suspension with which he was originally threatened. [166]

At West Virginia University, administrators created seven free speech zones scattered around campus, but most were small and tucked into remote, low-traffic parts of campus. Groups of fifteen or fewer students could protest at other locations with advanced permission of administrators.

In 2002, after months of negative publicity and the involvement of national free speech organizations, the university revised its policy to allow for protests outside of dormitories as long as they were not noisy and students did not block the entrances to buildings. Another policy tweak was that protest groups were no longer required to pay for security personnel. [167]

In 2002, Aaron Levine, a student at Syracuse University, wore blackface and golf attire to an on-campus party. When questioned about his costume, he responded that he was professional golfer Tiger Woods. The next day, more than sixty students demonstrated outside of the office of Chancellor Kenneth Shaw, demanding that Levine be expelled from the university and his fraternity, Sigma Alpha Epsilon, be suspended. Shaw agreed to the action against the fraternity but not that against Levine.

Both Shaw and leaders of the fraternity apologized to the university community for any offense that was perceived.

The incident came less than a year after two fraternities at Auburn University—Beta Theta Pi and Delta Sigma Pi—were suspended after members wore blackface and racially insensitive costumes in photographs posted on the Internet. With help from its national office, Beta Theta Pi sued the university and eventually reached a $100 million settlement that resulted in the fraternity being reinstated but not receiving university funding for the following school year. [168]

When Texas Tech University student Trevor Smith decided to organize a campus protest against the war in Iraq in 2003, he was unaware that such events were not allowed outside of the campus's "free speech area." His group was told it would have to schedule a day and time to use the zone, which was actually a gazebo measuring twenty square feet. That small structure was the only place on campus for any of the school's 28,000 students to distribute literature or make extemporaneous speeches on controversial topics. Lukianoff did the math and determined that the gazebo represented one square foot of protest space per 1,400 students, and an MIT mathematician estimated that if all of the school's students wanted to use the structure at the same time, they would have to squeeze themselves into the density of uranium in order to fit. With prompting from FIRE and weeks of negative publicity, the university expanded the free speech area to include surrounding grassy space and eliminated the reservation requirement. That was enough to satisfy Smith—who continued his antiwar activities—but not the Alliance Defense Fund, a Christian rights organization that questioned why the school needed a free speech zone at all. It also had problems with TTU's speech code, which prohibited speech that "insults" or "ridicules," so it joined FIRE in a lawsuit against the university. As a result, the school was forced to eliminate both the free speech zone and speech code. [169]

At the University of Houston in 1993, a student anti-abortion group calling itself the Pro-Life Cougars asked for permission to set up a display on Butler Plaza, a popular gathering place on campus where displays on a variety of topics—mostly non-controversial—were common. The proposed exhibit, titled "Justice for All," was to include information supporting their beliefs, and on alternatives to abortion, such as adoption. Dean of Students William F. Munson denied the application, claiming it was "potentially disruptive" and instead recommended the group set up its exhibit in one of five "speech zones" on campus. No permission was required for those other locations, but they could be used only between 11:30 a.m. and 1 p.m. and between 4 p.m. and midnight. Those were the university's preferred areas for activities of a "potentially disruptive nature," but they were also far away from the activity centers on campus.

The Pro-Life Cougars sued the university in Federal District Court, claiming the inability to use their preferred location and relegation to remote corners of campus violated their First Amendment rights. They also claimed that the application process for the Butler Plaza location gave far too much discretion to Munson, who could approve some applications and reject others without having to provide a reason and with no process for appeal.

The court decided in favor of the students and ordered the university to rescind its policy regarding designated free speech zones as well as Butler Plaza. As a result, the university was required to discontinue its permitting process and could only interfere with political speech events *after* they became disruptive and not *because they might become disruptive.* [170]

Donna Shalala served as President Clinton's Secretary of Health and Human Services from 1993 to 2001, but before and after served as the leader of two major American universities. Before her term at HHS, Shalala was chancellor at the University of Wisconsin-Madison, where she announced upon installation that "social justice is the mission of the university." A speech code followed. After leaving HHS, she served as president of the University of Miami, where she introduced another controversial speech code. [171]

Early in 2004, Case Western Reserve University student Jeffrey Wilson was the target of a cruel form of harassment, as classmates distributed posters across campus that labeled him as gay.

The posters, featuring Wilson's photo, contact information and the title, "In Search of a Male Companion." Wilson claimed the posters and the discussion they generated subjected him to embarrassment, humiliation, and ridicule and damaged his reputation and academic performance.

His suit against three classmates was filed within Ohio's state system, where a trial court and appeals court both ruled against him, claiming that "accusations of homosexuality were not libelous or indicative of any disease and was unlikely to injure him in a future trade or occupation." [172]

In 2004, University of New Hampshire sophomore Tim Garneau was annoyed by the long wait time to use the elevators in his residence hall. He blamed the problem on other students in the building and their unnecessary use of the elevators, sometimes for going up or down only one floor.

Garneau created a poster featuring a cartoon version of a college-age woman wearing workout clothing. The text of the poster read, "9 out of 10 freshman girls gain 10-15 pounds. But there is something you can do about it. If you live below the sixth floor, take the stairs. Not only will you feel better about yourself, but you will also be saving us time and won't be so sore on the eyes."

A residence hall director found the poster and didn't appreciate his artwork, his concern for the health of his female classmates, or his desire to make the building's elevators run more efficiently. UNH charged him with "harassment" under the school's affirmative action policy and, despite his repeated apologies, expelled him from the residence hall. FIRE intervened on Garneau's behalf and persuaded the university to drop the charges, allowing him to complete the semester. Until that decision was reached, however, Garneau spent several weeks living in his car. [173]

In 2005, it was the University of North Carolina system's turn to face national criticism over a speech code. The UNC system included the flagship school UNC-Chapel Hill as well as sixteen other institutions of various sizes and geographic settings. Most of the schools patterned their codes after those of the flagship school, but the Foundation for Individual Rights in Education found them to be vague and overbroad, constitutionally indefensible, and vulnerable to lawsuits.

The first cases of students challenging the codes occurred at UNC-Greensboro, where student groups were not allowed to protest administrative policies; and UNC-Chapel Hill, where a student group had been suspended after its faculty adviser and student leaders refused to sign the "anti-discrimination" policy required of all student organizations.

The Pope Center for Higher Education Policy worked with FIRE to research the situation at schools in that state and discovered that thirteen of the sixteen schools in the UNC system had at least one policy in effect that "clearly and substantially" restricts freedom of speech. Examples:

- Appalachian State University prohibited "insults" and "taunts" directed at another person.
- UNC Greensboro prohibited language that shows "disrespect for persons."
- UNC Asheville prohibited "taunting, challenging, or provoking any student or university official."
- UNC Pembroke prohibited "offensive speech of a biased or prejudiced nature related to one's personal characteristics, such as race, color, national origin, sex, religion, handicap, age, or sexual orientation."

The state's historically black institutions—Fayetteville State University and North Carolina Central University—had policies that prohibited "vulgar language" or "statements of intolerance."

"It is our hope that in the wake of publicity generated by this report, North Carolina's institutions of higher learning will not remain content to maintain such a low standard in the area of fundamental American rights," the report concluded. "Neither our nation's courts nor its people look favorably upon restrictions on basic American freedoms."[174]

The following year, FIRE conducted a similar study nationwide. Using lists of America's most popular universities compiled by *U.S. News & World Report*, the study divided the schools into three categories. "Red Light" schools were those at which at least one policy represented an overt infringement on free speech. "Yellow Light" schools were those at which policies did not overtly suppress free speech but were worded vaguely enough as to be abused by administrators. "Green Light" schools were those at which researchers did not find any problematic policies related to free speech. Of the 328 schools in the study, 229 were "Red Lights," ninety-one were "Yellow Lights," and eight were "Green Lights."[175]

In 2006, the editor-in-chief of *The Centurion*, a student-edited conservative magazine at Rutgers University, wanted to call attention to what he called "the absurdity of political correctness" that seemed to be prevalent at the school. He began writing editorials calling for the university to ban student dining halls from serving Lucky Charms breakfast cereal on the grounds the product was offensive to the Irish because of how it stereotyped Leprechauns.

The staffer who thought up the spoof? It was James O'Keefe, who after graduation went on to a career in what he called "investigative journalism," but others would call "gimmickry." O'Keefe's career included a number of semijournalistic stunts aimed at exposing political correctness and unethical behavior in government.[176]

In the months following the September 11, 2001, terrorist attacks, many college campuses banned displays of the American flag and the singing of patriotic songs in fear of offending international students.[177]

Students and professors are not the only targets of speech codes; at some schools even presidents are scrutinized for inappropriate or misconstrued comments. In 2005, for example, Harvard University President Lee Summers lost his job partly due to his public comments that gender differences explained the lack of women in professions related to science, math, and engineering.[178]

At the University of North Carolina at Greensboro in 2005, two students were disciplined for staging a protest about the school's "outdoor assembly policy" outside of the zones designated by the policy. Instead of using one of the zones, in remote parts of campus, Allison Jaynes and Robert Sinnott organized the gathering of about forty students on the lawn in front of the UNCG library.

The "official" zones also required protestors to seek permission two days in advance. Protests and other gatherings could be held in parts of campus other than the designated areas, but only with written permission. Administrators insisted the policy was in place to prevent conflicts between groups wanting to use the same space at the same time and was not based on content of the speech.[179]

Many universities require advance notice, ranging from twenty-four hours to ten days, before a student group can use a designated free speech zone. "Requiring people to wait to hold such a meeting detracts from the demonstrators' message by rendering it untimely," said a 2006 report from FIRE. "Moreover, requiring demonstrators to obtain a permit from the university, without explicitly setting forth viewpoint-neutral criteria by which permit applications will be assessed, is an invitation to administrative abuse."[180]

At numerous universities between 2003 and 2009, conservative student groups promoted "affirmative action bake sales" in order to protest their schools' offer of preferential treatment to minority students in admissions, scholarships, and other privileges. Under a typical sale, baked goods were offered to white and Asian male students for $1.00; white and Asian females for seventy-five cents; Latino, Black and Native American males for fifty cents; and Latino, Black and Native American females for twenty-five cents. According to one student leader at the University of California at Los Angeles, the purpose of such events was to "call attention to the controversy surrounding affirmative action and bring it down to everyday terms."[181]

At the University of Washington, student protestors demanded that the administration shut down such an event in 2009, but the school's president refused, even though he declared that the "statement being made was tasteless, divisive, and hurtful to many in the university community." *The Houston Chronicle* editorialized against a 2003 bake sale at Texas A & M University but praised the school's administration for respecting the students' First Amendment rights and not shutting it down.[182]

In contrast, administrators at Bucknell University in Pennsylvania terminated a similar sale, claiming that it violated the school's anti-discrimination policy.[183]

At the University of Illinois, the Students for Individual Liberty held an affirmative action bake sale, but instead of protesting it, another student group called Graduate and Professional Students of Color responded with a "white privilege popcorn giveaway" in which white males received a full bag of popcorn while white women and non-white male students received only one-third of a bag.[184]

In late February 2010, two students at the University of Missouri attempted to display their opinion of "Black History Month" by dumping hundreds of cotton balls at the entrance to the school's Black Culture Center. The university investigated the incident as tampering, but also as a hate crime. Both students were released from the Boone County Jail after posting bond of $4,500 each. The students were never charged with a crime but were suspended from the university.[185]

On September 11, 2011, students at Northern Arizona University were charged with a disciplinary offense for simply handing out American flags (outside of the campus's free speech zone) to commemorate the tenth anniversary of the terrorist attacks.[186]

In 2012, a Federal District Court in Ohio ruled against the University of Cincinnati and ordered administrators to eliminate the campus's free speech zones, which totaled less than 1 percent of the campus and required an application process and ten-day waiting period.[187]

In 2012, the national restaurant chain Chick-fil-A created national controversy when its chief executive officer stated in media interviews that he advocated only "traditional marriage." Numerous universities around the country, under pressure from pro-gay rights student groups, took steps to distance themselves from the company. At Emory University in Georgia and Duke University, administrators evicted the restaurants from their food courts. The Duke eviction was especially problematic, as the company had just spent thousands of dollars on renovations. At Davidson College in North Carolina, there was no restaurant to evict, but the administration banned the company from catering any events on campus.[188]

During the 2012 presidential election campaign, an Auburn University student supporting libertarian candidate Ron Paul was told he could not display his support with a poster in his residence hall window. When he complained that other students were similarly showing their support for other candidates in their windows, he was told the rule had "always been in place," but administrators failed to explain why it was apparently not enforced against other students.[189]

Within days of the re-election of President Obama in November 2012, hundreds of students at the University of Mississippi staged a protest on campus, hurling racist epithets and focusing national attention on the university reminiscent of that it received five decades earlier. It was in the early 1960s that the university was at the forefront of the civil rights movement, as James Meredith defied protestors to become the school's first black student.

"The university leadership strongly condemns this kind of behavior and is embarrassed that any students associated with the university would use this kind of language," Chancellor Daniel W. Jones told the media. "Our university creed calls for the respect of each individual and for fairness and civility."

Head football coach Hugh Freeze and prominent football alumni were also embarrassed and publicly worried that the negative publicity would harm the school's efforts to recruit black football players and that opposing coaches might use the school's negative reputation as a recruiting advantage. "I'm embarrassed as an alumnus and as a former athlete," said Deuce McAllister, a 2001 graduate who went on to a successful National Football League career. "I know how hard it is to get minority players to come and play here because of what's happened in the past. This does not put the school in the best light. And the biggest thing they fight a lot of the time is how much they've got to deal with the past and how they need to show how much they've changed."[190]

At Brandeis University in 2013, junior business major Daniel Mael ran afoul of the school's speech code for simply expressing support for Israel in his student newspaper column and conversations with faculty and fellow students. Mael had been cautioned on numerous occasions to "tone down" his speech, which his supporters described as "fairly benign compared to other voices on campus." But the situation escalated when Mael, representing one pro-Israel organization, attempted to respectively debate a representative from a different pro-Israel group on the finer points of the Israel-Palestine conflict. The other student filed a complaint, leading to a yearlong disciplinary proceeding that nearly resulted in Mael being expelled. Mael survived the ordeal, but not before spending thousands of dollars in legal fees.

Ironically, the administration at the Jewish-affiliated university named after Louis Brandeis, one of the strongest supporters of free speech to ever serve on the U.S. Supreme Court, stated that the goal of its speech code was to shield students from their sensibilities. "Rather than encourage debate, they try to intimidate students into being silent, in the interest of other people's feelings not being hurt," Mael said.[191]

In September 2013, a University of Kansas journalism professor responded to the shootings at the Washington Navy Yard with a tweet criticizing "America's gun culture" and the role of guns in recent tragedies. "Next time, let it be your sons and daughters," he stated, referring to the role of the National Rifle Association in opposing gun regulation.

The university placed David W. Guth on administrative leave and reassigned him to non-teaching duties. Following the controversy, the Kansas Board of Regents implemented a "social media policy" that prohibited employees from any online comments deemed to be "contrary to the best interests of their employer." Critics of the policy assumed that examples would include using profanity on a YouTube video, writing a blog about a school's improper handling of rape cases, or commenting on one's personal life on Facebook, or any other speech that could potentially embarrass the university.

"It's too broad, too vague, and it's already causing people to chill themselves in the way they use social media," said Doug Bonney, an attorney for the Kansas Chapter of the American Civil Liberties Union. [192]

In some cases the unusual campus rules on free speech come not from administrators, but from the students themselves.

In 2014, a student legislative council at the University of California-Irvine approved a resolution to ban the American flag from student government offices. Student leaders voting in favor of the resolution said those spaces needed to be "inclusive" and that the American flag had too often been flown "in instances of colonialism and imperialism." Discounting the free speech aspect of the issue, the student leaders added that "in a space that aims to be as inclusive as possible, free speech can be interpreted as hate speech." [193]

At Modesto Junior College in California in 2014, a student sued the administration after he was not allowed to distribute copies of the U.S. Constitution outside of the free speech zone. Before the case could go to trial, the school agreed to change its policies and pay the student $50,000 in damages and legal fees.

The same year, a conservative student group wishing to pass out copies of the Constitution at the University of Hawaii at Hilo sued the university after its members were told they could not do so outside of the free speech zone. Merritt Burch and Anthony Vizzone, members of Young Americans for Liberty, were seated at their assigned table outside the student center during an event designed to allow student groups to recruit members and promote their causes. Not pleased with their table assignment in the far corner of the event venue, Burch and Vizzone decide to walk around campus to hand out the pocket versions of the Constitution.

When administrators learned of their behavior, they told the students they could hand out their literature only at their designated table at that day's event, or at the campus's free speech zone, located in a small and often muddy part of campus.

Under the threat of a lawsuit, the university revised its speech-zone policy to allow distribution of materials in areas of campus "generally available to students and the community" without permission. It also paid the students' legal fees of about $50,000.[194]

In 2014, the Foundation for Individual Rights in Education filed suit against both Iowa State University and Ohio State University over their speech codes. At Iowa State, a student group that advocated the legalization of marijuana was charged with violating the university's speech code because it used the university's logo on its T-shirts, even though it had permission from the university's trademark office. At Ohio State, administrators reprimanded several individuals and groups for allegedly violating the school's speech code. When a new student group was formed solely for the purpose of opposing the code and providing legal aid to students accused of violating it, the administration "doubled down" on its code by charging that group with circulating T-shirts that violated the code. The shirts, which bore the message "we'll get you off for free," was deemed offensive by OSU administrators because of its reference to masturbation.[195]

At Middle Tennessee State University in 2014, the Sigma Pi Theta fraternity was suspended for a year after displaying a banner outside its house that read, "Freshman Girls Information Center." Fraternity leaders claimed it was "just a joke," but many students, as well as the staff of the Women's Center, said it was demeaning, especially considering the heightened awareness of the problem of sexual assault on college campuses nationwide.

"The sign in question is inconsistent with the values we promote as a university," said a statement released by the university. The year before at Old Dominion University in Virginia, the Sigma Nu Fraternity drew criticism, but no punishment, for displaying a banner outside of its house that read, "Freshman Daughter Drop Off. Go Ahead and Drop Off Mom, Too."[196]

In addition to campus-wide speech codes, individual professors often enact bans on certain political positions in their classrooms. In 2014, an instructor at Marquette University, a Catholic school in Wisconsin, announced that opposition to same-sex marriage is a topic unworthy of discussion. Cheryl Abbate told her students that "there are some opinions that are not appropriate, that are harmful." She further explained to students that questioning the legitimacy of same-sex marriage is the equivalent to sexism and racism. An investigation of the case by FIRE led to the discovery of material from a faculty training session on the school's "Guiding Values," which posed a hypothetical case of two students discussing their opposition to same-sex marriage outside of the classroom. When a third party overhears the conversation and complains, the university policy sides with the offended third party.[197]

In the days leading up to the Harvard-Yale football game in 2014, a student group at Yale was told by administrators it could not sell T-shirts with the slogan, "I think all Harvard men are sissies." The slogan, which was taken from F. Scott Fitzgerald's *This Side of Paradise*, might be offensive to gay men from both schools, the group was told.[198]

In 2014, a conservative student at Broward College near Miami was told that she must use the campus's free speech zone after they heard her ask fellow students if they agreed that "big government sucks."[199]

At Citrus College in Glendora, California in 2014, students wanted to gather signatures on a petition protesting the National Security Agency's domestic surveillance activities. But when they attempted to do so on September 13— Constitution Day—they were told they could not unless they went to the college's tiny free speech zone. The zone had supposedly been eliminated as a result of a FIRE lawsuit in 2003, but it had been reinstated after the negative publicity abated. Student Vincenzo Sinapi-Riddle sued the college, again with help from FIRE. The case was eventually settled, with the college agreeing to eliminate the zone again and pay Sinapi-Riddle $110,000 for attorney's fees and court costs.[200]

In July 2014, pro-life students at Boise State University were reprimanded for setting up a display and handing out literature outside of the free-speech zone.

The display, organized by Abolitionists4Life, featured photographs of aborted fetuses and one of a woman who died during a botched abortion. To avoid a lawsuit, the school agreed to eliminate the free speech zone and the student group agreed to post warning signs at the entrance to the display.

When the students learned that other campus groups distributed potential-ly upsetting material without posting warning signs, they went forward with their lawsuit, which forced the university to drop its "warning sign" require-ment.[201]

When an anti-abortion student group at the University of Alabama wanted to mark the forty-first anniversary of the Supreme Court decision in *Roe v. Wade*, its members set up a display in the Ferguson Student Center that included photographs of aborted fetuses and women who had died dur-ing abortions. Titled "Abortion: Not Safe, Not Rare, Just Legal," the display was created by Bama Students for Life and was up for less than a week when it was taken down by the staff of the center.

Group president Claire Chretien said the director of the center told her it was removed because of complaints from other students, but Chretien claimed the university's actions violated the group's First Amendment rights. Her complaint was based largely on the text of the Ferguson Center's policy that prohibited displays related to combustible materials, firearms, or alco-holic beverages, but made no mention of materials that were "offensive or graphic."

The university released a statement that stopped short of defending the removal of the display. "The university respects our students' First Amend-ment rights to express their opinions," the statement said. "As a result of this incident, we are reviewing our guidelines for the display boards in the stu-dent center."[202]

Returning from a fraternity event on a chartered bus on March 7, 2015, leaders of the Sigma Alpha Epsilon chapter at the University of Oklahoma didn't notice that one of their members was recording their singing perfor-mance.

"There will never be a nigger in SAE," the leaders sang. "You can hang him from a tree, but he can never sign with me. There will never be a nigger in SAE."[203]

A nine-second video of the incident was posted on the Internet within days, creating a national controversy and leading to the expulsion of two SAE members. University President David Boren said the fraternity had violated the school's "zero tolerance policy" and labeled the behavior as "racially threatening."[204]

Parker Rice, one of the two members expelled, apologized on behalf of the chapter, but it wasn't enough to save his academic standing at the university and prevent indefinite suspension of the fraternity. Boren told the national media that his suspensions of the students and the fraternity likely prevented the university from facing penalties from the Department of Justice's Civil Rights Division. The SAE chapter has sued the university in Federal District Court, but the case was not scheduled to be heard until fall 2016.[205]

The incident happened just a few months after the SAE chapter at Clemson University was suspended indefinitely by its national organization after members hosted a gangster-themed Christmas party seen by some groups on campus as racially insensitive. The event, held off-campus, was titled "Clemson Cripmas" and featured members dressed in gangster attire and singing parodies of Christmas carols for which the words had changed to support the theme. Hundreds of students, black and white, protested the event the following day, comparing the incident to other examples of campus racism of the previous year, and pointed out the fraternity had no black members.[206]

In May 2015, an international student at Duke University erected a noose on a tree near his residence hall so he and his friends could pose for pictures with it. The photographs then appeared on social media, accompanied by the caption, "come hang out with us." The student claimed he then "forgot" about the noose and left it attached to the tree, where it was discovered later that day by African American students. Treating the incident as a potential hate crime, the school immediately launched an investigation, and students organized protests outside of the administration building.

When the student was questioned by university officials, he claimed it was "just a joke" and as a student from another culture, he was not aware of the historical symbolism of the noose and its connection to the lynching of black Americans in the previous century.

The student was not identified, but was given an undisclosed sanction and allowed to apologize to the student body and faculty on the university's website.

Black students at Duke told local and national media they were upset about how quickly administrators accepted the student's defense that he "lacked cultural awareness" and changed their minds about the incident. Before they knew the student's nationality, administrators called it a "cowardly act of hatred," but the next day it appeared that all was forgiven. One black student penned a open letter titled "Did You Change Your Mind?" to administrators and posted it on social media. The student questioned how quickly the "cowardly act of hatred" became a "simple lack of judgment."[207]

In 2015, at Wesleyan University in Connecticut, the student newspaper ran an editorial questioning some of the tactics used by Black Lives Matter protestors. After the item, titled "Why Black Lives Matter Isn't What You Think" was published on September 14, the student government committee in charge of allocating fees to student organizations voted 27-0 to cut funding for the student newspaper in half. That caused the *Wesleyan Argus* to reduce circulation and eliminate twenty student jobs.[208]

That same year, at George Washington University in the nation's capital, the student government approved a measure requiring the leaders of all student organizations to take a sensitivity course related to LGBT issues and to use "proper gender pronouns" in their publications and other websites. One conservative student group refused to go along, publicly stating that it "already treats students with respect and doesn't need to be lectured on how to do so." The school's LGBT group, Allied in Pride, responded that "refusal to use the preferred gender pronouns is an act of violence."[209]

In the days leading up to Halloween in 2015, administrators, faculty, and students at Yale University were caught up in a controversy regarding costumes deemed to be "insensitive or inappropriate." The dustup began when the school's Intercultural Affairs Committee sent an email to the student body discouraging the display of insensitive costumes that played on stereotypes.

One of the first to take notice was Erika Christakis, a lecturer and administrator of Silliman College, a residential unit within Yale. After she sent her own residents a response questioning the institution's "exercise of implied control over its students," students accused her of overreacting and staged a protest outside of her office. They also attempted to have Christakis and her husband, also a Yale employee, censured and evicted from their home on campus.

They stopped short of meeting the demands of the protestors, but twelve other administrators echoed the sentiments of the original memo in a memo of their own, which drew the attention of critics across the country and portrayed the incident as yet another example of political correctness affecting universities campuses. "It is remarkable that these administrators took the time to compose, circulate, and co-sign a letter advising adult students on how to dress for Halloween, a cause that misguided campus activists mistake for a social-justice priority," wrote education reporter Conor Friedersdorf in a column in *The Atlantic.*

At the end of the fall semester, Christakis resigned from her teaching position but retained her administrative duties at Yale.[210]

Despite such well-publicized cases, university administrators (except those at the University of Kansas) are mostly reluctant to establish policies limiting the free speech rights of faculty members. In a 2014 survey conducted by *The Chronicle of Higher Education*, fewer than half of the schools responding indicated they had no specific policies in place to regulate the online activities of faculty members.[211]

At the University of Central Florida in Orlando, two unidentified students were seen leaving anti-Semitic stickers and fliers around campus on the evening of November 15, 2015. The materials featured images of the Star of David and swastikas and were found on bulletin boards and newspaper stands. The students were recorded by security cameras, but the two perpetrators were never identified.[212]

In 2015, a student at Michigan Technical University wrote a tongue-in-cheek op-ed for the school's satirical newspaper, the *Daily Bull*, in which he attempted to humorously examine the double standard that exists in sexual harassment cases based on the gender of the alleged victim.

Rico Bastian, editor-in-chief of the newspaper (which is not the school's official student paper), thought his piece, titled, "Sexually Harassed Man Pretty Okay with the Situation," would start a discussion about the issue. It did—but not the type of discussion he had in mind. Bastian simply wanted to call attention to fact that men's claims of sexual harassment were seldom taken seriously on his campus and his belief that in general, "It's considered more acceptable" for an attractive person to sexually harass someone. He concluded the article by quoting a male student who claims his recent complaint about being sexually harassed was "only because the woman was ugly."

The university's vice president for student affairs, Les Cook, sent out a campus-wide email denouncing the article and accusing the *Daily Bull* of "advocating criminal activity on campus." As in most cases, the administration's reaction to the article drew more attention than it otherwise would have received. "It became a really big deal after that," said Mike Jarasz, managing editor of the paper.

Neither Bastian nor any other individuals were punished, but the paper's faculty adviser resigned voluntarily and the paper was place on probation for two years, meaning that if another incident occurred, it could lose its funding permanently. The staff was required to take a training course in the university's non-discrimination policies. The paper also issued an apology and retraction.

Jarasz told local media the paper will avoid satirizing sensitive topics in the future because he "didn't want to stir up controversy." But he lamented the climate of political correctness the incident exposed. "Sometimes you gotta stretch the boundaries a little bit," he said. "There will always be pushback."[213]

At Miami University in April 2015, students vandalized a residence hall bulletin board with racist, sexist, anti-Semitic, and homophobic graffiti, but after being caught they said they didn't really believe what they wrote and were not racists.

"We wrote stupid shit on the board," the two nineteen-year-olds told university police. "We are not racist. We will accept responsibility. We regret what we did."

The graffiti included disparaging remarks about women, gays, lesbians, Jews, blacks, and even dwarfs. The students were charged under the criminal mischief, a misdemeanor. Under Ohio law, that charge was punishable by up to sixty days in jail and a $500 fine. The charges were eventually dropped, and the case was referred to the MU student judicial process, the results of which were protected under federal privacy laws.[214]

At Emory University in Georgia, students complained to administrators about the slogan "Trump 2016" (supporting republican presidential candidate Donald Trump) appearing in chalk around campus, then complained when the student newspaper, *The Emory Wheel*, did not editorialize against it. "I'm supposed to feel comfortable and safe here," one student told the paper. "But this man is being supported by students on our campus and our administration shows that they, by their silence, support it as well. I don't deserve to feel afraid at my school."

Emory president James Wagner at first resisted the idea of getting involved, but after days of protest, instructed the campus police to review security camera footage in an attempt to identify the chalkers. If they were students, he said, the case would be processed through the campus judiciary system; if they were outsiders, they would be charged with trespassing. None of the perpetrators could be identified, but many inside and outside the university were disappointed that the president gave in to student angst.

"His response was extremely creepy and a sign that something has gone terribly wrong," wrote *New York* magazine columnist Jesse Singal. Conservative pundit Robby Soave believed the student reaction was precisely the type of "political correctness" that Trump had been railing about. "No wonder so many non-liberal students are cheering for Trump," he wrote in *Reason.* "Not because they like him," but because he represents glorious resistance to the noxious political correctness and censorship that has come to define the modern college experience."[215]

In early 2016, conservative students at Dartmouth College recognized National Police Week with a display titled "Blue Lives Matter" that honored police officers killed in the line of duty. Almost immediately, the display was removed and replaced by fliers promoting the Black Lives Matter movement. The College Republicans had permission to set up the Blue Lives display and followed all university regulations applying to student organizations.

Members of the Black Lives Matter chapter admitted to taking down the display but claimed it was not meant to be "anti-police."

The display's removal drew sharp criticism from the school administration. "Freedom of expression is a fundamental value of the Dartmouth community," said an official statement released by the college. "By its very nature, the exercise of free speech will include views with which some of us disagree or which we find hurtful. The unauthorized removal on Friday of a student display for National Police Week in the Collis Center was an unacceptable violation of freedom of expression on our campus."[216]

School officials went on to say in their message to undergraduates that taking down the police display was an act of vandalism, and any students involved could face punishment. "Vandalism represents a silencing of free exchange, rather than open engagement," officials said.[217]

In response to a flurry of new speech restrictions at Princeton University in 2015 and 2016, students representing a variety of viewpoints—conservative, liberal, and libertarian—formed the Princeton Open Campus Coalition. In addition to diversity in political viewpoints, members were also diverse in demographics, as women, African Americans, and students with disabilities said they resented the university's view that need to be protected from offensive speech.

The group opposed administrative proposals to expand the school's speech code to cover "new forms of offense" as well as other student groups, including the Black Justice League. The BJL was a student group that claimed to represent the interests of African American students who claimed they faced racial discrimination and bias on a daily basis. Its specific proposals included requiring all incoming students to take a course titled "The History of Marginalized Peoples," mandating cultural sensitivity training for all faculty and staff, and removing the name of Woodrow Wilson, president of the university before becoming president of the United States, from a university building.

The position of the POCC was that students such as those affiliated with the Black Justice League were a vocal minority and did not represent the true opinions of minority students.[218]

NOTES

1. Alan C. Kors and Harvey A. Silverglate, *The Shadow University: The Betrayal of Liberty on America's Campuses.* New York. Harper Collins, 1998, p. 10.

2. Kors and Silverglate, *The Shadow University*, p. 10.

3. Ibid.

4. Rodney A. Smolla, *A Year in the Life of the Supreme Court.* Durham, NC: Duke University Press, 1995, pp. 188-9.

5. Sheldon Hackney, *The Politics of Presidential Appointment: A Memoir of the Culture War.* NewSouth Books, 2012, preface.

6. Vernon Jordan, "Foreword." In Sheldon Hackney, *The Politics of Presidential Appointment: A Memoir of the Culture War.* NewSouth Books. 2012, p. 9.

7. Kors and Silverglate, *The Shadow University*, p. 28.

8. NBC Nightly News, May 13, 1993.

9. Sheldon Hackney, *The Politics of Presidential Appointment: A Memoir of the Culture War.* NewSouth Books, 2012, preface.

10. Kors and Silverglate, *The Shadow University*, pp. 9-38.

11. Ibid.

12. James O'Neill, "Group Takes Aim at Speech Codes." *Daily Vanguard* (Portland State University), November 10, 2003.

13. Kors and Silverglate, *The Shadow University*, pp. 9-38.

14. "A Step Toward Civility." *Time*, May 1, 1989, p. 43.

15. "A Step Toward Civility."

16. "The State of the First Amendment in the University of North Carolina System." A Joint Report of the Pope Center for Higher Education Policy and the Foundation for Individual Rights in Education, 2006.

17. "Spotlight on Speech Codes." Foundation for Individual Rights in Education, 2015.

18. *Chaplinsky v. New Hampshire*, 315 U.S. 568 (1942). See also: Randy Bobbitt, *Exploring Communication Law.* Boston: Allyn & Bacon, 2008, p. 24.

19. Rodney A. Smolla, *Free Speech in an Open Society.* New York: Alfred A. Knopf, 1992, p. 158.

20. Stanley Fish, "There's No Such Thing as Free Speech and it's a Good Thing, Too." *Boston Review*, February 1992, p. 184.

21. Arati R. Korwar, *War of Words: Speech Codes at Colleges and Universities in the United States.* Nashville, TN: The Freedom Forum First Amendment Center, 1995, pp. 20-21.

22. Ibid., p. 20-21.

23. *Law of the Student Press*, Arlington, VA: Student Press Law Center, 1994, p. 70. See also: Rachele Kanigel, *The Student Newspaper Survival Guide.* Malden, MA: Wiley-Blackwell, 2012, p. 168.

24. *Corry v. Stanford University*, case 740309 (Santa Clara County Superior Court, February 27, 1995). See also: W. Wat Hopkins, ed. *Communication and the Law.* Northpoint, AL: Vision Press, 2000, p. 214.

25. Kirsten Powers, *The Silencing: How the Left Is Killing Free Speech.* Washington, DC: Regnery Press, 2012, p. 80.

26. Greg Lukianoff, *Unlearning Liberty: Campus Censorship and the End of American Debate.* New York: Encounter Books, 2014, p. 34.

27. Carnegie Foundation for the Advancement of Teaching, 1990.

28. "Spotlight on Speech Codes."

29. Ibid.

30. "Unfree Speech on Campus." *Wall Street Journal*, December 13, 2014, p. 12-A.

31. Sara Jerde, "Lawsuits Accuse Four Colleges of Unconstitutional Restrictions on Speech." *Chronicle of Higher Education*, July 2, 2014.

32. Walter Williams, "Tuition Pays for a Lot of Craziness." Syndicated newspaper column, August 25, 2014.

33. Bobbitt, *Exploring Communication Law*. Boston: Allyn & Bacon, 2008, p. 101.

34. Ibid.

35. Donald A. Downs, "Codes Say the Darnedest Things." *Quill*, October 1993, p. 19.

36. Ken Paulson, "How Free is Campus Speech?" Syndicated newspaper column, April 24, 2001.

37. Kors and Silverglate, "Suppression 101: A Quick Tour of Campus Speech Codes." *Reason*, November 1998.

38. Rodney A. Smolla, *A Year in the Life of the Supreme Court*. Durham, NC: Duke University Press, 1995, p. 188.

39. Franklyn Haiman, *Speech Acts and the First Amendment*. Carbondale, IL: Southern Illinois University Press, 1993, p. 28.

40. Gerald Gunther, "Good Speech, Bad Speech." In *Campus Wars: Multiculturalism and the Politics of Difference*, eds. John Arthur and Amy Shapiro, pp. 109-113. Boulder, CO: Westview Press, 1995.

41. John Frohnmayer, *Leaving Town Alive*. Boston: Houghton Mifflin, 1993, p. 185.

42. *Collin v. Smith*, 578 F.2d 1197 (Seventh Circuit 1978); *Village of Skokie v. National Socialist Party*, 373 N.E. 2d 21 (1978). See also Nadine Strossen, "Regulating Racist Speech on Campus: A Modest Proposal." *Duke Law Journal*, 1990, pp. 484-573.

43. *Texas v. Johnson*, 109 St. Ct. 2533 (1989).

44. James O'Neill, "Group Takes Aim at Speech Codes." *Daily Vanguard* (Portland State University), November 10, 2003.

45. Paulson, "How Free is Campus Speech?"

46. Melanie A. Moore, "Free Speech on College Campuses: Protecting the First Amendment in the Marketplace of Ideas." *West Virginia Law Review*, 1993-94, pp. 511-548.

47. Moore.

48. A. Barton Hinkle, "The Death of Free Speech on College Campuses." *Reason*, March 18, 2015.

49. O'Neill, "Group Takes Aim at Speech Codes."

50. Alison Alexander and Jarice Hanson, *Taking Sides: Clashing Views on Controversial Issues in Mass Media and Society*. Guilford, CT: Dushkin Publishing, 2013, p. 177.

51. Nat Hentoff, "Speech Codes on Campus," in Alexander and Jarice Hanson, *Taking Sides: Clashing Views on Controversial Issues in Media and Society*, p. 179.

52. Hentoff, "Speech Codes on Campus."

53. Lukianoff, p. 169.

54. Nadine Strossen, "Regulating Racist Speech on Campus: A Modest Proposal." *Duke Law Journal*, 1990, pp. 484-573.

55. Hentoff, "Speech Codes on Campus."

56. "Group Takes Aim at Campus Speech Codes." Associated Press report, April 30, 2003.

57. Lukianoff, p. 17.

58. *Chaplinsky v. New Hampshire*, 315 U.S. 568 (1942). See also: Bobbitt, *Exploring Communication Law*, p. 24.

59. Kors and Silverglate, *The Shadow University*, p. 116.

60. Bobbitt, *Exploring Communication Law*, p. 97.

61. Walter Williams, "Inspecting the Rot at the Top of our College Campuses." Syndicated newspaper column, October 19, 2007.

62. Bobbitt, *Exploring Communication Law*, p. 97.

63. Ibid.

64. Kors and Silverglate, "Suppression 101."

65. Ibid.

66. Ibid.

67. Williams, "Tuition Pays for a Lot of Craziness." Syndicated newspaper column, August 25, 2014.

68. Williams, "Tuition Pays for a Lot of Craziness."

69. Ibid.

70. Ibid.

71. Ibid.

72. Ibid.

73. "Spotlight on Speech Codes."

74. Ibid.

75. Ibid.

76. Ibid.

77. Ibid.

78. Ibid.

79. Powers, p. 80.

80. Ibid.

81. Ibid.

82. Charles R. Lawrence, "If He Hollers Let Him Go: Regulating Racist Speech on Campus. *Duke Law Journal*, 1990, pp. 431-483.

83. *Schenck v. United States*, 249 U.S. 47 (1919).

84. *Doe v. University of Michigan*, 721 F. Supp. 852 (1989). See also: Bobbitt, *Exploring Communication Law*, pp. 95-97.

85. Conor Friedersdorf, "Free Speech is No Diversion." *The Atlantic*, November 12, 2015.

86. John Arthur and Amy Shapiro, eds., *Campus Wars: Multiculturalism and the Politics of Difference*, pp. 109-113. Boulder, CO: Westview Press, 1995.

87. *Doe v. University of Michigan.*

88. Ibid.

89. Ibid.

90. Adam DeVore, "Poli Sci Professor Outlaws Free Speech." *Accuracy in Academia*, December 1992, p. 1. See also: Moore, "Free Speech on College Campuses."

91. Richard Miniter, "Campus Speech Wars: Waving the Tacky Shirt." *Insight*, Vol. 10, no. 4 (June 1994), pp. 18-21.

92. *UWM Post v. University of Wisconsin System*, 774 F.Supp. 1165 (1991). See also: *Chaplinsky v. New Hampshire*, 315 U.S. 568 (1942).

93. Ibid.

94. *Bair v. Shippensburg University*, 280 F.Supp. 2d 357 (2003). See also: James O'Neill, "Group Takes Aim at Speech Codes." *Daily Vanguard* (Portland State University), November 10, 2003.

95. Shannon P. Duffy, "Federal Judge Halts Use of University Speech Code." *The Legal Intelligencer*, September 9, 2003.

96. Ibid.

97. Scott Street, "Promoting Order or Squelching Campus Dissent." *Chronicle of Higher Education*, January 12, 2001, p. 38-A.

98. Bobbitt, *Exploring Communication* Law, p. 98-99.

99. In numerous free speech cases in the latter half of twentieth century, courts defined "traditional public forums" as those where controversial speech (either written or electronic) is common. They can be physical forums (such as public gathering places), passive forums (such as a bulletin board) or electronic forums (such as the Internet and social media). The courts defined "limited public forums" as places where speech and may be found but limited because of its potential to disrupt other activities. Examples include public libraries and areas of the university campus outside of the free speech zone.

100. Kors and Silverglate, *The Shadow University*, p. 149.

101. Ibid.

102. Tammy Bruce, *The New Thought Police: Inside the Left's Assault on Free Speech and Free Minds*. Roseville, CA: Forum Publishing, 2001, p. 230.

103. *Board of Trustees v. Fox*, 109 S.Ct. 3028 (1989). See also: Strossen, "Regulating Racist Speech on Campus."

104. Powers, p. 90.

105. Mary M. Kershaw, "West Virginia University to Open More Free Speech Zones." *USA Today*, April 22, 2002, p. 7-D.

106. "Unfree Speech on Campus."

107. Jerry Bledsoe, *Death by Journalism? One Teacher's Fateful Encounter with Political Correctness*. Asheboro, NC: Down Home Press, p. 41.

108. Bledsoe, pp. 77-78.

109. Alicia B. Shepherd, "Uncivil War." *American Journalism Review*, June 2002.

110. Ibid.

111. Ibid.

112. Moore, "Free Speech on College Campuses." See also: "An Interview with Alan Dershowitz." *The Defender*, March 1994, pp. 6-11. Nat Hentoff, "Academies of Fear," *The Washington Post*, December 18, 1993, p. 25-A.

113. Charles R. Lawrence, "If He Hollers Let Him Go: Regulating Racist Speech on Campus." *Duke Law Journal*, 1990, pp. 431-483.

114. Ibid.

115. Steven H. Shiffrin, "The Dark Side of the First Amendment," *UCLA Law Review*, 61 UCLA L. Rev 1480, 2014).

116. Eric Posner, "The World Doesn't Love the First Amendment." Slate.com, September 25, 2012.

117. The original source of this quote is unknown, but it appears in nearly every list of quotations attributed to Plato.

118. Jake MacAulay, "University Safe Zones, a Danger for the First Amendment." TheAmericanView.com, November 17, 2015.

119. Greg Lukianoff, *Unlearning Liberty*. pp. 9-10.

120. Philip Roth, *The Human Stain*. New York: Random House, 2000.

121. Perry Chiaramonte, "Florida Professor Who Denied Sandy Hook Shooting Now Claims Boston Bombings a Drill." Fox News.com, April 24, 2013.

122. Chiaramonte. See also: Carl Hiaasen, "Firing of FAU Professor Long Overdue." Syndicated newspaper column, January 17, 2016.

123. Robert Mackey, "Professor's Angry Tweets on Gaza Cost Him a Job." *The New York Times*, September 12, 2014.

124. . Laura Krantz, "Controversy Trails New Professor to BU." *The Boston Globe*, June 27, 2015.

125. Rem Reider, "Mizzou Prof: One Mistake Shouldn't End My Career." *USA Today*, February 16, 2016.

126. Rachel Kyler, "Is it Censorship or Sensitivity?" *The Northwest Florida Daily News*, October 25, 2007, p. 1-A. See also: "Mockingbird Quarrel Calls for Courage." *The Northwest Florida Daily News*, October 30, 2007, p. 7-A and "The Right Decision on Mockingbird." *The Northwest Florida Daily News*, November 4, 2007, p. 7-A.

127. "The Right Decision on Mockingbird."

128. Victor Davis Hanson, "The Hypocrisy Behind the Campus Renaming Craze." Townhall.com, March 24, 2016. See also: "A Year of Protest." *USA Today*, February 28, 2016, p. 1-A.

129. Maximilian Longley, "Speaker Ban Continues to Resonate." *MetroMagazine*, July 2005, pp. 28-31. See also: Don Campbell, "Dissent v. Patriotism on Campus." *USA Today*, December 6, 2001. Reider, "Obama's Support for Free Speech on Campus Welcome." *USA Today*, May 27, 2016, p. 2-B.

130. Campbell, "Dissent v. Patriotism on Campus."

131. Lukianoff, p. 31.

132. Bob Beckel and Cal Thomas, "Only Puppets Get Free Speech." *USA Today*, May 2, 2013, p. 7-A.

133. Pat Toomey, "Vermont College Made Bad Choice in Commencement Speaker." *Daily Signal*, October 2, 2014.

134. "Land of the Free, Home of the Wuss." *USA Today*, December 26, 2014.

135. Powers, p. 92.

136. Ibid., p. 93.

137. Ibid., p. 94.

138. Ibid.

139. *Stanley v. Magrath*, 719 F. 2d 279 (Eighth Circuit, 1983). See also: *Law of the Student Press*, p. 57.

140. *Kania v. Fordham*, 702 F.2d 475 (Fourth Circuit, 1983).

141. *Board of Regents of the University of Wisconsin System v. Southworth*, 120 S.Ct. 1346 (2000).

142. *Board of Regents of the University of Wisconsin System v. Southworth.*

143. Derek P. Langhauser, Leonard M. Niehoff, and Lawrence White, "Forums, Zones, and Codes: The First Amendment and Free Speech on Campus." National Association of College and University Attorneys teleconference, June 3, 2004.

144. "Supreme Court Upholds Student Fees." *SPLC Report*, Spring 2000, p. 4.

145. Ibid.

146. "Hump Day Now Banned at Connecticut Middle School." *Time*, October 4, 2013.

147. Greg Lukianoff and Jonathan Haidt, "The Coddling of the American Mind." *The Atlantic*, September 2015.

148. Susie Pakoua Vang and Christina Vance, "Schools Grapple with 'So Gay' Term." *The Fresno Bee*, March 11, 2007. See also: Bobbitt, *Decisions, Decisions: Case Studies and Discussion Problems in Communication Ethics*. Dubuque, IA: Kendall-Hunt, 2015, p. 75.

149. Lori Kersey, "St. Albans High 'Hobo Day' Draws Criticism." *The Charleston Gazette-Mail*, October 4, 2015.

150. Todd Starnes, "The Wussification of Wisconsin." FoxNews.com, January 13, 2016.

151. "Principal Fired Over Racist Comments." *USA Today*, May 15, 2015.

152. John Taylor, "Are You Politically Correct?" *New York*, January 21, 1991, p. 34.

153. Alexander and Hanson, p. 178.

154. Ibid.

155. Jeffrey Hart, "Mr. Freedman's Moral Suicide." *National Review*, November 5, 1990, p. 23.

156. Hentoff, *Free Speech for Me, But Not for Thee*. New York: Harper Perennial, 1993, pp. 193-196. See also: Laurence R. Stains, "Speech Impediment." *Rolling Stone*, August 5, 1993, pp. 46-48.

157. Ibid., p. 198-201.

158. Moore, "Free Speech on College Campuses."

159. *Sigma Chi Fraternity v. George Mason University*, 993 F.2d 346 (1993). See also: Moore, "Free Speech on College Campuses."

160. Hentoff, "Fear and Deliverance at the University of Nebraska." *Village Voice*, January 18, 1994.

161. Kors and Silverglate, *The Shadow University*, p. 183.

162. Richard Miniter, "Campus Speech Wars: Waving the Tacky Shirt." *Insight*, January 24, 1994.

163. Susan Philips, "Student Journalism: Are Free Speech Rights in Danger?" *CQ Researcher*, June 5, 1998, pp. 481-504.

164. Bruce, p. 230.

165. "Students Sue Community College District for Putting Restrictions on Free Speech," *SPLC Report*, Spring 2000, p. 6.

166. Scott Street, "Promoting Order or Squelching Campus Dissent." *Chronicle of Higher Education*, January 12, 2001, p. 38-A.

167. Mary M. Kershaw, "West Virginia University to Open More Free Speech Zones." *USA Today*, April 22, 2002, p. 7-D.

168. "Syracuse Suspends Fraternity After Blackface Incident." *Diverse Issues in Higher Education*, June 6, 2002

169. *Roberts v. Haragan*, 346 F.Supp. 2d 853 (N.D. Texas, 2004). See also: Lukianoff, *Unlearning Liberty*, pp. 62-63.

170. *Pro-Life Cougars v. University of Houston*, 259 F.Supp. 2d 575 (2003).

171. Donald A. Downs, "Codes Say the Darnedest Things." *Quill*, October 1993, p. 19. See also: O'Neill, "Group Takes Aim at Speech Codes."

172. *Wilson v. Harvey*, Case 85829 (Ohio Appeals Court Dist. 8, Oct. 27, 2005).
173. "Spotlight on Speech Codes."
174. Jane Stancill, "Report Blasts UNC's Speech Codes." *Raleigh News & Observer*, January 19, 2006.
175. "Spotlight on Speech Codes."
176. Scott Shane, "A Political Gadfly Lampoons the Liberal Left." *New York Times,* September 18, 2009.
177. Williams, "Inspecting the Rot at the Top of our College Campuses."
178. Bobbitt, *Decisions, Decisions*, p. 75.
179. "Free Speech Zones Protested." Associated Press report, December 17, 2005.
180. "Spotlight on Speech Codes."
181. "Cookie Sale Was Half-Baked Affirmative Action Protest." *The Houston Chronicle*, October 19, 2003, p. 4-D. See also: Ashby Jones, "Bucknell and the Affirmative Action Bake Sale." *The Wall Street Journal*, June 23, 2009.
182. Ibid.
183. Ibid.
184. Ibid.
185. Janese Heavin, "Two Arrested in Cotton Ball Incident." *Columbia Daily Tribune*, March 3, 2010.
186. Lukianoff, *Unlearning Liberty*, p. 66.
187. Powers, pp. 89-90.
188. Ibid.
189. Will Rahn, "Auburn Student Ordered to Take Down Ron Paul Sign Shares His Story." *The Daily Caller*, December 22, 2011. See also: Greg Lukianoff, *Unlearning Liberty*, p. 30.
190. Paul Myerberg, "Racist Protest Hurts Mississippi Football." *USA Today*, November 18, 2012, p. 1-C.
191. Sohrab Ahmari, "How to Fight the Campus Speech Police: Get a Good Lawyer." *The Wall Street Journal*, January 3, 2105, p. 9-A.
192. Ken Paulson, "Professor's Tweet Was Crass, But It's His Right." *USA Today*, September 27, 2013, p. 9-A. See also: Peter Schmidt, "Colleges are Divided on Need for New Speech Policies," *Chronicle of Higher Education*, March 10, 2014. Lauren C. Williams, "Kansas State Schools Reserve the Right to Fire Professors For Using Social Media." ThinkProgress.com, May 21, 2014.
193. "Unfree Speech on Campus." *The Wall Street Journal*, December 13, 2014, p. 12-A.
194. A. Barton Hinkle, "The Death of Free Speech on College Campuses." *Reason*, March 18, 2015.
195. Sara Jerde, "Lawsuits Accuse Four Colleges of Unconstitutional Restrictions on Speech." *Chronicle of Higher Education*, July 2, 2014.
196. "MTSU Frat Removes 'Freshman Girls' Sign." WKRN-TV, August 15, 2015.
197. Powers, pp. 54-55.
198. Ibid., p. 80.
199. George F. Will, "Thanks For the Laughs, America." Syndicated newspaper column, November 29, 2014.
200. "Free Speech Suits Target Universities." *USA Today*, July 2, 2014.
201. *Abolitionists4Life v. Kustra* (Case 14-257, District Court of Idaho). See also: "BSU Stops Making Pro-Life Groups Post Warning Signs." News release from the Foundation for Individual Rights in Education, June 3, 2015.
202. "Group Upset by Removal of Anti-Abortion Display." Associated Press report, February 15, 2015.
203. Eliott C. McLaughlin, "University of Oklahoma Student Apologizes for Racist Chant." CNN, March 11, 2015.
204. Ibid.
205. Ibid.
206. Abby Ohlheiser, "Clemson Fraternity Suspended Over Gang-Themed Party." *The Washington Post*, April 6, 2015.
207. Scott Jaschik, "Ignorance or Bigotry?" *Inside Higher Education*, May 4, 2015.

208. Lydia Wheeler, "Colleges Are Restricting Free Speech on Campus, Lawmakers Say." TheHill.com, June 2, 2015.

209. A. Hinkle, "The Death of Free Speech on College Campuses."

210. Conor Friedersdorf, "The New Intolerance of Student Activism." *The Atlantic*, November 9, 2015. See also: Rahel Gebreyes, "Yale Student Explains Why Students Were Offended by Halloween Costumes Email." *The Huffington Post*, November 12, 2015.

211. Peter Schmidt, "Colleges are Divided on Need for New Speech Policies," *Chronicle of Higher Education*, March 10, 2014.

212. "Anti-Semitic Fliers Posted on UCF Campus." Associated Press report, November 28, 2015.

213. Madeline Will, "Student Satire Publication on Probation After Article on Sexual Harassment." SPLC News, December 15, 2015.

214. Hannah Sparling and Michael D. Clark, "Miami Graffiti Suspects: We Are Not Racists." *The Cincinnati Enquirer*, April 7, 2015.

215. Glenn Harlan Reynolds, "PC Culture is Killing Higher Education." Syndicated newspaper column, March 30, 2016.

216. Steve Annear, "Blue Lives Matter Display Removed at Dartmouth College." *Boston Globe*, May 17, 2016.

217. Ibid.

218. Sarah Brown, "In Era of Campus Activism, Student Group Seeks to be the Face of Free Speech." *Chronicle of Higher Education*, April 8, 2016, A-17.

Chapter Six

Disruption, Fighting Words, and True Threats

Real and Imagined

INTERNATIONAL TERRORIST

In 2003, Bretton Barber, a junior at Dearborn High School in Michigan, wore to school a T-shirt bearing the likeness of President George W. Bush and the phrase, "international terrorist." Barber attended his first three classes without anyone noticing or mentioning the shirt. During his lunch period, however, one student noticed it and complained to the principal, citing his family's tradition of military service, including his brother's current military service in Iraq, as grounds for being offended.

Barber was told to change shirts, turn it inside out, or go home. The school's justification was that the shirt might cause a disruption, despite the fact that he had already worn it for four hours without incident.

Administrators based much of their position on the *Tinker* standard, believing that Barber's provocative T-shirt could be disruptive to the orderly operation of the school in ways that the rather passive black armbands worn by Mary Beth Tinker and her friends were not.

The American Civil Liberties Union came to Barber's aid, asking for an injunction in Federal District Court. Judge Patrick J. Duggan ruled in favor of Barber, agreeing with the ACLU position that the shirt generated no threat of disruption. "The record does not reveal any basis for the administrators' fear other than their belief that the T-shirt conveyed an unpopular political message," Duggan wrote in his opinion. In rejecting the school district's argument that the campus was "an inappropriate place for political debate,"

Duggan countered that "students benefit when school officials provide an environment where they can openly express their diverging viewpoints and when they learn to tolerate the opinions of others."[1]

Barber told local media after the victory that he was pleased with the outcome of the case but nevertheless puzzled by the degree of angst it created on both sides.

"I wore the shirt to spark discussion among the students on an issue I cared deeply about," he said. "I haven't decided when I will wear the shirt again, but now I have the confidence of knowing I have the right to wear it."[2]

ADVENTURES IN DRESS CODES

Even before the Columbine tragedy in 1999, court rulings tended to favor school administrators in cases involving any unusual or nonconformist behavior in the form of dress, demeanor, or disturbing writings in class assignments.

One of the most common areas for controversy is student dress. Judges in both state and federal courts have backed up school districts as they have expanded dress codes to include bans on images of the Confederate flag, slogans critical of the war in Iraq or American presidents, or messages supporting or opposing abortion, gay rights, or other controversial issues.[3]

Limitations on student clothing have taken place at both ends of the political spectrum. Students have been sent home—or ordered to turn T-shirts and sweatshirts inside out—for displaying the Confederate flag or anti-abortion messages, as well as slogans denouncing President George W. Bush and the war in Iraq. The American Civil Liberties Union often provides legal support for students in such cases, but courts typically side with school principals and rule that dress codes are constitutional because of the potentially disruptive nature of some clothing.

Since the mid-1990s, the ACLU and other free speech advocates have reported several cases each month of students being suspended for wearing the Confederate flag on their clothing. The precedent for supporting the position of school administrators came in two cases in the 1970s in which Circuit Courts of Appeal ruled that ongoing racial tensions in public schools justified the elimination of symbols that perpetuated those problems. Similar decisions continued through the 1990s and into the new century, as courts ruled in Confederate-flag cases that "schools are not required to wait until disorder or invasion occurs" but only need "the existence of facts which might reasonably lead school officials to forecast substantial disruption."[4]

In general, courts were more likely to cite the *Bethel* case (giving the benefit of the doubt to administrators) rather than the *Tinker* case (giving the benefit of the doubt to the students).

One morning in 1988, ninth-grader Mark Vice Jr. wore a denim jacket to school bearing a Confederate flag on the back. Principal Janet Stevens of North Garner Middle School in Garner, North Carolina, asked him to keep the jacket at home and warned that he would not be allowed to wear it inside the school building in the future.

Vice's parents asked the local office of the American Civil Liberties Union for help. Instead of litigation, ACLU attorney William Simpson suggested working with school officials on staging an assembly during which opposing viewpoints on the meaning of the flag could both be heard.

About one-third of the North Garner student body was black, and there had been racial tensions at the school before. Vice's jacket was looked upon unfavorably by the majority of classmates and teachers. Simpson worked with Stevens and school district attorney George Rogister to organize the event and allow "cooler heads to prevail."[5] The speakers included Simpson, Rogister, and other individuals on both sides of the issue. When it was Simpson's turn to speak, he told the audience that his organization was against what many believed the flag stood for, but also that while school administrators did not like the symbolism of the flag either, their counterparts of the 1960s did not like the symbols of the civil rights movement.

Most of the audience at the assembly, which also attracted parents and local media, appeared to leave the building satisfied, and Vice continued to wear his jacket, and about fifteen other students also did so. *The Raleigh News & Observer*, the major daily newspaper in the area, covered the event but questioned its necessity, editorializing that in light of *Tinker*, the question of symbolic speech was settled two decades earlier and in favor of the students.

After a week of smaller-scale debates in classes, there were no substantial disruptions, and without fanfare Stevens eliminated the Confederate flag ban from the school's dress code.[6]

In 1996, middle school student Jamie Kinley was suspended from his school in Anderson, South Carolina, for wearing a jacket bearing the Confederate flag.

"We have a duty and an obligation to remove anything from a school campus that causes a disruption, so teachers can teach and students can learn," said Bill Dillard, assistant school superintendent. But Kinley claimed his jacket never caused a disruption and was not as offensive as the Malcolm X images worn on the clothing of African American students. "When you are talking about teenagers, fashion and appearance are a crucial part of self-expression," added Loren Siegel, director of public education for the ACLU.[7]

In 2015, the issue of the Confederate flag made national headlines following a mass murder, carried out by a white supremacist, in a black church in Charleston, South Carolina. After months of controversy, political leaders in the state decided to remove the Confederate flag from the grounds of the state capitol building, and across the South, numerous other city and county governments made similar decisions.

Educators feared the media stories of those controversies would make the Confederate flag a more desirable part of student wardrobes, but as of this writing, no such cases have been reported in the media. But in media interviews, school administrators have expressed concern over the potential for a double standard emerging: if they suspend white students for wearing the Confederate flag, do they also suspend black students for wearing images of Malcolm X, or Latino students for wearing images of Cesar Chavez?[8]

Another problem area for school administrators are T-shirts and jackets bearing the logo of the National Rifle Association. One such case occurred at Jack Jouett Middle School in Albemarle, Virginia, in 2002. Twelve-year-old Alan Newsom wore a T-shirt promoting the National Rifle Association's Sport Camp. Just three years following the deaths of twelve students and teachers at Columbine High School in Colorado, Assistant Principal Elizabeth Pitt told Newsom he would have to turn the shirt inside out or go home to change.

He agreed to do so, but a few months later when the school revised its dress code to include a ban on any depiction of weapons, Newsom's father took the matter to court. A Federal District Court issued an injunction preventing the school from enforcing the new part of the code, and on appeal the Fourth Circuit Court told the school the ban was constitutionally unenforceable. The justices on the appellate court said they sympathized with the administrators' desire to ban messages on clothing that were offensive or provocative, but ruled that the students' constitutional rights took priority. The justices also pointed out the irony that the Virginia state flag flying in front of the school included an image of an Amazon warrior bearing a spear, and across the street the flag flying in front of a high school included the image of the school's mascot—a patriot armed with a musket. That same year, however, a court in Ohio sided with school administrators when they barred a student from wearing a T-shirt bearing a likeness of serial killer Charles Manson.[9]

In 2013, fourteen-year-old Jared Marcum was arrested and suspended from Logan Middle School in West Virginia after refusing to take off a National Rifle Association shirt. Despite being asked several times by school officials to remove the garment, Marcum kept it on, reportedly saying he was not violating the school's dress code and was exercising his First Amendment rights.

Applying the *Tinker* standard, school officials claimed the message conveyed by his shirt had the potential to "materially disrupt the educational process," and they suspended him for a day.

Although the school's dress code made no mention of the NRA logo, it did state that, "If in the judgment of the administration, a student is dressed inappropriately, the student will be required to change clothes or cover up inappropriate clothing before returning to classes."[10]

Following Marcum's arrest, students across Logan County wore similar NRA shirts to show their support for him.

ADVENTURES IN SCHOOL UNIFORMS

In 1996, following a rash of school shootings across the country (but still three years before Columbine), officials at the U.S. Department of Education dusted off old data regarding school uniforms. The idea had been floated as far back as the 1980s by Washington, DC, Mayor Marion Berry, who believed school uniforms could help public school students achieve as much as their counterparts in Catholic schools.[11]

Based on their belief that clothing choices stratified students into the "cool kids" and "uncool kids" and that relieving peer pressure to wear designer labels on their clothing might decrease school violence perpetrated by the "uncool kids," officials suggested putting the issue back in the public debate. The DOE developed a manual for local school districts that offered numerous proposed policy statements. In order to prevent legal challenges, the manual suggested that policies have "opt-out" clauses by which students, with their parents' approval, would not be required to wear the uniforms.

Loren Siegel, director of public education for the ACLU, believes school uniforms represent the government's overreaction to the problem of school violence. Other critics point out suggestions to make uniforms optional would simply worsen the divide between "in" students and "out" students and make students wearing the uniforms targets of increased ridicule.[12]

President Bill Clinton endorsed the idea of school uniforms in his 1996 State of the Union Address. "If it means that teenagers will stop killing each other over designer jackets, then our public schools should be able to require school uniforms," Clinton said. "If it means that the schoolrooms will be more orderly, more disciplined, and that our young people will learn to evaluate themselves by what they are on the inside instead of what they're wearing on the outside, then our public schools should be able to require their students to wear school uniforms."[13]

Proponents of school uniforms believe they not only reduce the peer pressure students feel to wear designer brands, but also prepare students to "dress for success" in the real world. In school districts that have began requiring student uniforms, anecdotal evidence indicates a reduction in absences and disciplinary problems and an increase in academic performance.[14]

ADVENTURES IN DISRUPTION

In the fall of 1998, James LaVine was a junior at Blaine High School in Blaine, Washington. Teachers knew him as a "bright kid, but somewhat of a loner." They also noticed inconsistencies in his dress—some days as a cowboy, other days in a trenchcoat, even in warm weather. One day he wore a T-shirt that read, "Eat shit and die," and that earned him a trip to the office of assistant principal Tim Haney. On other occasions, LaVine disclosed to school counselors that was having problems at home, had broken up with his girlfriend, and had considered suicide.[15]

At some point during the previous summer, LaVine had written the first draft of a poem, titled "Last Words," in which he reflected on recent school shootings, including one in nearby Springfield, Oregon. It was a first-person account of an armed student who roamed the halls of his high school, and with his heart pounding, killed twenty-eight classmates. He put the poem aside until late September, when he revised it and showed it to his mother. Concerned about the school's "zero tolerance" policy on violence or even the slightest threat of violence, his mother cautioned him against showing it to anyone at school.[16]

But LaVine looked at English teacher Vivian Bleecker as a mentor he could trust, so he showed it to her on a Friday afternoon—not for extra credit, as he had other poems—but simply for feedback. The poem included a number of disturbing passages, including:

"As I approached the classroom door, I drew my gun and threw open the door. Bang, Bang, Bang-Bang. When it was all over, 28 were dead, and all I remember was not feeling any remorce (sic), for I felt, I was, cleansing my soul. Two years have passed, and now I lay 29 roses down upon these stairs, as now, I feel I may strike again."[17]

Later that evening, Bleecker read the poem at home and saw it as a cry for help. The next morning, she called LaVine's counselor, Karen Mulholland, to discuss the contents of the poem. Mulholland set up a meeting for that evening between herself, Bleecker, and Haney.

Haney contacted the Blaine Police Department for guidance. Believing LaVine was a suicide risk, police suggested that Haney refer LaVine to the Community Mental Health Crisis Center. LaVine was then picked up by the police and taken to the office of a psychologist for evaluation. The psychologist reported back to Haney that he found that LaVine was not a threat to himself or anyone else, had no access to weapons, and had no thoughts of carrying out any of the actions he had described in his poem.[18]

On Sunday, Haney met with Principal Dan Newell, and the two men decided that regardless of the positive outcome of the psychologist's report, in light of recent school shootings, they would emergency expel LaVine under an applicable Washington law. In a meeting on Monday morning at the school, LaVine and his father were informed of the suspension, and according to court documents, both went into a profanity-laden tirade and then left the building.

The LaVine family hired attorney Breean Beggs to appeal the suspension. Beggs and school district attorney Timothy Slater agreed that if LaVine agreed to be evaluated by a psychiatrist, he would be eligible to return to school. After three meetings with LaVine, the psychiatrist determined that he be allowed to return to school, which he did after missing seventeen days.

LaVine wanted to enter the military after high school and was concerned that having the suspension in his academic file would be a detriment. With Beggs's help, the family sued the school district, claiming it had violated the First Amendment by suspending LaVine and maintaining the documentation in his file.

"The expulsion of James LaVine for the mere content of his poetry, which expressed thoughts and feelings about teen violence, violated James' right to free speech," Beggs wrote in a preliminary brief. Beggs based much of the case on the *Tinker* principle, analogizing LaVine's reacting to school violence by writing poetry to Mary Beth Tinker's reacting to the Vietnam War by wearing a black armband to school.[19]

School district officials had argued that it was the combination of the poem and other factors—mostly LaVine's previous disciplinary history—that led to the suspension, but Rothstein said the district had overreacted in expelling LaVine.

"There were far less restrictive ways to ensure the safety of students and school personnel," she wrote. "A temporary suspension pending psychiatric examination would have accomplished the [district's] purpose."[20]

The following February 24, U.S. District Judge Barbara J. Rothstein of Seattle ruled in favor of the family, determining that LaVine was disciplined solely for the evocative nature of his poem. She ordered the suspension vacated and all references to the penalty or the controversial poem be expunged from his records.

Rothstein ruled that the poem was not written as part of a class assignment, but instead a personal reflection on the issue of school violence. "Although the district need not wait until the school experiences an actual disturbance before taking corrective action, neither may it preemptively silence a student unless a reasonable person under similar circumstances would conclude that the poem constitutes a true threat of physical violence," Rothstein wrote.[21] LaVine completed his senior year at Blaine without further incident.

THE 1960S: FREE SPEECH ON CAMPUS, OR MAYBE NOT

In the 1960s, cases involving discipline on the high school campus introduced terms such as "disruption of the educational process" and "orderly operation of the school." More specifically, cases were measured against the standard of fighting words—a term taken from the 1942 case of *Chaplinksy v. New Hampshire* and defined as "words which by their very utterance tend to inflict injury or incite an immediate breach of the peace."[22]

Although the 1969 *Tinker* case holds the distinction for setting the precedent for disruption on a K-12 campus, a lesser-known case—argued in the Fifth Circuit Court of Appeals three years earlier—produced a similar outcome. The case of *Burnside v. Byars* began when about thirty students at a historically black school in Philadelphia, Mississippi, wore "freedom buttons" to protest racial segregation in the state and draw attention to disparity in voting rights. The buttons carried the slogan, "One Man, One Vote," which referred to the push for black voting rights across the Southeast.

The buttons had been distributed off campus by the local chapter of a civil rights group, the Council of Federal Organizations. Principal Montgomery Moore announced to the school that the buttons violated the school's conduct policy because they were unrelated to any educational topics discussed in classes and would "cause commotion."

On September 21, four students defied the ban by wearing the buttons to school. After being summoned to Moore's office, one student took off the button, while three kept them on and went home. The following day all three returned to school without the buttons, but two days later, an entire class of more than thirty students were wearing the buttons. Moore gave them the same choice—remove the buttons or return home and face suspension. Most of them left campus and were suspended for a week.

After receiving letters explaining the principal's actions, three parents filed suit against the school in Federal District Court, charging administrators with violating their children's First and Fourteenth Amendment rights.

In their defense, school officials could only respond that their actions in prohibiting the buttons were necessary to "maintain discipline and order" in the school.

The Court sided with the parents, claiming that simply wearing a button, regardless of what controversial message it may have contained, was unlikely to disrupt the school's academic mission and was not in the same category as carrying banners, disseminating leaflets, and extemporaneous speaking, which are protected forms of speech in adult settings but could be reasonably prohibited in a classroom. The Court added that it recognized the role of school officials in maintaining order, but in this case they had overstepped their bounds. Two years later, the Fifth Circuit Court of Appeals upheld the ruling of the lower court, claiming that the buttons caused only "mild curiosity" at worst and that the regulation prohibiting them was "arbitrary and unreasonable."[23]

One evening in early December, 1965, a group of adults and students met at a private home in Des Moines, Iowa, to discuss their opposition to the Vietnam War. Among the students present were fifteen-year-old John Tinker, his thirteen-year-old sister, Mary Beth, and their friend, sixteen-year-old Christopher Eckhardt, whose parents hosted the meeting.

The Tinker children told their friends that before the school closed for Christmas break, they were going to wear black armbands at their respective schools as a "passive protest" of the war. On December 14, school officials heard about their plans and enacted an emergency policy banning armbands and other forms of symbolic speech.

Mary Beth and Christopher wore black armbands on December 15, and John Tinker joined the protest the next day. The armbands bore no message other than the "peace sign" that was popular at the time. Early on the second day, the three students were sent to the principal's office and asked to remove the armbands. When they refused, they were each suspended for three days. Their parents sued to have their suspensions overturned, which began a three-year battle that eventually reached the U.S. Supreme Court.

A Federal District Court dismissed the complaint, so Tinker's family took the case to the Eighth Circuit Court of Appeals. That court was equally divided, which meant the lower court's dismissal stood. The next stop was the U.S. Supreme Court, which agree to hear the case during its 1968-1969 session.

The school district's central contention was that principals should have the sole responsibility for determining what is potentially disruptive and it was inappropriate for the courts to second-guess the principal's authority. During the proceedings, Justice Thurgood Marshall expressed the skepticism of the Court when he asked the school district's attorneys if they were really concerned about seven students creating a disturbance among combined student populations of 18,000.

On February 24, 1969, the Court announced it was siding with Tinker and students in general, determining that school administrators could not infringe on students' free speech rights unless such speech could be proven to be disruptive. Student speech, the courts ruled, "was protected under the First Amendment as long as it did not materially and substantially interfere with the requirements of appropriate discipline and without colliding with the rights of others."[24]

The Court added that "undifferentiated fear or apprehension of disturbance is not enough to overcome the right to freedom of expression." In the majority decision, Justice Abe Fortas wrote that, "It can hardly be argued that either students or teachers shed their constitutional rights to freedom of speech at the schoolhouse gate." Later in the opinion, he added, "In our system, state-operated schools may not be enclaves of totalitarianism. School officials do not possess absolute authority over their students. Students in school as well as out of school are 'persons' under our Constitution. They are possessed of fundamental rights which the state must respect, just as they themselves must respect their obligations to the state. In our system, students may not be regarded as closed-circuit recipients of only that which the state chooses to communicate. They may not be confined to the expression of those sentiments that are officially approved. In the absence of a specific showing of constitutionally valid reasons to regulate their speech, students are entitled to freedom of expression of their views."[25]

The justices also noted that the school had not prohibited other forms of passive speech—including buttons that supported political candidates and even the Iron Cross, a symbol of Nazism—and there was no discussion of "disruption." Therefore, no claim of the armband band being content-neutral could be supported.[26]

In the *Tinker* ruling, the USSC determined that in order for a school official to suppress student expression, the school must be able to show that the action was prompted by "something more than the mere desire to avoid the discomfort and unpleasantness that always accompany an unpopular viewpoint."[27]

The only surprise in the case was the dissent filed by Justice Hugo Black, usually a strong advocate of free speech rights, who warned of a "slippery slope" that might result from the decision and lead to a "new era of permissiveness." Black wrote that courts should defer to the expertise of school officials in deciding when expression needs to be prohibited and punished and that judicial review should be used sparingly because it undermines the necessary authority of the school.[28]

The *Tinker* case represented the final step in the court's gradual shift from placing the "burden of proof" in campus free speech cases on the administrator rather than the student. Or to put it the other way around, it shifted the "benefit of the doubt" from the administrator to the student. The shift was similar to the one seen in off-campus free speech cases, in which the attitude during the first half of the twentieth century—when the government cracked down on even the slightest case of speech critical of the military or government—to the era of strict scrutiny in the latter half of the century, in which the burden of proof in free speech cases was placed on the government and the benefit of the doubt was given to the speaker. Many viewed the *Tinker* case, and similar cases that followed it, as a reminder that classrooms at all grade levels should be both safe havens for constitutional freedoms and places where students could learn about their rights. [29]

The case of *Grayned v. Rockford* began on April 25, 1969, when students from West Senior High School in Rockford, Illinois, demonstrated, along with their parents and community leaders, outside the office of the principal. The demonstration was based on complaints that the principal was unresponsive to the concerns of black students. Specifically, the protestors complained that there were no black cheerleaders at the school, despite its large black student population; there were no black guidance counselors; and the school's Black History class was taught by a white instructor. More than forty of the protestors were arrested and charged with violating a local noise ordinance.

Despite the defendants' protests that the police response to the protest caused much more disruption than the protest itself, the trial court ruled in favor of the City of Rockford. Richard Grayned, one of the students arrested, appealed his conviction to the U.S. Supreme Court, where the case was decided in 1972. The Court upheld the conviction, determining that city officials were within their rights to break up the demonstration, based on its disruption of the academic activity taking place inside the building. Even though the speech-limiting actions in the case were taken by the police and not school officials, the case is still significant because it was believed to be the first of its type to be decided after the better-known case of *Tinker v. Des Moines Independent Community School District*. [30]

BETHEL V. FRASER: HOOTING, YELLING, EMBARRASSMENT, AND BEWILDERMENT

After *Grayned*, it would be another fourteen years before another case involving the free speech rights of K-12 students would reach the U.S. Supreme Court. The case of *Bethel School District v. Fraser* (1986) began in 1983 when parents in Washington State sued the school district after their son, who had previously been suspended for using indecent language when speaking at a school assembly, was denied the opportunity to speak at commencement ceremonies, even though the student body had elected him to do so. Matthew Fraser's earlier nominating speech for a friend running for a position in student government included the following:

> I know a man who is firm—he's firm in his pants, he's firm in his shirt, his character is firm—but most of all, his belief in you, the students of Bethel, is firm. Jeff Kuhlman is a man who takes his point and pounds it in. If necessary, he'll take an issue and nail it to the wall. He doesn't attack things in spurts—he drives hard, pushing and pushing until finally—he succeeds. Jeff is a man who will go to the very end—even to the climax, for each and every one of you. So vote for Jeff for A.B.S. vice-president—he'll never come between you and the best our high school can be.[31]

Approximately 600 students attended the mandatory assembly. The next day, Fraser was called to the assistant principal's office, notified of the accusations against him, and was given a chance to tell his side of the story. Fraser admitted to intentionally using sexual innuendos in his speech. Although no profanity (the most common rationale for punishing speakers) was included, administrators suspended Fraser for ten days based on student reaction to the speech, which they described in court testimony as "hooting, yelling, embarrassment, and bewilderment."[32]

He was also informed that his name would be deleted from a list of candidates for graduation speaker at the school's commencement exercises. He appealed to the school district's grievance committee, which agreed with the assistant principal that the speech was obscene and disruptive.

Fraser and his father then sued in Federal District Court, which sided with the family, ordering the school district to return his name to the list of candidates for commencement speaker and compensate the Frasers for their legal fees.[33]

The school district appealed to the Ninth Circuit, which upheld the decision of the lower court in 1985, determining that Fraser's speech was similar to the black armbands worn by the students in *Tinker*. The appeals court noted that the resulting disruption was minor and difficult to document. It added the "slippery slope" nature of its ruling, expressing concern that if it found in favor of the school district, it would criminalize behavior better categorized as merely adolescent rather than disruptive.[34]

The following year, the case went before the U.S. Supreme Court, which disagreed with the *Tinker* comparison and ruled in favor of the school district, claiming that unlike the black armbands in *Tinker*, Fraser's speech was both obtrusive and delivered to a captive audience. The Court added that the school district was within its rights to punish students for speech that is "inconsistent with its educational mission" and that society has "an interest in teaching students the boundaries of socially appropriate behavior."[35]

Chief Justice Warren Burger wrote that there was a marked difference between the passive political speech in the *Tinker* case and the vulgar speech in *Bethel*. "The constitutional rights of students in public schools are not co-existent with the rights of adults in other settings," Burger wrote.[36] Burger also noted the need for the courts to defer to school administrators in disciplinary matters, stating that, "The undoubted freedom to advocate unpopular or controversial views must be balanced against the society's countervailing interest in teaching students the boundaries of socially appropriate behavior."[37]

In his dissent, Justice John Paul Stevens cited a line from the movie *Gone With the Wind*, uttered by Clark Gable, "'Frankly, my dear, I don't give a damn.' When I was a high school student, the use of these words in a public forum shocked the nation," Stevens wrote. "Today that four-letter expletive is less offensive than it was then."[38]

Jeffery T. Haley, Fraser's lawyer, criticized the decision largely because his client's speech was part of the student government process (despite its vulgar content) and was thereby deserving of the highest level of First Amendment protection. In subsequent cases, the Courts have used the *Bethel* decision in supporting the rights of school administrators in a variety of "disruption" cases, including those involving books in the school library, content of student publications, and controversial slogans or images on student clothing.

Civil libertarian Daniel A. Farber described the speech as "filled with clumsy sexual innuendos that today might earn a movie a PG-13 rating."[39]

IN THE SHADOW OF COLUMBINE

On April 20, 1999, two mentally troubled students at Columbine High School in Littleton, Colorado, executed a mass shooting they had planned for months and had foreshadowed in various writing assignments and conversations with teachers and guidance counselors. Missing the "red flags" led to the loss of life for twelve students and one teacher. In the seventeen years that has elapsed since, it has also compelled administrators to "err on the side of caution" and scrutinize the ramblings and rants that students have expressed in the form of class assignments, videos, and social media postings.

As a result of Columbine, civil libertarian David L. Hudson Jr. wrote in 2005, "some school administrators have reacted swiftly to student expression that contains harsh language, violent themes or similar content . . . 'zero tolerance' has spread from drugs and weapons to controversial student speech. Students have been punished for dark poetry, rap songs, Halloween essays, doodles of teachers and students with sticks in their heads or other material. In some cases, intervention was necessary, justified, or wise. At other times, the fear for safety has led to the suppression of constitutional rights."[40]

In fact, Hudson claims that many courts ruling against student free speech rights in cases involving "true threats" to school safety specifically cite the Columbine tragedy in giving the benefit of the doubt to school administrators.

Student expressions that in prior decades might have been dismissed as flights of imagination, normal teen angst, or "blowing off steam" are now scrutinized by school counselors, and in some cases, local law enforcement officers in honest attempts to prevent the next tragedy.

Ken Trump, president of the National School Safety and Security Services, a consulting firm, sides with school administrators in their responses to "red flags" that show up in student writings and behavior. "Art and English teachers are often in the best position to recognize early warning signs of potential violence, as students who are troubled may communicate these 'red flags' in their drawings and writings," Trump said. "School officials should be alert to such communications and treat them seriously—meaning that they investigate further with an emphasis on providing support to students determined to be legitimately troubled prior to an incident occurring. Some initial concerns may turn out to be unfounded, but this cannot be determined if the initial signs are overlooked or dismissed."[41]

Factors that go into the "true threat" decision include whether a specific person (classmate, teacher, or principal) is mentioned, a student's previous disciplinary history, and the degree to which the artistic or written expression is accompanied by angry demeanor or other physical conduct.[42]

Columbine has cast such a large shadow over America's high schools, contends First Amendment attorney Lawrence Fischmann, that "the Tinker case might be decided differently today."[43]

In the 1990s, even before Columbine, many of the school rules limiting free speech were enacted in response to issues such as school shootings and gang activity. In the first decade of the new century, added to the list of reasons was the phenomenon of cyberbullying.

Most educators realize that very few cases or troubling artistic or written expression will eventually result in violence, but they fear being second-guessed or held liable for *not acting* when violence does happen. But critics say what the schools gain in the perception of safety they lose in the chilling effect it creates among students at a time in their lives when they should be learning about the benefits of self-expression rather than its dangers. "We used to defer to the professional discretion of teachers and administrators," said Richard Arum, a professor of sociology at New York University and author of a 2005 book, *Judging School Discipline*. "Now our schools are run increasingly by lawyers and judges, and that has profound consequences in undermining the moral authority of school discipline."[44]

One legal expert expressing concern over the court's tendency to over-reach is Jonathan Turley, professor of law at Georgetown University and a frequent contributor to *USA Today*. Following a series of cases in late 2013 and early 2014 that were decided mostly in favor of school administrators, Turley chastised the courts for backing away from the 1969 *Tinker* standard.

"Since *Tinker*, the federal courts have not only stripped students of their free speech rights at the schoolhouse gate, they also have done so at their bedroom doors," Turley wrote. "Federal courts have upheld a series of cases where school officials have punished students for statements they make out-side school on social media."[45]

First Amendment attorney Charles C. Haynes is one of many free speech advocates who question the value of using limitations on student expression in the effort to combat bullying. "Rather than shutting down speech about politics or religion, schools should help students master the skills of civil discourse, including the skill of listening to speech with which one profound-ly disagrees," Haynes wrote in a 2012 op-ed piece. "Censorship doesn't make schools safer (from bullying). On the contrary, suppressing speech depends on divisions and fuels intolerance. To prepare students for citizen-ship in a pluralistic society that values the First Amendment, schools should be places that are both safe and free."[46]

MORSE V. FREDERICK: HALFWAY DOWN THE SLIPPERY SLOPE

When the Olympic Torch made its way through the streets of Juneau, Alaska, on January 24, 2002, students at Juneau-Douglas High School, on the route of the parade, were excused from class in order to witness the historic event. Among them were Joseph Frederick and several friends, who unfurled their home-made, fourteen-foot banner carrying the phrase "Bong Hits 4 Jesus," which was captured by print and broadcast cameras recording the event.

The banner was confiscated by school officials, and Frederick was suspended for ten days by principal Deborah Morse. The principal claimed that Frederick's behavior violated school policy regarding the "promotion of drug use" and was punishable because while off school property, the students' participation in the event was part of a school-sanctioned activity.

When Frederick sued Morse in district court, the court ruled in favor of the principal, validating both of her points. Frederick appealed to the Ninth Circuit, who reversed the lower court's ruling, determining that Morse had violated Frederick's First Amendment rights. In its written ruling, the appeals court leaned heavily on the *Tinker* ruling, determining that despite the principal's initial claims, the event at which the speech took place was outside of school and did not disrupt an official school activity. The panel also dismissed the principal's claim that the *Bethel* ruling—allowing the school to punish speech inconsistent with its educational mission—should apply in this case. The SPLC called the case a "turf war" between the *Tinker* and *Hazelwood* cases and was pleased that the legacy of the *Tinker* case prevailed.[47]

The principal, backed by the George W. Bush administration and assisted by former Solicitor General Kenneth Starr, appealed to the U.S. Supreme Court. Filing supporting briefs on behalf of the principal were the National School Board Association, two other educational associations, and several anti-drug organizations.

Backing Frederick were the American Civil Liberties Union and the National Coalition Against Censorship. Many conservative political groups filed amicus curie briefs as well, including the American Center for Law and Justice, the Christian Legal Society, the Alliance Defense Fund, and the Liberty Institute. While offended by Frederick's message, they nonetheless were concerned about the potential "slippery slope" that might result if the Court ruled in favor of the school. If the speech of liberal students was limited, they reasoned, the speech rights of conservative students would be at risk in the future.

The Court reversed the ruling of the appeals court, reinstating the opinion of the original trial court. Chief Justice John Roberts, in one of the first cases over which he presided, wrote in the court's decision that "schools may take steps to safeguard those entrusted to their care from speech that can reasonably be regarded as encouraging illegal drug use . . . we conclude in this case that school officials did not violate the First Amendment by confiscating the banner and suspending the student responsible for it."[48]

Justice Anthony Kennedy voted in the majority, but said he was a bit skeptical, pointing out that speech cases that "took place outside of a formal classroom setting were difficult to classify as disruptive." In his dissenting opinion, Justice David Souter called Frederick's speech "just a kid's provocative statement."[49]

Chief Justice Roberts emphasized that neither *Bethel* nor *Morse* should be interpreted as allowing schools to restrict speech merely because it is offensive. Political and religious speech is often offensive; Roberts pointed out, but would nevertheless be protected. Although the speech given by Fraser was on the surface an act of political speech, its offensiveness and potential to disrupt the educational process disqualified it from First Amendment protection.[50]

IN THE SHADOW OF VIRGINIA TECH

While high school administrators claim to make decisions regarding student free speech and disruption under the "shadow of Columbine," university administrators do so citing a more recent case.

On April 16, 2007, a mentally disturbed student at Virginia Polytechnic University killed thirty-two students and faculty members and himself in what is to date the worst mass murder affecting an educational institution. In the decade that has passed since, university administrators concerned about similar crimes often overreact to even the slightest aberration in student behavior.

Many threats, made online and elsewhere, cite the Virginia Tech tragedy, the name of the killer, or simply the term "4/16." Such references that appear in English class essays or poetry or on social media messages are enough to cause administrators to expel students, order psychiatric evaluations, or both.

THE MEMORIAL PARKING GARAGE

In the spring of 2007, Valdosta State University student Hayden Barnes objected to the university's plan to spend $30 million to build a parking garage on campus. Believing the per-space price of $15,000 was exorbitant and more environmentally friendly options were available, Barnes made his feelings known to the student body through a letter to the editor and the university president and board of trustees through personally addressed letters. When he got no response, he took his case to Facebook, creating a collage of photos showing smog, a bulldozer, and an asthma inhaler. What got the attention of university administrators and campus police was the heading he had chosen: "the Zaccari Memorial Parking Garage." Barnes claimed the headline referred only to President Ronald Zaccari's public comments that the garage would be part of his legacy, but the president interpreted it differently.

On May 7, Barnes received a notice that he had been administratively withdrawn from the university, effective that day. The president had taken the word "memorial" as a threat on his life. Coming just three weeks after the

April 16 tragedy at Virginia Tech, Zaccari and administrators and mental health counselors at other universities across the country were reacting—some say overreacting—to even the slightest sign of unclear thinking among students.

Barnes was locked out of his residence hall and ordered to leave campus. He was told he could return only after he provided a "certificate of mental health" from a psychiatrist. He provided that documentation, along with a lengthy and detailed written appeal in which he pointed out that he was expelled with no hearing, no formal explanation of the charges, and no opportunity to appeal—all of which violated the university's due process procedures. More importantly, he claimed the school had violated his First and Fourteenth Amendment rights. [51]

The Foundation for Individual Rights in Education (FIRE) came to Barnes's defense, along with noted First Amendment lawyer Robert Corn-Revere. After a formal lawsuit was filed in January 2008, other university employees testified that Zaccari was so incensed that Barnes would not go away quietly that he began a personal vendetta against him that included having staff "look into his academic records, his religion, and registration with VSU Access." The latter was a program to help students with disabilities, including anxiety and depression. [52]

Zaccari used the fact that Barnes had sought counseling through the Access program as a justification for considering him a threat to campus safety. Again, he cited Virginia Tech. Counselors in the Access program, as well as the original psychiatrist Barnes had visited the previous summer, assured Zaccari that Barnes was not a threat to him or anyone else. As it turned out, Barnes was a successful emergency medical technician and a strong believer in non-violence.

None of that seemed to matter to Zaccari, who moved ahead with defending the suit. The VSU Board of Regents eventually interceded and voted to reinstate Barnes in exchange for him dropping the suit. By that time Barnes was already close to completing his degree at another institution, so he respectfully declined and continued the suit. A Federal District Court sided with Barnes and against the university, and in 2012 that decision was upheld on appeal to the Eleventh Circuit. The university eventually settled with Barnes and agreed to pay him $50,000. [53]

KILLING SPREE

In 2014, a professor at the University of Central Florida was suspended for making a tasteless joke during an optional test-review meeting for his accounting class. The controversy began when Professor Hyung-il Jung noticed the pained look on students' faces, and asked, "Am I on a killing spree or what?"[54]

Jung apologized to the students and later to the administration. "It was purely a joke, of course," he said. "I thought all of the students laughed together with me."[55]

Coming just a few weeks after a former UCF student shot himself as police thwarted what university officials believe was a planned killing spree on campus, UCF spokesman Chad Binette called the comment "completely inappropriate."[56]

"The student who reported the comment to us interpreted it as a threat to her class, and we will always take any reported threat very seriously," Binette said. "This is not an acceptable topic to joke about, particularly in light of recent events around the country and on our campus."[57]

A group of about twenty students e-mailed a letter to the UCF administration, explaining that they knew the comment was meant as a joke. Sophomore Marina Reasoner, one of the students who added their names to the letter, said she and others were upset that Jung's reputation as an excellent teacher was being called into question over a comment that was taken out of context.

"Yes, there are jokes and sometimes they are taken too far," Reasoner said. "But if you know this man he would never mean anything in that way."[58]

Jung was originally told he had been suspended until the end of the semester, but the suspension was later nullified after days of negative publicity.

THE WORLD ACCORDING TO YIK YAK

During "Free Speech Week" in October 2015, a coalition of women's and civil rights groups announced a campaign to pressure colleges and universities, through the U.S. Department of Education, to be more aggressive in investigating and possibly closing down online forums such as Yik Yak. The site is one of many anonymous Internet sites where members—mostly college students—can defame and harass friends and enemies, mostly without fear of every being identified, much less punished.

The groups wanted the DOE to require schools to investigate the sites and charge their more obnoxious members with violating federal civil rights laws. If the schools don't comply, the groups insist, the DOE should withhold the schools' federal funding.

Although most college students were already aware of Yik Yak since its debut in 2013, it first gained national fame in April 2015 when a student at the University of Mary Washington in Fredericksburg, Virginia, was murdered. Twenty-year-old Grace Mann and several other members of Feminists United, a student group, had been targets of sexist threats on Yik Yak for several weeks.

Following Mann's death, attorney Lisa Banks filed a complaint on behalf of the group with the DOE, alleging the group's members had been threatened and "cyberstalked" after speaking out about gender issues on campus. Banks accused UMW administrators of ignoring the group's complaints about the threats. On multiple occasions, Banks said, she and the group's president had met with university officials about the threats. At minimum, they said, the school should have blocked access to Yik Yak through the campus's Wi-Fi network and attempted to identify those responsible for the threats. Instead of doing so, administrators sent an email to students saying the university "had no recourse for cyberbullying" and urged them to report threatening situations to the social media site. In cases of more direct and specific threats, however, students were encouraged to contact university police.

Police charged Mann's male roommate with first-degree kidnapping and murder, but did not speculate on whether Mann's death was connected with her political activities. Because she was one of several members who were targets of more than seven hundred threatening Yik Yak messages, however, women's groups across the country found it unlikely that any other motive was possible.

About the same time at Clemson University in South Carolina, racially offensive and threatening Yik Yak messages were posted after authorities in Ferguson, Missouri, failed to indict the police officer responsible for the death of an unarmed African American man. [59]

In Atlanta, an eighteen-year-old college student started a petition asking Yik Yak to strengthen its monitoring procedures after she became aware of threatening messages posted following her suicide attempt. Within a few months, the petition had more than 78,000 signatures, but as of early 2016, the site had not changed its procedures or policies. [60]

The high school equivalent of Yik Yak is a social media application called After School, which its founders refer to as "Funny Anonymous School News for Confessions and Compliments." Founded in 2014, the program includes graphic and sexually explicit videos and comments from anonymous members about their friends, teachers, and principals. At first, Apple limited its availability through its app store to users age twelve or older, but once it became aware of the content, it deleted the app from its offerings.

School districts around the country are not allowing it to be accessed on school computers and are warning parents to watch for the icon—a tiger wearing yellow striped sunglasses—showing up on their child's home computer or portable devices. [61]

ADVENTURES IN CYBERSPACE

In late 2005 in Hermitage, Pennsylvania, Hickory High School senior Justin Layshock posted a fake MySpace page parodying Eric Trosch, the school's principal. Layshock posted a picture of Trosch and answered the questions asked by the site's profile template by riffing on the word "big" because Trosch was apparently a large man. Answers included phrases like "big faggot," "big hard ass," and "big dick." To the question, "What did you do on your last birthday?" Trosch answered "Too drunk to remember." Layshock created the profile from a computer at his grandmother's home.

School administrators discovered the profile and suspended Layshock for ten days.

In addition, the administration ordered him to finish high school in the Alternative Education Program and forbid him from attending his own graduation in the spring. The school eventually permitted Justin to attend his regular classes, and he graduated in spring 2006.

The following year, in a federal court case filed by Justin's parents and the American Civil Liberties Union of Western Pennsylvania, a judge ruled that the school's suspension was unconstitutional.

At the same time Layshock's case was proceeding through the appeals process, a similar case was unfolding on the opposite side of the state. An eighth-grader at Blue Mountain Middle School in Orwigsburg, Pennsylvania, disliked the school's principal so much that she created a parody profile of him and posted it on MySpace. It identified principal James M. McGonigle by title rather than name, but it did use his official photograph the student copied from the school's website. The profile listed his interests as "hitting on students and their parents" and claiming in the "About Me" section that the principal was a "sex addict."

Because MySpace and other social networking sites could not be accessed through school computers, she used her parents' home computer. The daughter later admitted that she created the fake profile in retaliation for the principal having cited her for a dress code violation. The student used the network's privacy settings to limit access to only twenty of her friends, but one showed it to the principal, who didn't find it amusing and suspended the student, identified in court documents simply as J. S., for ten days.

Her parents immediately sued the school district to have the suspension overturned, but a Federal District Court ruled in favor of the school district, determining that the principal correctly applied the *Bethel* standard in assessing the potential for the site to affect the orderly operation of the school. [62] The court added that because the site was vulgar and had "some effect" on campus, it was not necessary to demonstrate "substantial disruption." The court rejected the parents' claims that their daughter's First Amendment rights had been infringed.

It took four years for the parents' appeal to be heard, and because the case was so similar to the Layshock case and it reached the Third Circuit Court of Appeals at the same time, the cases were consolidated. In its 2011 ruling, the appeals court overturned the lower court's decision and sided with both families on their First Amendment claims. The court decision relied heavily on *Tinker*, claiming the school district was unable to prove that the postings created disruptions at the respective schools.[63]

The appeals court also rejected the lower court's application of *Bethel*, primarily because the speech in that case occurred on campus. With the speech in the *Layshock* and *Snyder* cases taking place primarily off campus and communicated to limited audiences, the court determined that they were cases involving hurt feelings more than disruption. The court also labeled the content of the profiles as "so juvenile and nonsensical" that no reasonable person could have taken them seriously." The following year, both school districts appealed the rulings to the U.S. Supreme Court but failed to get hearings.[64]

IT MUST BE TRUE BECAUSE I SAW IT ON FACEBOOK

As the Internet and social media became increasingly popular among teenagers and pre-teens in the first decade of the new century, school administrators as well as the courts were faced with new disciplinary questions. When students use their own computers and their own time to ridicule their teachers, administrators, and peers, how much can the school do to regulate it? To what degree is such speech protected by the First Amendment?

Early case law resulted in findings on both sides. In some cases, the courts cited the *Tinker* standard and placed the burden of proof on school administrators to explain how the speech in question was disruptive of the educational process, which in most cases they could not do. As with many post-*Tinker* cases, judges ruled that simple vulgarity, distastefulness, or adolescent ranting was not sufficient grounds for the courts to interfere.

In other cases, administrators and courts cited the *Bethel* standard, which states a school did not have to "tolerate speech that is inconsistent with its educational mission."[65]

"Students once limited to sharing their thoughts about school with each other or on the bathroom wall now share them on the Web," wrote University of Houston professor Ashley Packard in her 2013 textbook, *Digital Media Law*. "This has created a new challenge for school and courts. While it is clear that student speech on campus may be restricted and that speech off campus is protected, Internet posts—made off school property but accessible on campus—fall into a gray area in between on-campus and off-campus speech."[66]

Ken Paulson, president of the Nashville-based First Amendment Center, points out the principles underlying the free speech rights of high school students haven't changed since the 1969 case of *Tinker v. Des Moines Independent Community School District*, but the methods used to exercise those rights certainly have. "Four decades later (since *Tinker*), the stakes have changed," Paulson wrote in a 2010 op-ed piece in *USA Today*. "The black armbands have been supplanted by the Internet, a potent tool for information, education, and character assassination. For young people, the Web presents an unprecedented opportunity to share their views with their friends, school-mates, and the community beyond. Some use it more wisely than others."[67]

Paulson rejects the double standard applied to regulation of comments posted on the Internet by students and adults, questioning why students are punished or expressing legitimate opinions about the operation of their schools, while their parents—or other adults—are free to express nastier and more obnoxious comments about the government and public officials. "The best legal path to take in these cases is to treat young people posting ugly and potentially defamatory content the way we would adults," Paulson wrote. "If the content is illegal or threatening, charge them. If the content is libelous, sue them, as some teachers and principals have done. And if the content is neither criminal nor libelous, accept a provocative posting as the free speech that it is."[68]

Law school student Mickey Lee Jett was one of a number of observers pointing out the difference between yesterday's form of disruption and that of today. Instead of rude comments made orally or on paper that reached a limited audience, it's now a case of students venting in cyberspace about even the most trivial perceived injustice.

"Anyone reflecting on his or her days in secondary school will probably recall a teacher or administrator who students ridiculed," wrote Jett in a 2014 article in *Catholic University Law Review*. "Students may have whispered comments about this person during lunch and passed notes behind his or her back during class. Fast forward to the present. Today a student has the ability to create a social media profile about a school administrator, allowing the student to ridicule that principal or teacher within a digital social environment."[69] What Jett left out of his article is that many such attacks take place from behind the veil of anonymity.

First Amendment attorney Ann Beeson identifies the censoring of student websites—created on their own time and using their home computers—as one of the "most disturbing trends" on the free speech landscape. "If a student publishes (offensive) material on his home computer, that is the parents'

jurisdiction, not the school's. It is an intrusion on the parent-child relationship."[70]

About the same time the *Layshock* and *Snyder* cases were being argued in the
appeals court, a sixth-grader at Minnewaska Area Middle School in Minnesota was learning a similar legal lesson about the dangers of ridiculing school
administrators on social media. Riley Stratton published a Facebook post
about one of her school's hall monitors, saying she hated that particular
teacher's aide for "being mean."[71]

News about the posting soon reached school administrators. Even though
it was published off school grounds, Stratton was given an in-school suspension.

Attorney Wally Hilke, who took the case pro bono for the American Civil
Liberties Union, said that the school's actions were a violation of Stratton's
rights to free speech.

"They punished her for doing exactly what kids have done for 100
years—complaining to her friends about teachers and administrators," Hilke
told local media. "She wasn't spreading lies or inciting them to engage in bad
behavior, she was just expressing her personal feelings."[72]

In order to find out which of her classmates snitched on her, Riley turned
to her favorite research tool—Facebook. She never found out. Then the
mother of one of Stratton's classmates discovered that the young girl was
having sexual discussions with her son on Facebook. The mother complained
to school officials about the racy chat, which caused administrators to call
Stratton to the office.

With a sheriff's deputy present, school officials pressured the teen into
disclosing her password, then searched through her Facebook profile. Her
mother, Sandra Stratton, told local media she was furious that, at minimum,
she was not notified about the interrogation and allowed to be present. "They
never once told me they were going to bring her into the room and demand
her Facebook password," her mother said. "I'm hoping schools kind of leave
these things alone so parents can punish their own kids for things that happen
off school grounds."[73]

School superintendent Greg Schmidt defended the administrators' actions, citing concern for school discipline and the prevention of cyberbullying.

"The school's intent wasn't to be mean or bully this student, but to really
remedy someone getting off track a little," Schmidt told local media.[74] "But
the situation was so distressing to Stratton that she was taken out of the
public school system in order to be home-schooled."[75]

"Riley's really a hero to me, it's really quite a brave thing she's done," Hilke told local media. "It was very upsetting to her. And, you know, for days she couldn't return to school, and she lost a tremendous amount of trust in adults through this process."[76] Riley's parents eventually sued the school district for violation of their daughter's First Amendment rights and were awarded $70,000 in damages.

As part of the settlement, Minnewaska schools agreed to retrain teachers and change the policy about social media usage. The policy now says students' electronic records can only be searched if there is a "reasonable suspicion" that school rules were violated.

"Educators can still be involved in the lives of young people, they can look out for the interests of young people," Hilke said. "They just can't punish them for exercising their constitutional rights."[77]

In 2007, high school senior Katie Evans established a Facebook page to rant about her English teacher, who she labeled on the page as "the worst teacher I've ever met." She expected her peers at Pembroke Pines Charter High School near Miami, Florida, to join in by becoming "friends" and supporting her opinion, but most defended the teacher and attacked Evans.

She took the page offline, but the school's principal later found out about it and suspended the student for three days and removed her from her Advanced Placement classes. He called the student's behavior "disruptive behavior" and "cyberbullying." In the surrounding community, the student became known as the "Ferris Bueller of Facebook," a reference to the 1986 movie that that focused on the exploits of an academic underachiever who thumbed his nose at the authority of his teachers and principal.

A nearby chapter of the ACLU came to the student's defense, claiming that her suspension was a form of punishing speech protected by the First Amendment. A federal judge ruled in the student's favor and ordered the principal to expunge the suspension from the student's file. She also received $1 in damages and $15,000 in legal fees. In his written opinion, the judge wrote that the student's expression "fell under the wide umbrella of protected speech . . . it was an opinion of a student about a teacher that was published off-campus, did not cause any disruption on-campus, and was not lewd, vulgar, threatening, or advocating illegal or dangerous behavior."[78]

When twenty-four-year-old high school teacher Ashley Payne returned from her summer vacation in Europe in 2009, she thought nothing of posting photographs of the trip on her Facebook page. Her photos included shots of her drinking wine and beer in cafes in Italy, Spain, and Ireland, and one photo included the word "bitch" on a banner in one of the bars—a reference to a Irish bar trivia game called "Bitch Bingo." Her employer, the Barrow County School System in Georgia, had a rule prohibiting teachers from "unacceptable online activities." Payne believed her privacy settings would limit access to her friends and would not be available to students or their parents.

But in late August, only a few weeks into the new school year, Payne was called into her principal's office and confronted with the visual evidence. An email that her principal said came from a "concerned anonymous parent" prompted the inquiry.[79]

Citing the school system's policy, the principal gave her two choices—suspension or resignation. Payne chose the latter, but a few months later filed a lawsuit against the school system, claiming that the principal had violated a state law dealing with the due process that must be provided to teachers before they could be dismissed. Payne and her attorney asked for reinstatement to her position, back pay for the time she spent out of the classroom, and reimbursement for her legal fees.

Payne later learned that the anonymous email did not come from a parent, but from another unidentified person. She based her legal complaint partially on that detail and partially on the fact that she had conformed with school board policy of not communicating with her students using social networking sites. But the school board contended that regardless of the privacy settings, Payne's Facebook page "promoted alcohol use" and "contained profanity."

"Yes, I put it on the Internet, so you can make that argument," Payne told CBS News in a February 2011 interview. "But it sort of feels like the same thing as if I had put the pictures in a shoebox in my house and someone came in and took them and showed one of them to the principal."[80]

Her attorney, Richard Storrs, added, "It would be like I went to a restaurant and saw my daughter's teacher sitting there with her husband having a glass with some kind of liquid. Is that frowned upon by the school board? Is that illegal? Is that improper? Of course not. It's the same situation in this case."[81]

Frederick Lane, an attorney not involved in the case, believes that while unfair on the surface, the situation is evidence to support his contention that once individuals post something online, they surrender part or all of their privacy. "All it takes is one person making a copy of what you've posted and it's out in the wild, and you no longer have control," Lane told CBS News. "And we're not losing that control, we're giving it away. Every time we buy with credit cards, use cellphones which signal our location, or post pictures on social networks like Facebook. Just sending an email may make private information public."[82]

CYBERBULLYING, CYBERSTALKING, AND CYBER HARASSMENT

Another serious issue for parents and school administrators is the use of social networking sites for online pranks and other forms of cruelty, a problem that sociologists have termed *cyberbullying*. Related issues are that of *cyberstalking* and *cyberharassment*. "When Oscar Wilde observed that the only thing worse than being talked about is not being talked about, he could not have imagined the Internet," wrote syndicated columnist Kathleen Parker in a 2009 piece.[83]

One of the earliest known cases of cyberbullying occurred in 2006, when students at a St. Louis high school created a list titled "Who's Hot and Who's Not" that included the names of one hundred classmates, along with racist and sexist comments. They posted it on Facebook and signed the name of a seventeen-year-old classmate, who discovered it only after one of the girls mentioned asked him about it. After a lengthy investigation, school officials were unable to determine who was responsible. More serious cases of cyberbullying have caused at least two teen suicides.

In 2010, the tragedy of gay teens committing suicide after years of harassment and abuse from other teens prompted syndicated newspaper columnist Dan Savage to establish the "It Gets Better" project. Beginning with a YouTube video and then expanding to a website and book, the project is aimed at providing a support system for gay, lesbian, bisexual, and transgendered teens and young adults. The website, which claims to have more than 330,000 members, features testimonials from successful adults who survived adolescence while questioning their sexual identity.[84]

ACCEPTABLE USE POLICIES

As many college newspapers began publishing online editions in the late 1990s, advisers became concerned with the level of control that administrators might attempt to exercise. Most institutions have "acceptable use" policies that prohibit the use of university-owned computer networks to transmit pornography, indecency, and other objectionable material, and advisers worried that such policies might be used to limit speech in the online newspapers. While no such cases have yet reached the courts, the Student Press Law Center issued a report in 1998 that predicted that no acceptable use policy could be used to circumvent rights guaranteed by the First Amendment.

"A school's AUP, just like any school policy, must be in compliance with state and federal laws," the report stated. "Courts have suggested that online expression should receive the same protection as print, and traditional rules regarding print publications dictate that 'viewpoint discrimination' is not allowed. When school administrators pick sides in a debate and target only one side with restrictions, they are engaging in viewpoint discrimination." The report pointed to the hypothetical example of a university that penalized students for criticizing academic programs, faculty members, or the school's sports teams or coaches on Internet forums (the term "social media" was not used at the time). The SPLC stated those restrictions would be determined by the courts to violate the students' First Amendment rights, unless they could be proven to be defamatory or otherwise disruptive. [85]

BEST OF THE REST

While administrators were rarely able to meet the "disruption" standard in the 1970s and 1980s, some case law does exist. In the 1981 case of *Dodd v. Rambis*, for example, a Federal District Court in Indiana upheld the suspensions of students who distributed leaflets calling for a classroom walkout the following day. A similar walkout the previous week was organized in protest of the school's new disciplinary policies, and fifty-four students left their classrooms. Administrators based their "disruption" claim in the precedent set by the previous walkout, an atmosphere of "excitement" about the next day's planned walkout, and an increase in tardiness and absenteeism. [86]

In the 1987 case of *Gano v. School District No. 411*, a Federal District Court in Idaho upheld the suspension of a student who produced and wore a T-shirt depicting three school administrators inebriated. [87]

Seven years later, in *Baxter v. Vigo County School Corporation*, the Seventh Circuit Court of Appeals upheld the suspension of high school students for wearing T-shirts protesting racism at the school and the school's new grading policy. [88]

In early 1990, Jamie Brown, principal of Cambridge Elementary School in Orange, California, announced plans to ban Bart Simpson-themed T-shirts. Claiming the shirts, bearing a likeness of the animated television character and bearing messages such as "I'm Bart Simpson, Who the Hell are You?" and "Underachiever and Proud of It" celebrated underachievers. Brown told students and parents that he "didn't want kids thinking that being an underachiever was cool." He claimed that phone calls to his office were 100 percent positive, even though local media found several parents who intended to challenge the ban.

That same school year, Simpson T-shirts were banned at five schools in Freemont, Ohio. But when principals in West Palm Beach and Boca Raton, Florida announced a similar ban, a principal at nearby Allamanda Elementary School in nearby Palm Beach Gardens recognized a "teaching moment" and suggested an alternative strategy. "If faced with that question, I would not ban the shirts," said Amelia Murgio. "Instead, I would ask the children if they understood the message and how they feel about it."[89]

In 1992, the Ninth Circuit Court of Appeals ruled that two students attending a McMinnville, Oregon, high school were unlawfully suspended for wearing buttons supporting teachers who were participating in a lawful strike. The students' fathers were both among the striking teachers, and the students were simply showing support for their fathers as well as their displeasure with the replacement teachers.[90]

In 1995, a student at Newport High School in Newport, Washington, used his home computer to create a satirical website that parodied events at the school and poked some gentle fun at teachers and administrators. Those administrators didn't find it amusing, but instead of simply suspending senior Paul Kim, they withdraw his nomination as a National Merit Scholar and contacted numerous colleges on his wish list. With help from the ACLU, Kim sued the school district for violating his First Amendment rights. The two parties reached an out-of-court settlement in which the school paid Kim $2,000 to partially compensate for the loss of the scholarship and issued a public apology.[91]

In the 1996 case of *Pyle v. South Hadley School Committee*, a Massachusetts court ruled in favor of three brothers who repeatedly wore to school shirts bearing offensive images and slogans. After being disciplined, the boys appealed to the school district's disciplinary committee, which determined that officials of a public school do not need to prove the potential for disruption in order to enforce a dress code; it had to prove only that the appearance of the clothing, or the messages conveyed, were offensive. The Court, however, reverted to the *Tinker* standard and determined that the messages, while offensive, were not disruptive. [92]

In 1997, Nicholas Boroff was a senior when he arrived at Van Wert High School in Van Wert, Ohio, wearing a Marilyn Manson T-shirt. The front of the shirt depicted a three-faced Jesus and the back of the shirt said "believe" with the letters "lie" highlighted.

A school administrator told Boroff the shirt was offensive and told him to either turn it inside out, go home and change, or leave and be considered truant.

Boroff left, and returned each of the next four school days wearing other Marilyn Manson T-shirts. Each time he was told he could not attend class wearing the shirt.

Boroff sued, saying school officials violated his constitutional rights to free speech and due process. A federal judge ruled for the school district, and the Sixth U.S. Circuit Court of Appeals in Cincinnati agreed. The following year, the U.S. Supreme Court declined to hear his appeal. [93]

In May 1998, an eighth-grade student at Nitschmann Middle School in Bethlehem, Pennsylvania, used his home computer to create a website that ridiculed his algebra teacher, principal, and others. The comments directed toward the algebra teacher included, "She's a bitch" and "I need only $20 for a hitman." School officials considered those comments threats, and contacted local law enforcement, including the FBI.

The student, identified in court document only by the initials J. S., voluntarily deleted the website, but that wasn't enough to avoid being suspended. He sued the school district in the Pennsylvania court system, where a trial court, appeals court, and Supreme Court found in favor of the school district. The Supreme Court determined that the website represented a "disruption of the school's orderly operation" and rejected the student's contention that the school could not regulate speech taking place off-campus. The latter opinion was based on the fact that word of the website's existence spread across campus by word of mouth. [94]

In 1998, T. J. West was a seventh-grader at Derby Middle School in Derby, Kansas. During math class, he drew a four-inch by six-inch sketch of the Confederate battle flag. West was sent to the school office, where he told the principal that he knew what the image was but nothing about its cultural significance.

West was charged with violating the school's racial harassment policy, in place since 1995, which banned students from possessing "any written material, either printed or in their own handwriting, that is racially divisive or creates ill will or hatred." West was suspended for three days. West's father challenged the suspension in court, accusing the school of violating his son's First Amendment right of free expression. A Federal District Court ruled in favor of the school district, and the Tenth Circuit Court of Appeals upheld it, determining that T.J. was old and mature enough to understand the nature of his drawing and the rationale of the school policy that prohibited it.

"We're greatly disappointed," said lawyer John Whitehead, who represented the boy on behalf of the Rutherford Institute. "You don't teach democratic values by slamming a hammer down on someone's free expression."

On the first day of its 2000-2001 session, the U.S. Supreme Court declined to hear the father's appeal, leaving the decision of the two lower courts in place. [95]

In April 1999, Jennifer Boccia and about ten other students at Allen High School in Allen, Texas, wore black armbands to mourn the victims of the Columbine tragedy.

No administrators reacted at first because they believed it was a short-term act of symbolic speech. But when they learned that the students had continued to wear the armbands to protest the new school rules passed in light of Columbine (including random locker searches and changes to the school's dress code), they suspended Boccia and several classmates.

The ACLU assisted Boccia in her lawsuit against the school district, which ended in an out out-of-court settlement that included the removal of the records of suspensions from the students' files. [96]

In 2000, at high schools in Chesapeake, Virginia, and Ledford, North Carolina, students were suspended for refusing to remove Confederate flags from their trucks driven to school and parked in the student parking lots. [97]

In 2000, fifteen-year-old Michael Demers was taken out of his class at Northwest High School in Leominster, Massachusetts, for talking out of turn. When another student asked how he felt about being removed, he responded by drawing two sketches—one showing the school building surrounded by explosives and another showing a gun pointed at the superintendent's head.

The principal did nothing until the next day, when Demers returned to class and wrote on a paper, "I want to die" and "I hate life." School officials recommended a visit to a psychiatrist, but he refused, and the school suspended him for the balance of the school year. His parents sued the school district, claiming it had violated their son's First Amendment right to "express himself through creative writing," but a Federal District Court ruled in favor of the school, determining that Demers should have anticipated that his drawings and writings could be perceived as a "true threat." The Court added that the school was not required to demonstrate that the student had the ability or intention to carry out a threat. [98]

In 1999, at Timberline High School in Thurston County, Washington, student Kurt Beidler created a website, titled "Lehnis Web," that mocked assistant principal Dave Lehnis. Altered photographs showed Lehnis participating in Nazi book-burning, drinking beer, and spray-painting graffiti on a wall.

The school's principal suspended Beidler on an emergency basis, citing reports from teachers that they were not comfortable having the student in class after knowing about the content of the website. Beidler sued the school district in Washington State Court and won, as school officials were unable to prove the website caused any disruption of school activities. "Schools can and will adjust to new challenges created by such students and the Internet, but not at the expense of the First Amendment," the decision read. [99]

At Kentlake High School in Washington in the spring of 2000, senior Nick Emmett created a website that included photographs of himself and classmates, along with a list of fake obituaries of classmates. Each obituary was done only after the subject consented, and the site became so popular that hundreds of students started "voting" online about who they wanted to see listed next. The administration of the school was unaware of the site until a local television station broadcast a story about it and erroneously called the fake obituaries a "hit list."

Less than a year after the 1999 tragedy at Columbine, the principal considered the list a "real threat" and suspended Emmett for five days. In media interviews, the school principal defended the suspension by calling the website "intimidating and harassing" to students and staff at the school. He further claimed it has created a "disruption" because "multiple classrooms were taken off task and (the site) became a focus of student activity."

Emmett immediately sued in Federal District Court and obtained an injunction preventing the school from enforcing the punishment. In a preliminary hearing, Judge John Coughenour, chief judge for the U.S. District Court for the Western District of Washington, began his decision by admitting that he understood the plight of teachers and school administrators in the post-Columbine world.

"The school district argues, persuasively, that school administrators are in an acutely difficult position after recent school shootings in Colorado, Oregon, and other places," Coughenour wrote. "Websites can be early indicators of a student's violent inclinations, and can spread those beliefs quickly to like-minded or susceptible people." The judge found, however, that the school district had failed to demonstrate that the mock obituaries "were intended to threaten anyone, did not actually threaten anyone, or manifested any violent tendencies whatsoever."

Coughenour agreed with Emmett's contention that the "hit list" moniker was a mischaracterization on the part of the television station and nothing on the site could be considered a threat to anyone at the school. The judge added that the content of the website was in poor taste, but nonetheless ruled that the principal had overreacted based on the Columbine tragedy and other school shootings. The bottom line, Coughenour ruled, was that the website contained "no true threat" and was developed entirely off school grounds and during non-school hours.

Before the case could go to trial, the school district reached a settlement with Emmett, waiving the suspension, paying him $1 in damages, and paying his attorney's fees. [100]

In 2000, seventeen-year-old Sarah Boman created a pen-and-ink poster titled "Who Killed my Dog?" for her art class at Bluestem High School in Leon, Kansas. The poster featured a first-person narrative in which Boman threatened to kill the person or persons responsible for the death of her dog.

Instead of reading from left to right, the text of the poster appeared in a clockwise spiral and was difficult to read. Boman said she created the poster to be part of a portfolio of work samples she hoped to use in applying to art school.

At first, it was hung in the school hallway, but after the school's principal read it, he seized it and ordered an investigation. School administrators suspended Boman for the last four months of the school year and ordered her to undergo a psychological evaluation before returning the following school year. Boman sued the school in Federal District Court, which found in her favor, determining that her artwork neither constituted a threat nor caused a substantial disruption at the school.

"There is simply no factual basis for believing that Ms. Boman threatened harm to other students or that her return to school would constitute a threat," U.S. District Court Judge Wesley Brown wrote in his written opinion. "As such, there is no basis for requiring her to undergo a psychological evaluation."

The school district did not contest the ruling and agreed to pay Boman's legal fees of $15,000. One of her attorneys commented that the judge's decision, combined with having to pay the legal fees, "will provide some incentive for schools not to act so irrationally the next time around."[101]

In 2001, Andrew Breen brought to Galvez Middle School in Louisiana a drawing showing nearby East Ascension High School under attack by a missile launcher, armed individuals, and explosives. The drawing also contained disparaging and racist remarks about the principal at East Ascension. The drawing did not belong to him; it was later determined to have been the work of his older brother, Adam Porter, an East Ascension student who created it two years earlier.

After Breen showed the drawing to a classmate and then a bus driver, he was called into the principal's office and suspended for three days. Officials at Galvez notified their counterparts at East Ascension, who searched Porter's locker and found nothing unusual other than a box cutter. Not accepting Porter's contention that he used the tool for his job at a local grocery store, officials had him expelled from school and arrested. After spending four nights in jail, Porter was allowed to enroll at an alternative school.

After their mother declined to appeal her sons' suspensions, the boys filed suit against the school board in Federal District Court. The school board defended its actions by claiming that, in light of Columbine and other school shootings, it believed the drawing constituted a "true threat" and it could "reasonably forecast that the drawing would create a substantial disruption of school activities."

The Court decided in favor of the school. In his decision, U.S. District Judge Frank J. Polozola wrote that "schools cannot operate in a vacuum or in a fantasy world and must be aware of the events occurring at other schools to properly protect their students and faculty." Polozola agreed with the school's contention that "warning signs had been missed in the Columbine case," and therefore their actions did not violate the students' First Amendment rights.[102]

While courts tend to side with high school principals in the majority of cases involving student speech, that tendency is not an absolute. In the 2001 case of *Saxe v. State College Area School District,* for example, two Christian high school students were charged under the school district's speech code for stating publicly their belief that homosexuality was a sin. The trial court ruled in favor of the school, but the Circuit Court of Appeals reversed that decision, ruling that the school's code was unconstitutional because administrators failed to meet their burden of proving that the code was necessary to protect other students or maintain order.[103]

In 2002, administrators at a high school in Beaver County, Utah, resorted to the state's 1876 criminal libel statute in asking the courts to punish sixteen-year-old Ian Lake for a website on which he disparaged his classmates, teachers, and the school principal. Lake described the principal as a drunk who was having an affair with the school secretary and suggested that a teacher at the school was gay and leading a double life. Although there were no threats posted on the website, the county sheriff's office arrested him and held him in detention for a week to avoid a "Columbine-like" tragedy.

On appeal to the Utah Supreme Court, Lake was eventually vindicated when the court found the 1876 law was unconstitutional because it covered protected speech and included no standard for determining malice.[104]

In Vermont in 2003, middle school student Zachary Guiles was suspended for wearing a T-shirt that portrayed President Bush as "Chicken-Hawk in Chief." Guiles told school officials he was simply protesting the war in Iraq, but they considered it disruptive. With help from the ACLU, Guiles sued the school district in Federal District Court, which upheld the suspension and determined that the shirt was "offensive" under the standard established by the *Bethel* case. Guiles and the ACLU took to the Second Circuit Court of Appeals, which reversed and ruled in his favor.

According to the appeals court, "the shirt used harsh rhetoric and imagery to express disagreement with the president's policies and impugn his character," but the shirt did not cause any disruption, and the censorship was unwarranted.[105]

In the 2003 case of *Smith v. Mount Pleasant Public Schools*, a Federal District Court in Michigan upheld the school's punishment of a student who delivered an extemporaneous speech in the school cafeteria in which she criticized the school's tardy policy and referred to one administrator as a "skank" and a "tramp" who cheated on her husband and another as "confused about his sexuality." Administrators justified the punishment by claiming that many students in the "captive audience" were upset by the speech and that the *Tinker* ruling regarding "disruption" should be applied.[106]

In September 2004, seventh-grader James Nixon caused controversy at Sheridan Middle School in Thornville, Ohio, with his T-shirt that carried a Bible verse on the front and comments on the back that were anti-gay, anti-Muslim, and anti-abortion. School officials ordered him to stop wearing the shirt, so he sued in Federal District Court, claiming that the school district violated his First Amendment rights. Judge George Smith ruled that just because some students were offended did not mean the shirts created the potential for disruption as defined by the *Tinker* standard.[107]

In 2005, the school district in New Hanover County in southeastern North Carolina was faced with controversial T-shirts bearing messages such as "If you can read this, you need another cocktail," "I see drunk people," "Candy is dandy but liquor is quicker," and "It's happy hour somewhere." Officials added a clause to the district dress code that banned messages that promoted the use of alcohol, tobacco, or illegal drugs. Over the objections of local civil rights leaders, the new policy went into effect and as of this writing has not faced any legal challenges.[108]

A Providence, New Jersey, high school student who photographed the school's principal smoking, and then posted the pictures on the Internet, was suspended by the school. It was early 2005, shortly after the school district changed its smoking rules to require that faculty and administrators who wanted to light up had to do so at least twenty-five feet from the nearest building. Central High School Principal Elaine Almagno was leaning against the building, clearly in violation of the rule, and sophomore Eliazar Velasquez posted the photographic evidence online within hours.

Following the suspension, the ACLU of New Jersey came to Velasquez's defense, prompting the school district to reinstate him, wipe the incident from his record, and drop the requirement that he take down the website.[109]

In 2006, a middle school student in Ft. Myers, Florida was denied the right to distribute anti-abortion literature at her school. [110]

In 2007, a teacher at the prestigious Horace Mann Preparatory School in New York discovered she had no support from administrators when faced with cyberharassment (a few years before the term was coined) at the hands of her students. Danielle McGuire discovered students had created a Facebook page, titled "McGuire Survivors 2006," that described her as a "witch" and "liberal brainwasher." When she complained to administrators, she was told that she violated the students' privacy by accessing their Facebook page, even though the students made no attempt to use the available privacy settings. The students were given minor disciplinary notations in the files, and McGuire's contract was not renewed. She discovered later that many of the students who created the page were children of members of the school's board of trustees. [111]

In 2007, two high school students in Newark, New Jersey, wanted to protest the school's dress code, so they printed and wore to school buttons bearing a likeness of German dictator Adolph Hitler. The students were threatened with suspension, but when their parents took the case to Federal District Court, Judge Joseph A. Greenaway Jr. sided with them. Citing *Tinker*, Greenaway wrote in his decision that "a student could not be punished for merely expressing views unless the school has reason to believe that the speech or expression would materially and substantially disrupt the work and discipline of the school." The judge did rule, however, that the students could not distribute the buttons to their classmates on school grounds. [112]

In the fall of 2007 at Ponce de Leon High School in Panama City, Florida, junior Heather Gillman wanted to wear homemade T-shirts supporting her fellow students who were gay or lesbian.

Principal David Davis told her apparel violated the school's dress code that barred attire that "expressed political beliefs through words or symbols." But what outraged Gillman, fellow students, and their parents, was Davis's statement that the messages were "disruptive to the educational process and were indicative of membership in a secret society or illegal organization."

Gillman and her friends agreed to stop wearing the shirts, but then wrote phrases such as "Gay Pride" and "GP" on their arms and the covers of the notebooks. When Davis expanded school rules to prohibit those messages as well, Gillman and her mother decided in was time to go to court.

In court documents and media interviews, Gillman identified herself as straight, but said she wore the T-shirts to support her gay and lesbian friends. Examples of phrases on her T-shirts included "Equal Rights, Not Special Rights" and "Gay? Fine By Me."

After Gillman sued and won in Federal District Court, the judge ordered the principal and Holmes County School Board to notify all students in the district in writing that they had the right to "express their support for their gay and lesbian classmates in an appropriate and non-disruptive way."

A few months after the case was resolved, Gillman participated in a panel discussion on campus free speech issues held at Gulf Community College. Also on the panel were her lawyers, representatives of the ACLU, a local journalist who covered the story, and Mary Beth Tinker, the plaintiff in the groundbreaking 1969 Supreme Court case.[113]

The problem of cyberbullying and suicide is not limited to high school students. In 2010, a Rutgers University freshman jumped to his death off the George Washington Bridge after a roommate and his friend secretly videotaped him having sex with another man and posted the video on the Internet.[114]

At the beginning of the new school year in 2010, administrators at high schools in Pennsylvania and Indiana ordered students to remove wristbands that read, "I Love Boobies." The messages were distributed by a national organization supporting breast cancer research and treatment, but administrators believed they would be disruptive because of the maturity level displayed by other students.

Students at both schools filed lawsuits, but the two courts reached different conclusions. In Pennsylvania, the court ruled in favor of the students, citing the obvious similarity to the *Tinker* case and its belief that the messages were neither lewd nor disruptive, but rather useful conversation-starting messages about an important topic.

In Indiana, however, the court reached the opposite conclusion, ruling in favor of the school district. The court stopped short of agreeing that the bracelets were disruptive, claiming instead that its ruling was based on a reluctance to second-guess the motives of school administrators.

School administrators in Pennsylvania appealed the district court's ruling to the Third Circuit Court. Principal Angela DiVietro, herself a breast cancer survivor, never claimed the bracelets were lewd or obscene, but rather "trivialized" what was a serious issue for her and other cancer survivors. School district attorney John Freund III added that the intent of the ban was not to stifle expression, but rather to prevent disruption and "discourage the sexualization of clothing and to keep kids focused on learning."[115]

On Cinco de Mayo in 2010, students who arrived at Live Oak High School near San Jose, California, were called into the principal's office for engaging in what the school labeled as "offensive speech." Their offense? They were wearing the T-shirts bearing the American flag, which administrators considered offensive to the school's Hispanic students, who preferred that only the Mexican flag be displayed that day.

Principal Miguel Rodriguez ordered the students to change their shirts or turn them inside out in order to hide the flag. Those who did not comply were sent home, but the controversy didn't end there. The students and their parents took the case to federal court, which sided with school administrators and allowed the T-shirt ban to remain in place.

In one the few examples of the *Tinker* standard working in favor of school administrators, the district court determined that because there was "ongoing racial tension and gang violence at the school" as well as a "near-violent altercation (in the past) over display of the American flag," the *Tinker* standard had been met.

On appeal, the Ninth Circuit Court upheld the lower court's ruling, claiming it would be inappropriate to "second guess the school's precautions put in place to avoid violence." One legal expert to criticize the outcome of the case was Jonathan Turley, professor of law at Georgetown University. In an op-ed in *USA Today*, Turley claimed that "removing any display of the flag in the face of violence is akin to removing gay students to prevent them from being harassed or girls to prevent them from being assaulted." Instead of focusing on limiting the free speech rights of students, administrators should have instead prepared to punish the perpetrators of any violence that took place.[116]

In Wesley Chapel, Florida, in 2010, senior Alex Fuentes was voted out of his high school's National Honor Society's chapter by a panel of six teachers angry that he created a Facebook page critical of the school's low academic ratings.[117]

Late in 2010, officials at several universities in the southeast, including Flori-da State, Alabama, Auburn, Tennessee, and Louisiana State, investigated numerous cases of "cyberstalking" involving female students seeking mem-bership in various sororities. Contacting the women on Facebook, the anony-mous individuals claimed to be officers or alumni of the sororities and sug-gested ways the women could improve their chances of being accepted, including posting nude photos and answering questions of an intimate nature. When the women refused to comply, they were verbally abused and threat-ened.[118]

In 2011, a thirteen-year-old student at Rundlett Middle School in Concord, New Hampshire was suspended after posting on her Facebook page that she wishes "Osama bin Laden had killed her math teacher." The girl's mother unsuccessfully appealed the suspension, claiming that she didn't approve with the content of the post but thought the punishment was excessive. "They are denying her an education based on something she did at home," Kimberly Dell'isola told local media. "That's my business, not theirs."[119]

In 2012, brothers Steven and Sean Wilson created a website and blog, titled NorthPress, through which they and a handful of friends anonymous insults at their teachers, administrators, and classmates at Lee's Summit North High School in Missouri. According to court documents, the content of the site included "a variety of sexually and racially offensive comments as well as explicit comments about particular female classmates." Other comments al-legedly mocked the school's black students.

Even though the material was created on the Wilsons' own time and using their own computers, administrators suspended them for ten days. Upon further investigation, the suspension was extended to six months, during which the brothers were allowed to transfer to another school in the district.

Their parents sued the school district in Federal District Court, and in preliminary hearings administrators claimed they had met the "substantial disruption" standard from the *Tinker* case, based on anecdotal evidence, including teachers' observations of campus disturbances (with varying de-grees of verification) and the phone calls from parents who contacted the school with concerns about student safety and bullying.

The court ruled in favor of the school district, prompting the students to appeal to the Eighth Circuit. That court acknowledged that most speech produced outside the school was generally outside of the purview of school administrators, but in this case the administrators were within their rights because the location from which the speech was located was less important than where it was targeted. The judges on the appeals court also acknowledged that the nationwide problem of cyberbullying, which had generated news coverage and resulted in many teen suicides, factored into their decision. "The repercussions of cyberbullying are serious and sometimes tragic," their decision stated.[120]

In December 2012, just a few weeks after the killing of twenty-six students and employees at Sandy Hook Elementary School in Newtown, Connecticut, a high school English teacher at Life Learning Academy in San Francisco suggested that her students to write personal essays reacting to the tragedy. Seventeen-year-old Courtni Webb wrote a poem she titled, "I Know Why he Pulled the Trigger" in which she wrote that "the government is a shame; society never wants to take the blame" and "I understand the killings in Connecticut; I know why he pulled the trigger."

Officials at the San Francisco Unified School District suspended Courtni for violating its "zero-tolerance" policy regarding threats of violence against students or teachers.

In her defense, Webb said she was attempting to emulate the style of her favorite writer, Stephen King. "He writes weird stuff all the time; that doesn't mean he's gonna do it or act it out," Webb said. Her mother pointed out that Courtni often submitted poems dealing with "dark issues," but none caused any concerns until the one in question. She also claimed her daughter was a good student with no disciplinary issues on her record.

As of summer 2016, Webb's family was still working through the court system to have her suspension overturned.[121]

In early 2013, a seven-year-old boy student at Park Elementary School in Baltimore, Maryland, was suspended after he chewed a Pop-Tart into the shape of a gun in the school cafeteria.

Andrew Nussbaum, a lawyer who serves as a hearing examiner for several school systems surrounding Washington, looked into the case and issued a thirty-page opinion that agreed that principal Sandra Blondell acted properly when she removed Josh Welch from school.

The boy, according to Nussbaum's opinion, told his classmates, after nibbling the breakfast pastry: "Look, I made a gun." The incident took place in March, 2013, only months after the school shooting at Sandy Hook.

Nussbaum reported that the suspension was based not only on that incident, but on a pattern of disciplinary problems. "As much as the parents want this case to be about a 'gun,' it is, rather, a case about classroom disruption from a student who has had a long history of disruptive behavior," Nussbaum wrote in his opinion.

"Had the student chewed his cereal bar into the shape of a cat and ran around the room, disrupting the classroom and making 'meow' cat sounds, the result would have been exactly the same," Nussbaum wrote in the report, the highlights of which were published in the local media.

Welch's lawyer, Robin Ficker, unsuccessfully appealed the two-day school suspension. In the appeal, Ficker included pictures of the states of Idaho and Florida because "they looked more like guns than Josh's Pop-Tart."

Welch finished the school year after his suspension and was transferred to another school. The following spring, he was awarded an honorary membership in the National Rifle Association. [122]

In 2003 at the University of Northern Colorado, a student created a satirical website called *The Howling Pig* that included fictional news stories about the university and its employees. At first administrators dismissed it as juvenile but not harmful, but the turning point came when website creator Thomas Mink posted a digitally altered photograph of Junius Peake, a finance professor. The image showed Peake as resembling KISS singer Gene Simmons with an Adolf Hitler mustache. A caption described its subject as "Junius Puke," a roadie who made a fortune by "riding the tech bubble of the nineties like a $20 whore."

On orders from local prosecutor Susan Knox, police from the city of Greeley, Colorado, confiscated Mink's computer and accused him of violating the state's criminal libel statute. With help from the ACLU of Colorado, Mink filed suit in Federal District Court, which ruled partially in his favor and partially against. The court ordered Knox to return his computer (on the grounds that it never should have been taken away), and drop the criminal libel charges. But the court also ruled that Mink couldn't challenge the confiscation of his computer based on the Fourth Amendment's "search and seizure" clause because the prosecutor was immune to such lawsuit. Mink appealed that portion of the trial court's ruling to the Tenth Circuit, which ruled in 2010 that the because the charges of criminal libel were unsubstantiated—as no reasonable reader would believe them—Knox had violated Mink's constitutional rights. In 2012, after nearly nine years in and out of court, Mink reached a settlement with the prosecutor's office, which paid Mink $425,000 in compensatory damages and legal fees. [123]

In 2014, administrators at Howell High School in Howell, Michigan, reprimanded several students for posting racially offensive tweets after the school's all-white basketball team defeated a team representing its mostly black cross-town rival, Grand Blanc. Among the comments were "All hail white power," "Light the cross," and "Hitler is my dad." Administrators did not specify what punishment was applied, but local media reported the students were allowed to stay in school while being banned from attending athletic events. No team members were involved in the incident, but Principal Jason Schrock and Coach Dan Schell nevertheless apologized to the Grand Blanc coaches, players, and fans.[124]

At Dr. Phillips High School near Orlando, Florida, Jack Englund was told he could not wear a costume for the school's 2014 Homecoming Week based on the "Trojan Man" from television commercials for Trojan brand costumes. His costume, which included a red cape and giant foil condom wrapper, was not allowed for three reasons, administrators told him. One concern was a potential violation of trademark law, but larger concerns were the violation of the school's dress code (that prohibited any clothing that promoted sex) and the costume's potential for "disrupting the learning environment." Englund did not contest the first two issues but complained that his costume was no more disruptive than those characters from video games and television cartoons. And despite his mother being a lawyer, he said he had no plans to sue. "All I want is an apology," he told local media.[125]

In early 2014, Kamryn Renfro, a nine-year-old student at Caprock Academy in Grand Junction, Colorado, wanted to show support for friend Delaney Clements, who had been stricken with cancer. She shaved her head to match the appearance of her ill friend.

The school's board of directors claimed that violated the school's dress code and barred Kamryn from attending class.

Delaney, meanwhile, told reporters that knowing her friends had shaved their heads as a show of support made it easier to withstand teasing about her appearance. For the week that followed, the telephone in the administrative office at Caprock didn't stop ringing, and the school's website and Facebook page were flooded with comments supportive of Kamryn. School administrators told the local media that many of the online comments were "too profane" to repeat and that none of the comments were supportive of the school's position.

After days of negative news coverage, both local and national, the board voted 3-1 to grant Kamryn a waiver from the dress code. Several of Delaney's other friends then shaved their heads.[126]

———

At Talbott Elementary School in Widefield, Colorado, in 2014, a class was taken outside and told to look up at the sky and describe the shapes of clouds they saw. Eight-year-old Kody Smith told the teacher that he imagined a cloud in the shape of a gun. That earned him a trip to the principal's office, where a "behavioral report" was filed.

His mother, Angel Rivers, complained that he was simply "doing what was required for the assignment," and his father, Jeff Smith, was incensed that his son was being punished just for "having an imagination." The Widefield School District agreed not to have a record of the incident in the boy's file, but defending the trip to the principal's office by claiming that its "primary responsibility as a school district is to ensure the safety of all staff, students, and the community. Our response was in line with routine procedures focused on school safety."[127]

———

In Summerville High School in South Carolina in 2014, sixteen-year-old Alex Stone and his classmates were asked to write "a few sentences about themselves" for an English class assignment. When he wrote that he fantasized about killing his neighbor's pet dinosaur with a gun, he was taken out of the classroom and arrested by local police. School officials contend that he was not arrested for his imagination but for resisting arrest and disorderly conduct.[128]

———

In 2015, sixteen-year-old Taylor Victor wanted to celebrate her sexuality with a T-shirt bearing the slogan, "Nobody Knows I'm a Lesbian." Administrators at Sierra High School in Manteca, California, citing the school district's dress code, ordered her to go home and change. She complied, but within days she and her mother, aided by the ACLU, took legal action.

After weeks of negative publicity, the school district agreed to settle the case out of court, not admitting wrongdoing but revising its dress code to allow clothing that "supported their or their classmates' identities on the basis of race, gender, religion, sexual orientation, or other characteristics." The district also paid the ACLU's court costs of $63,000 and agreed to provide training to school administrators on issues related to student free speech and free expression.[129]

In 2015, Claudietta Love was a seventeen-year-old high school junior at Carroll High School in Monroe, Louisiana, and was told by the principal and other school officials that would not be allowed to wear a tuxedo to the prom. Prior to the controversy, the school's dress code specified that prom attire included "dresses for girls and tuxedos for boys." When the openly gay Love declared that she would not attend the prom unless she could dress as she pleased, the first reaction of the administration was, "fine." But after her mother threatened to sue, the superintendent of schools ordered that the dress code be revised to allow students to dress in their "formal wear of choice."[130]

High school students are not the only young scholars finding themselves on the wrong side of disciplinary proceedings based on their musings on social media. College students, presumably more mature and less likely to inappropriately vent in cyberspace, nonetheless do so and draw unwanted attention to themselves and their institutions.

In the fall of 2015, following a series of incidents across the country in which white police officers were accused of excessive force, a police officer in Texas was shot and killed while pumping gas into his patrol car. Monica Foy, a student at nearby Sam Houston State University, posted on Twitter that she "couldn't believe so many people care about a dead cop and NO ONE has thought to ask what he did to deserve it." After fellow tweeters blasted her with threatening responses, Foy deleted the tweet, and within a few days deleted her entire account and apologized to university officials.

University President Dana Hoyt released a statement indicating the institution was disappointed in Foy's comment but would take no action against her.

"The path of least resistance would be to take disciplinary action against Ms. Foy, but the legal rights conferred on every American citizen and the code of conduct that governs SHSU students say otherwise," Hoyt said in a statement released by the school's media relations office. "A personal comment made on a private social media account, as offensive as it was, remains protected by the First Amendment. Offensive speech is protected speech. As an institution that is responsible for educating generations of students in criminal justice and the order of law, we must stand behind those teachings."[131]

One need not actually harm another individual to be charged with criminal activity; recent cases indicate that merely making online threats draws the attention of law enforcement agencies. In 2006, for example, U.S. Secret Service agents showed up at the door of a University of Oklahoma freshman after he joked on his Facebook profile about assassinating President George W. Bush. And in 2010, a twenty-three-year-old student at Faulkner State University in Alabama posted on his Facebook page threats to carry out a "Virginia Tech style" mass murder at the university and "break the record of thirty-two" deaths that took place at the Virginia school three years earlier. The student was originally charged with making a terrorist threat, a felony under federal law. The charge was later reduced to a misdemeanor in exchange for his guilty plea.[132]

As the 2014-2015 school year neared its end for students at Wicomico High School in Salisbury, Maryland, school administrators expelled a sixteen-year-old student after he allegedly used his Twitter account to make threats against the school. The Wicomico County Sheriff's Office then arrested him and charged him with four counts of making terrorist threats. In his Twitter post, the teen claimed having ties to ISIS, an Islamic terrorist group, and threatened to "shoot up" his school.

Schools administrators and the sheriff's office were notified of the threats by local television station WBOC. After station officials responded that both they and the sheriff's office determined the threats to be "not credible," the tweeter responded, "Doubt the credibility as you please."

Despite its initial findings, the WCSO decided to err on the side of caution and arrest the teen. Because he was treated as a juvenile offender, the results of the investigation are not known.[133]

Less than a year later, a seventeen-year-old senior at Ithaca High School in New York was charged with a felony after he threatened on Facebook to "shoot up" his school with an assault rifle. His postings included a photo of the school and a warning to other students to avoid the "day of mass death." Another photo showed a tombstone showing a classmate's name.[134]

Because of the popularity of social media among college athletes and their fans, numerous universities have enacted policies aimed at preventing athletes from embarrassing those schools with their cyberspace vents or musings. Some athletic departments impose outright bans on all forms of social media, while others allow their use but assign athletic department staffers to monitor the content.

At first, coaches and athletic directors were concerned about players using social media to disparage their fans, game officials, or opposing teams or coaches. But some administrators also worried that players might inadvertently reveal game strategy or violate National Collegiate Athletic Association rules by releasing inside information about potential recruits.

The first of these cases generated national publicity in 2012. Western Kentucky University suspended a football player after he tweeted comments critical of the team's fans, Lehigh University suspended a player after he retweeted a racial slur, and the University of North Carolina was sanctioned by the NCAA after a player's tweet led to an investigation of its academic standards. That same year, a star football player was expelled from Bosco Preparatory School in Ramsey, New Jersey, and lost a scholarship offer to attend the University of Michigan after his Twitter account was found to include graphic and racially insensitive material. He eventually accepted a scholarship offer at the University of Colorado.

Many observers believed the universities were within their rights, based on their view that benefiting from a college scholarship is a privilege, and in exchange for that privilege they surrender some of their free speech rights. But others disagree, including Ken Paulson, president of the First Amendment Center in Nashville, Tennessee, who believes that schools that prohibit athletes from using social media are not doing a good job of preparing those players for their lives after college, regardless of whether or not they become professional athletes.

"Coaches who impose blanket bans or chill players' speech by watching everything they post are not doing their athletes any favors," Paulson wrote in a 2012 op-ed in *USA Today*. "The handful of athletes who go on to professional sports will have to deal with social media throughout their careers, and they won't learn anything if they're not given any latitude. The best approach is to give student-athletes the education they need to enter the workplace and to become well-rounded citizens. That includes the smart and responsible use of social media. There's no better place to learn those lessons than in America's high school and colleges."[135]

NOTES

1. *Barber v. Dearborn Public Schools*, 286 F. Supp 2d 847 (E.D. Mich. 2003).

2. *Barber v. Dearborn Public Schools*. See also: Tamara Lewin, "High School Tells Student to Remove Anti-War Shirt," *New York Times*, February 26, 2003; Don R. Pember and Clay Calvert, *Mass Media Law*, Boston: McGraw Hill, 2009, pp. 87-88.

3. Jonathan Zimmerman, "Let Students Keep Their Opinions on Their Chests." *USA Today*, March 17, 2003, p. 11-A.

4. Tony Mauro, "Teenagers, T-Shirts, and the First Amendment." *First Amendment News,* May 1996.

5. Nat Hentoff, *Free Speech for Me, But Not for Thee.* New York: Harper Perennial, 1993, pp. 361-363.

6. Ibid.

7. Mauro, "Teenagers, T-Shirts, and the First Amendment."

8. "Re-Birth of Confederate Flag Controversy Poses Problems for Educators." Associated Press report, February 8, 2016.

9. James J. Kilpatrick, "Free Speech and T-Shirts at School." Syndicated newspaper column, January 19, 2004.

10. "NRA Supports Student in T-shirt Case." Associated Press report, April 14, 2013.

11. Greg Toppo, "What to Wear Back to School." *USA Today*, August 19, 2013, p. 3-A.

12. Mauro.

13. David L. Hudson, Jr. *The Silencing of Student Voices*, Nashville, TN: The First Amendment Center, 2003, pp. 60-61.

14. Ibid.

15. *LaVine v. Blaine School District,* 257 F.3d 981 (2001).

16. Ibid.

17. Ibid.

18. Ibid.

19. "The First Amendment vs. School Safety." *SPLC Report*, Spring 2000, pp. 18-21.

20. Mark Walsh, "Legal Update." *Education Week*, May 16, 2016.

21. Ibid.

22. *Chaplinsky v. New Hampshire*, 315 U.S. 568 (1942).

23. *Burnside v. Byars*, 363 F.2d 744 (1966).

24. Richard Arum, *Judging School Discipline.* Cambridge, MA: Harvard University Press, 2005, p. 77.

25. *Tinker v. Des Moines Independent Community School District*, 393 U.S. 503 (1969).

26. William W. Van Alstyne, *The First Amendment: Cases and Materials.* Westbury, NY: The Foundation Press, 1995, p. 282.

27. *Tinker v. Des Moines Independent Community School District.*

28. Ibid.

29. Erwin Chemerinsky, "Students Do Leave Their First Amendment Rights at the Schoolhouse Gates: What's Left of Tinker?" *Drake Law Review*, vol. 57 (2000), pp. 527.

30. *Grayned v. Rockford,* 408 U.S. 104 (1972).

31. *Bethel School District v. Fraser*, 478 U.S. 675 (1986)

32. *Bethel School District v. Fraser.* See also: Erum H. Shahzad, *First Amendment Constraints of Public School Administrators to Regulate Off-Campus Student Speech in the Technology Age.* Doctoral dissertation, University of North Texas, 2003. p. 12-13.

33. Ibid.

34. *Bethel School District v. Fraser.* See also: Mickey L. Jett, "The Reach of the Schoolhouse Gate: The Fate of Tinker in the Age of Digital Social Media." *Catholic University Law Review*, 2014, pp. 895-919.

35. Ibid.

36. Ibid.

37. Ibid.

38. *Bethel School District v. Fraser.* See also: Hudson, *The Silencing of Student Voices*, p. 26.

39. Daniel A. Farber, *The First Amendment*. New York: Foundation Press, 1998, p.188.

40. Hudson, *Student Expression in the Age of Columbine*. Nashville, TN: First Amendment Center, 2005, p. 21.

41. Ibid., p.1

42. Ibid., p. 21

43. Hudson, *The Silencing of Student Voices*, p. 7.

44. Arum, *Judging School Discipline*. See also: Reynolds Holding, "Speaking up for Themselves." *Time*, May 27, 2007, pp. 65-67.

45. Jonathan Turley, "Courts Kill Student Rights." *USA Today*, March 4, 2014, p. 9-A.

46. Charles C. Haynes, "Schools Must Stop Bullying, Not Speech." Syndicated newspaper column, June 5, 2012.

47. "Suspension Violated Alaska Student's Rights," *SPLC LegalAlert*, April, 2006.

48. *Morse v. Frederick*, 551 U.S. 393 (2007).

49. Ibid.

50. Ibid.

51. *Morse v. Frederick*. See also: Linda Greenhouse, "Free Speech Case Divides Bush, Religious Right." *The New York Times*, March 18, 2007. Stephen Henderson, "Court Hears Free Speech Case," McGlatchey Newspapers, March 20, 2007. Joan Biskupic, "High Court Case Tests Limits of Student Speech Rights." *USA Today*, March 1, 2007, p. 1-A.

52. Ashley Packard, *Digital Media Law*. Malden, MA: Wiley-Blackwell, 2013, pp. 41-42.

53. Greg Lukianoff, *Unlearning Liberty: Campus Censorship and the End of American Debate*. New York: Encounter Books, 2014, pp. 1-4 and 247.

54. Denise-Marie Ordway, "UCF Instructor Placed on Leave After "Killing Spree" Comment." *Orlando Sentinel*, April 25, 2013. See also: Kirsten Powers, *The Silencing: How the Left is Killing Free Speech*. Washington, DC: Regnery Press, 2012, p. 80-1.

55. Powers, pp. 80-81.

56. Ibid.

57. Ibid.

58. Ibid.

59. Justin Jouvenal and T. Rees Shapiro, "Feminists at Mary Washington Say They Were Threatened on Yik Yak." *Washington Post*, Mary 6, 2015.

60. Gene Policinski, "Join the Newest Speech Debate." Syndicated newspaper column, October 23, 2015. See also: Jouvenal and Shapiro, "Feminists at Mary Washington Say They Were Threatened on Yik Yak."

61. "School District Issues Warning About App." *Pensacola News Journal*, December 19, 2014, p. 3-B.

62. *Bethel v. Fraser*.

63. *Tinker v. Des Moines Independent Community School District*.

64. *Snyder v. Blue Mountain School District*, 650 F.3d 915 (2011) and *Layshock v. Hermitage School District*, 650 F.3d 207. See also: "Recent Cases: Snyder v. Blue Mountain School District," *Harvard Law Review*, vol. 125 (2012), pp. 1064-1071.

65. *Tinker v. Des Moines Independent Community School District*.

66. Packard, p. 40.

67. Ken Paulson, "Sophomoric Speech is Free Speech, Too." *USA Today*, July 20, 2010, p. 9-A.

68. Paulson, "Sophomoric Speech is Free Speech, Too."

69. Mickey L. Jett, "The Reach of the Schoolhouse Gate: The Fate of Tinker in the Age of Digital Social Media." *Catholic University Law Review*, 2014, pp. 895-919.

70. Hudson, *The Silencing of Student Voices*, p. 55.

71. Vicki Glembocki, "The Case of the Facebook Fracas." *Reader's Digest*, March 2015, pp. 21-22.

72. Ibid.

73. Ibid.

74. Ibid.

75. Ibid.

76. Ibid.

77. Randy Leonard, "The Ferris Bueller of Facebook." *Florida Today*, January 20, 2008, p. 7-A.

78. "Did the Internet Kill Privacy?" *CBS Sunday Morning*, February 13, 2011.

79. Ibid.

80. Ibid.

81. Ibid.

82. Kathleen Parker, "Internet Freedom Sacrifices Decency." Syndicated newspaper column, August 30, 2009.

83. Randy Bobbitt, *Decisions, Decisions: Case Studies and Discussion Problems in Communication Ethics.* Dubuque, IA: Kendall-Hunt, 2013, p. 383.

84. "Cyberlaw and the Student Media." Report from the Student Press Law Center, 1998.

85. *Dodd v. Rambis,* 535 F. Supp. (S.D. Indiana 1981). See also: *Law of the Student Press,* Arlington, VA: Student Press Law Center, 1994, p. 33.

86. *Gano v. School District No. 411,* 674 F. Supp 796 (1987).

87. *Baxter v. Vigo County School Corporation,* 26 F.3d 728 (Seventh Circuit, 1994).

88. Steven R. Biller, "Dress Codes Ban 'Bart' T-Shirts." *Fort Lauderdale Sun-Sentinel,* August 12, 1990.

89. *Chandler v. McMinnville School District,* 968 F. 2d. 524 (Ninth Circuit, 1992). See also: Erum H. Shahzad, *First Amendment Constraints of Public School Administrators to Regulate Off-Campus Student Speech in the Technology Age.* Doctoral dissertation, University of North Texas, 2003. p. 16-17.

90. Hudson, *The Silencing of Student Voices,* p. 54.

91. *Pyle v. South Hadley School Committee,* 423 Mass. 283 (1996). See also: Shahzad, *First Amendment Constraints of Public School Administrators to Regulate Off-Campus Student Speech in the Technology Age.*

92. *Boroff v. Van Wert City Board of Education* (Sixth Circuit Court of Appeals, case 98-3869).

93. *J.S. v. Bethlehem School District,* 807 A. 2d 412 (Pennsylvania Court, 2000). See also: Hudson, *The Silencing of Student Voices,* pp. 58-59.

94. Laurie Asseo, "High Court Lets Suspension Stand for Drawing Rebel Flag." Associated Press report, October 3, 2000.

95. "ACLU Helps Student Fight Suspension." Associated Press report, May 21, 1999. See also: Hudson, *The Silencing of Student Voices,* pp. 6-7.

96. "Re-Birth of Confederate Flag Controversy Poses Problems for Educators." Associated Press report, February 8, 2016.

97. *Demers v. Leominster School Department,* 263 F.Supp 2d 195 (2003). See also: Reynolds Holding, "Speaking up for Themselves." Hudson, *Student Expression in the Age of Columbine,* pp. 12-13.

98. *Beidler v. North Thurston School District,* No. 99-2-00236-6 (Washington Superior Court, 2000).

99. *Emmett v. Kent School District,* 92 F.Supp. 2d 1088 (Western Dis. Washington, 2000). See also: Carl Kaplan, "Judge Says School May Have Overreacted to Student's Site." *Cyberlaw Journal,* March 3, 2000. "The First Amendment vs. School Safety." *SPLC Report,* Spring 2000, pp. 18-21.

100. *Boman v. Bluestem Unified School District,* 650 F.3d 915 (Third Circuit, 2011). See also: "The First Amendment vs. School Safety." *SPLC Report,* Spring 2000, pp. 18-21.

101. Hudson, *Student Expression in the Age of Columbine,* pp. 12-13.

102. *Saxe v. State College Area School District,* 77 F.Supp. 621 (2001).

103. *Lake v. Utah,* 2002 UT 110 (2002). See also: Ashley Packard, *Digital Media Law,* p. 246. "The First Amendment vs. School Safety." *SPLC Report,* Spring 2000, pp. 18-21.

104. Joan Biskupic, "High Court Case Tests Limits of Student Speech Rights." *USA Today,* March 1, 2007, p. 1.

105. Ibid.

106. *Smith v. Mount Pleasant Public Schools,* 285 F. Supp. 2d 987 (E.D. Michigan 2003); see also, Frank D. LoMonte, Adam Goldstein, and Michael Hiestand, *Law of the Student Press.* Arlington, VA: Student Press Law Center, 2013, p. 31.

107. "Ohio Student Can Wear Anti-Gay, Anti-Muslim, Anti-Abortion T-Shirt, Court Rules." *SPLC LegalAlert,* October 2005.)

108. Angela Mack, "Addressing the Dress Code." *Wilmington Star-News,* May 22, 2003, p. 1-B.

109. New Jersey Principal Caught Smoking on School Grounds Suspends Student That Photographed Her." SPLC *LegalAlert,* March 2005.

110. *Heinkel v. School Board of Lee County* (2005 WL 1571077). See also: "Federal Court Finds Florida School's Distribution Policy Unconstitutional." SPLC Legal Alert, October 2015.

111. John Freeman, *The Tyranny of Email*. New York: Scribner Publishing, 2009, p. 157.

112. "Judge OKs Hitler Buttons." Associated Press report, September 21, 2007.

113. *Gillman v. Holmes County Board of Education*, 5:08-CV-34 (2008).

114. Bobbitt, *Decisions, Decisions: Case Studies and Discussion Problems in Communication Ethics*. Dubuque, IA: Kendall-Hunt, 2013, p. 324.

115. Tony Mauro, "Why the First Amendment Still Matters to Students." *USA Today*, August 28, 2013, p. 6-A.

116. *Dariano v. Morgan Hill Unified School District*, 822 F. Supp. 2d 1037 (N.D. Cal. 2011). Jonathan Turley, "Courts Kill Student Rights." See also *USA Today*, March 4, 2014, p. 9-A.

117. Paulson, "Sophomoric Speech is Free Speech, Too."

118. Bobbitt, *Decisions, Decisions*, p. 324.

119. "Concord Student Wishes bin Laden Had Killed Her Teacher, Gets Suspended." *Concord Telegraph*, May 18, 2011.

120. *S. J. W. v. Lee's Summit School District*, 696 F. 3d 771 (2012).

121. "High School Student Defends Poem on Sandy Hook Shooting." MSNBC.com, December 31, 2012.

122. Deborah Hastings, "Boy Who Chewed Pop-Tart into the Shape of a Gun Gets Honorary NRA Membership." *New York Daily News*, May 31, 2013.

123. *Mink v. Suthers*, 613 F.3d 995 (Tenth Circuit, 2010). See also: Packard, *Digital Media Law*, p. 246. Brian Schraum, "Former Colorado Student Publisher Reaches Settlement with Prosecutor." *SPLC Report*, December 2011.

124. "Students Punished After Racial Tweets." WJBK-TV report, March 18, 2014.

125. Lauren Roth, "Dr. Phillips Bars Student From Wearing Condom Costume." *Orlando Sentinel*, October 2, 2014.

126. Martha Irvine, "Where Should Schools Set Limits?" Associated Press report, April 27, 2014.

127. George F. Will, "Thanks For the Laughs, America." Syndicated newspaper column, November 29, 2014.

128. Will.

129. Hailey Branson-Potts, "Girl Can Wear 'Nobody Knows I'm a Lesbian' T-Shirt at School." *Los Angeles Times*, February 17, 2016.

130. Barbara Leader, "Gay Student's Stand on Prom Dress Code Changes Rules." *The News Star*, April 7, 2015.

131. "Student Under Fire for Goforth Tweet Apologizes." *The Houston Chronicle*, September 2, 2015.

132. Bobbitt, *Decisions, Decisions*, p. 324.

133. Bill Mich, "Wicomico High Student Arrested for Twitter Threats." *Baltimore Sun*, May 18, 2015.

134. Kelsey O'Connor, "Ithaca High Threat: 17-Year-Old Charged." *Ithaca Journal*, March 15, 2016.

135. Ken Paulson, "College Athlete Tweet Ban? Free Speech Sacks That Idea." *USA Today*, April 16, 2012, 9-A.

Epilogue

Where Are They Now?

CHAPTER 2

Hazelwood School District v. Kuhlmeier: Student Newspapers are not Public Forums: Cathy Kuhlmeier Frey (*Hazelwood v. Kuhlmeier*, 1988) graduated from Hazelwood East High School in 1984, earned a journalism degree from Southeast Missouri State University in 1988, and today works in management for Bass Pro Shops in Springfield, Missouri. Robert Reynolds retired as principal of HEHS in 2002. Howard Emerson left the position of faculty adviser to *Spectrum*, the school newspaper at HEHS, in 2001. Today he is an independent communications professional in St. Louis, Missouri. Supreme Court Justice Byron White, who wrote the majority opinion in the case, retired from the Court in 1993 and died in 2002.

CHAPTER 3

Marshall Mess: Former *Parthenon* editor Kevin Melrose lives in Parkersburg, West Virginia, and is the editor of Comic Book Resources, a web-based industry publication. Former Managing Editor Bill Gardner teaches in the Information Technology Department at Marshall. Dwight Jensen, the journalism professor whose lawsuit against the university set the legal process in motion, died in 2006. Journalism school Director Harold C. Shaver, who reached the compromise with MU President J. Wade Gilley, held that position until his death in 2004. Gilley left Marshall in 1999 to become the president of the University of Tennessee. He retired from that job in 2001 and today is working with his son in the real estate business in Virginia.

Hosty v. Carter: The "Threat of Censorship" and "Actual Censorship": Margaret Hosty taught English at Tarrant County College in Fort Worth, Texas, until her retirement in 2012. Co-plaintiff Jeni Porche attended the seminary and today is a hospice chaplain in the Chicago area.

Disrupting the Educational Process, or Maybe Not: Gary Dickey (*Dickey v. Alabama State Board of Education*, 1967) graduated from Troy State University in 1967 and worked for the Internal Revenue Service until his retirement in 2011. Ralph Adams retired as president of Troy University in 1989 and died in 1998. He is buried on campus.

John Antonelli (*Antonelli v. Hammond*, 1970) graduated from Fitchburg State University in 1970, worked as a producer for Public Broadcasting Service, and today owns Mill Valley Film Group, a documentary film company in San Francisco. James Hammond served as president of FSU until 1976, when he became chancellor of the statewide community college system in Massachusetts. He retired from that job in 1982 and died in 1998.

Johnnie Joyner (*Joyner v. Whiting*, 1973) is retired and living in Henderson, North Carolina. Albert Whiting served as president at North Carolina Central University until his retirement in 1983. Today he is ninety-nine years old and living in Columbia, Missouri.

Going Underground: Barbara Papish (*Papish v. Board of Curators of the University of Missouri*, 1973) never returned to UM, and instead transferred to Bowling Green State University in Ohio. She worked as a freelance writer, covering women's issues and the performing arts, until her death in 2013.

Access to Information: Howard and Connie Clery formed the Clery Center for Security on Campus in 1987 and remain the leaders of that organization today. They live and work in Wayne, Pennsylvania.

Sometimes a Stagecoach, Sometimes Not: David Horowitz is the founder of the Horowitz Freedom Center, a free speech think tank in Sherman Oaks, California. Bradley Smith is the founder of the Committee for an Open Debate on the Holocaust, located in Visalia, California.

Best of the Rest: John W. "Knocky" Parker retired from the University of South Florida in 1985 and died in 1986.

Laura Ingraham is a nationally syndicated talk radio host and frequent critic of higher education.

Ronald Rosenberger (*Rosenberger v. Rector and Visitors of the University of Virginia*, 1995) graduated from the University of Virginia in 1991 and has worked for a variety of nonprofit and political organizations, including the Young America's Foundation and the Ethics and Public Policy Center.

David Kalwinski is an insurance broker in Sarasota, Florida.

Loni McKown remains on the journalism faculty at Butler University but is no longer adviser to the student newspaper.

CHAPTER 4

Gobitis and Barnette: William Gobitis (*Minersville School District v. Gobitis*, 1940), one of three Jehovah's Witnesses suspended for refusing to salute the American flag and recite the Pledge of Allegiance, died in 1989. One of the other students was his sister, Lillian Gobitis. She attended an international Jehovah's Witness conference in 1951, where she met Erwin Kluse, a survivor of a World War II concentration camp who was tortured for refusing to salute the Nazi flag. They were married in 1954 and spent the rest of their lives as missionaries. Lillian Gobitis died in 2014. Supreme Court Justice Robert Jackson, who wrote the majority opinion, died in 1954.

School Prayer and Bible Reading: Steven Engel, the student at the center of the school-prayer case of *Engel v. Vitale*, became an attorney for the New York Civil Liberties Union, where he worked until his death in 2008.

Edward Schempp (*Schempp v. Abington School District*), died in 2003. Madalyn Murray O'Hair, founder of American Atheists, was murdered in 1995 by a former employee she had accused of stealing money from the organization. Her son, William J. Murray III, was a co-plaintiff in the *Schempp* case, but he renounced atheism and became a Christian in 1980. Today he is a Baptist minister and chairman of the Religious Freedom Coalition.

CHAPTER 5

Free Speech at the University of Pennsylvania, or Maybe Not: Eden Jacobowitz graduated from the University of Pennsylvania in 1996. He briefly attended Fordham University Law School but did not graduate. Today he works in human resources for a national hotel chain. Alan C. Kors, the history professor who advised him during the appeal of his suspension, remains on the faculty at UP and in 1999 co-founded the Foundation for Individual Rights in Education. Former Penn President Sheldon Hackney served as chairman of the National Endowment for the Humanities under President Bill Clinton from 1993 to 1997. He then returned to Penn, where he taught as a history professor until his death in 2013.

Uncivil War: adjunct instructor and historical reenactor Jack Perdue died shortly after his controversial class at Randolph Community College was canceled.

Professors Behaving Badly: James Tracy was fired from Florida Atlantic University in 2016 and immediately founded the James Tracy Legal Defense Fund, which he describes as an organization that "defends the free-speech rights of university faculty and other intellectuals."

Saida Grundy remains on the faculty at Boston University.

Melissa Click was fired from her teaching job at the University of Missouri and as of the summer of 2016 was still searching for a teaching job.

Student Fees and Compelled Speech: Scott Southworth (*Board of Regents of the University of Wisconsin System v. Southworth*, 2000) completed his law degree at the University of Wisconsin and today practices law in central Wisconsin, specializing in adoption and criminal defense. He also serves in the Wisconsin Army National Guard.

Best of the Rest: Tim Garneau earned his law degree from the University of New Hampshire and today serves as corporate counsel for Oracle America.

Daniel Maers earned his bachelor's degree in business from Brandeis University in 2015 and today is an account executive for MGP Promotions, a marketing and advertising firm in New York.

David Guth remains as an assistant professor at the University of Kansas.

Erika Christakis retained her position as a lecturer in the Department of Early Childhood Education at Yale University.

CHAPTER 6

International Terrorist: Bretton Barber (*Barber v. Dearborn Public Schools*, 2003) earned a law degree from the University of Arizona and today practices law in Phoenix, Arizona, specializing in First Amendment and civil liberties cases.

The 1960s: Free Speech on Campus, or Maybe Not: Mary Beth Tinker (*Tinker v. Des Moines Independent Community School District*, 1969) became a pediatric nurse but today spends most of her time directing the "Tinker Tour" with First Amendment attorney Mike Hiestand. The pair travels around the country promoting the concepts of free speech and free press on K-12 campuses. Christopher Eckhardt, another student involved in the case, died in 2012. Justice Abe Fortas, who wrote the majority opinion, retired from the Supreme Court at the end of the 1968-1969 session and died in 1982.

Morse v. Frederick: Halfway Down the Slippery Slope: Joseph Frederick (*Morse v. Frederick*, 2007) was the subject of a book titled *Bong Hits 4 Jesus*, written by James C. Foster, a political history professor at Oregon State University, and was a consultant on a documentary film of the same name. Deborah Morse retired as principal at Juneau-Douglas High School and today still lives in Douglas, Alaska.

The Memorial Parking Garage: Hayden Barnes completed his degree at Kennesaw State University, and instead of continuing his career as an emergency medical technician, he earned a law degree at the University of Baltimore and today practices law in Columbus, Georgia. He does not list his attendance at Valdosta State University on his résumé or the website for his law firm. Ronald M. Zaccari retired as president of Valdosta State University in 2008, and in 2015 was honored by the Cancer Coalition of Southern Georgia for surviving cancer and supporting cancer-related nonprofit organizations.

Killing Spree: Hyung-il Jung is still a popular accounting professor at the University of Central Florida.

It Must Be True Because I Saw it on Facebook: Ashley Payne lost her lawsuit against the Barrow County School System. She earned her master's degree in education at the University of Georgia in 2012 and today is an administrator for the Fulton County School System in suburban Atlanta.

Best of the Rest: Heather Gillman was honored by the Playboy Foundation with its 2008 Hugh Hefner First Amendment Award, which included a $10,000 college scholarship.

Bibliography

Alexander, Alison, and Jarice Hanson. *Taking Sides: Clashing Views on Controversial Issues in Mass Media and Society.* Guilford, CT: Dushkin Publishing, 2013.

Arthur, John, and Amy Shapiro, eds. *Campus Wars: Multiculturalism and the Politics of Difference.* Boulder, CO: Westview Press, 1995.

Arum, Richard. *Judging School Discipline.* Cambridge, MA: Harvard University Press, 2005.

"Battle Brews Over Alcohol Ads in College Media." *SPLC Report,* Fall 1999.

Beckel, Bob, and Cal Thomas. "Only Puppets Get Free Speech." *USA Today,* May 2, 2013, p. 7-A.

Berley, Marc. "Campuses Silence Free Speech." Syndicated newspaper column, April 2, 2001.

Bernstein, David E. *You Can't Say That!* Washington, DC: Cato Institute, 2003.

Biskupic, Joan. "High Court Case Tests Limits of Student Speech Rights." *USA Today,* March 1, 2007, p. 1-A.

Bledsoe, Jerry. *Death by Journalism? One Teacher's Fateful Encounter with Political Correctness.* Asheboro, NC: Down Home Press, 2000.

Bobbitt, Randy. *Decisions, Decisions: Case Studies and Discussion Questions in Communication Ethics.* Dubuque, IA: Kendall-Hunt, 2015.

———. *Exploring Communication Law.* Boston: Allyn & Bacon, 2008.

———. "Lou Grant in Sweat Socks." *The Tampa Tribune,* September 1, 1981, p. D-1.

———. *Us Against Them: The Political Culture of Talk Radio.* Lanham, MD: Lexington Books, 2010.

Bosmajian, Haig, ed. *The Freedom to Publish.* New York: Neal-Schuman Publishers, 1989.

Bruce, Tammy. *The New Thought Police: Inside the Left's Assault on Free Speech and Free Minds.* Roseville, CA: Forum Publishing, 2001.

Buss, William G. "School Newspapers, Public Forums, and the First Amendment." *Iowa Law Review,* vol. 74 (1989), pp. 505-543.

Campbell, Geoffrey C. "Trials, Tribulations, and Ongoing Litigation." *Fort Worth Star-Telegram,* October 2, 2005.

Chemerinsky, Erwin, and Howard Gillman. "What Students Think About Free Speech." *Chronicle of Higher Education,* April 8, 2016, p. 4-B.

Chemerinsky, Erwin. "Students Do Leave Their First Amendment Rights at the Schoolhouse Gates: What's Left of Tinker?" *Drake Law Review,* Vol. 48 (2000), pp. 527-46.

Click, J. William, Lillian L. Kopenhaver, and Larry Hatcher. "Attitudes of Principals and Teachers Toward Press Freedom." *Journalism Educator,* Vol. 48 (1993), pp. 59-70.

"Cyberlaw and the Student Media." Report from the Student Press Law Center, 1998.

Dardenne, Robert. *A Free and Responsible Student Press.* St. Petersburg, FL: The Poynter Institute, 2000.

Death by Cheeseburger: High School Journalism in the 1990s and Beyond. Washington, DC: The Freedom Forum, 1994.

Devol, Kenneth S. *Major Areas of Conflict in the Control of College and University Student Daily Newspapers in the United States.* PhD dissertation, University of Southern California, 1965.

Dickson, Tom. "Attitudes of High School Principals About Press Freedom." *Journalism Quarterly*, vol. 66 (1989), pp. 169-173.

———. "Preparing Scholastic Press Advisors for Roles After Hazelwood Decision." *Journalism & Mass Communication Educator*, Winter 1997, pp. 4-15.

——— "Self-Censorship and Freedom of the High School Press." *Journalism Educator*, vol. 49, no. 3 (1994), pp. 56-63.

Duscha, Julius, and Thomas Fischer. *The Campus Press: Freedom and Responsibility.* Washington, DC: American Association of State Colleges and Universities, 1973.

Farber, Daniel A. *The First Amendment.* New York: Foundation Press, 1998.

Feldman, Samuel N. *The Student Journalist and Legal and Ethical Issues.* New York: Rosen Press, 1968.

Fish, Stanley. "There's No Such Thing as Free Speech and it's a Good Thing, Too." *Boston Review*, February 1992.

Friedersdorf, Conor. "The New Intolerance of Student Activism." *The Atlantic*, November 9, 2015.

———. "Free Speech is No Diversion." *The Atlantic*, November 12, 2015.

Frohnmayer, John. *Leaving Town Alive.* Boston: Houghton Mifflin, 1993.

Gillmor, Donald M., Jerome A. Barron, Todd F. Simon, and Herbert A. Terry. *Mass Communication Law: Cases and Comment.* St. Paul, MN: West Publishing Company, 1990.

Goodman, Mark. "Freedom of the Press Stops at the Schoolhouse Gate." *Nieman Reports*, Spring 2001.

Greenhouse, Linda. "Free Speech Case Divides Bush, Religious Right." *New York Times*, March 18, 2007.

Gunther, Gerald. "Good Speech, Bad Speech." In *Campus Wars: Multiculturalism and the Politics of Difference*, eds. John Arthur and Amy Shapiro, pp. 109-113. Boulder, CO: Westview Press, 1995.

Haiman, Franklyn. *Speech Acts and the First Amendment.* Carbondale, IL: Southern Illinois University Press, 1993.

Hanson, Victor Davis. "The Hypocrisy Behind the Campus Renaming Craze." Townhall.com, March 24, 2016.

Haynes, Charles C. "Schools Must Stop Bullying, Not Speech." Syndicated newspaper column, June 5, 2012.

Hentoff, Nat. "Academies of Fear." *The Washington Post*, December 18, 1993, p. 25-A.

———. *Free Speech for Me, But Not for Thee.* New York: Harper Perennial, 1993.

———. *Living the Bill of Rights: How to be an Authentic American.* Berkeley, CA: University of California Press, 1999.

———. "Speech Codes on Campus," in Alison Alexander and Jarice Hanson, *Taking Sides: Clashing Views on Controversial Issues in Media and Society.* Guilford, CT: Dushkin Publishing, 2013.

Hentoff, Nat, and Stanley Fish. "Do Speech Codes Suppress Freedom of Expression?"

Hinkle, A. Barton. "The Death of Free Speech on College Campuses." *Reason,* March 18, 2015.

Hudson, David L., Jr. *The Silencing of Student Voices*, Nashville, TN: The First Amendment Center, 2003.

Hunker, Christopher J. "From Hazelwood to Hosty: Student Publications as Public Forums." *Communication Law Review*, Vol. 7, no. 1 (2007), pp. 74-97.

Ingelhart, Louis E. *Freedom for the College Student Press.* Westport, CT: Greenwood Press, 1985.

———. *Press Law and Press Freedom for High School Publications.* Westport, CT: Greenwood Press, 1986.

Jett, Mickey L. "The Reach of the Schoolhouse Gate: The Fate of Tinker in the Age of Digital Social Media." *Catholic University Law Review*, 2014, pp. 895-919.

Johnson, John W. *The Struggle for Student Rights*. Lawrence, KS: University of Kansas Press, 1997.

Kanigel, Rachele. *The Student Newspaper Survival Guide*. Malden, MA: Wiley-Blackwell, 2012.

Kilpatrick, James J. "Free Speech and T-Shirts at School." Syndicated newspaper column, January 19, 2004.

Kleiman, Howard E. "Student Electronic Media and the First Amendment." *Journalism & Mass Communication Educator*, Summer 1996, pp. 4-14.

Knight, Robert P. "High School Journalism in the Post-Hazelwood Era." *Journalism Educator*, vol. 43, no. 2 (1988), pp. 42-47.

Kors, Alan C., and Harvey A. Silverglate. *The Shadow University: The Betrayal of Liberty on America's Campuses*. New York: Harper Collins, 1998.

———. "Suppression 101: A Quick Tour of Campus Speech Codes." *Reason*, November 1998.

Korwar, Arati. *War of Words: Speech Codes at Colleges and Universities in the United States*. Nashville, TN: The Freedom Forum First Amendment Center, 1995.

Kristof, Nicholas D. *Freedom of the High School Press*. Lanham, MD: University Press of America, 1983.

Kurtz, Howard. "A Trash Course in Free Speech." *The Washington Post*, July 29, 1993, p. 1-C.

Langhauser, Derek P., Leonard M. Niehoff, and Lawrence White. "Forums, Zones, and Codes: The First Amendment and Free Speech on Campus." National Association of College and University Attorneys teleconference, June 3, 2004.

Law of the Student Press, second edition. Arlington, VA: Student Press Law Center, 1994.

Lawrence, Charles R. "If He Hollers Let Him Go: Regulating Racist Speech on Campus." *Duke Law Journal*, 1990, pp. 431-483.

Lewis, Lionel. "The Limits of Faculty Freedom." *St. Petersburg Times*, December 29, 2002, p. 1-D.

LoMonte, Frank D., Adam Goldstein, and Michael Hiestand. *Law of the Student Press*. Arlington, VA: Student Press Law Center, 2013.

Longley, Maximilian. "Speaker Ban Continues to Resonate." *MetroMagazine*, July 2005, pp. 28-31.

Lukianoff, Greg, and Jonathan Haidt. "The Coddling of the American Mind." *The Atlantic*, September 2015.

Lukianoff, Greg. *Freedom from Speech*. New York: Encounter Books, 2014.

———. *Unlearning Liberty: Campus Censorship and the End of American Debate*. New York: Encounter Books, 2012.

MacAulay, Jake. "University Safe Zones, a Danger for the First Amendment." TheAmericanView.com, November 17, 2015.

"Making Schools Safe for the First Amendment." *Student Press Law Center Report*, Spring 2000.

Mauro, Tony. "Teenagers, T-Shirts, and the First Amendment." *First Amendment News*, May 1996.

———. "Why the First Amendment Still Matters to Students." *USA Today*, August 28, 2013, p. 6-A.

McMasters, Paul. "Teaching Freedom Where it Does Not Exist." *SPLC Report*, Spring 2000, p. 2.

McMurtrie, Beth. "War of Words." *Chronicle of Higher Education*. May 23, 2003, p. A-31.

Middleton, Kent R, and William E. Lee. *The Law of Public Communication*. Boston: Pearson, 2013.

Miniter, Richard. "Campus Speech Wars: Waving the Tacky Shirt." *Insight*, vol. 10, no. 4 (June 1994), pp. 18-21.

Moore, Melanie A. "Free Speech on College Campuses: Protecting the First Amendment in the Marketplace of Ideas." *West Virginia Law Review*, 1993-94, pp. 511-548.

Nelson, Jack. *Captive Voices: The Report of the Commission of Inquiry into High School Journalism*. New York: Schocken Books, 1974

O'Neill, James. "Group Takes Aim at Speech Codes." *Daily Vanguard* (Portland State University), November 10, 2003.

Overbeck, Wayne. *Major Principles of Media Law*. Fort Worth, TX: Harcourt Brace, 1999.

Packard, Ashley. *Digital Media Law*. Malden, MA: Wiley-Blackwell, 2013.

Parker, Kathleen. "Internet Freedom Sacrifices Decency." Syndicated newspaper column, August 30, 2009.

Paulson, Ken. "How Free is Campus Speech?" Syndicated newspaper column, April 24, 2001.

Pember, Don R., and Clay Calvert. *Mass Media Law*. New York: McGraw Hill, 2015.

Philips, Susan. "Student Journalism: Are Free Speech Rights in Danger?" *CQ Researcher*, June 5, 1998, pp. 481-504.

Pisciotti, Lisa M. "Beyond Sticks and Stones: A First Amendment Framework for Educators Who Seek to Punish Student Threats." *Seton Hall Law Review* (2000), pp. 635-677.

Policinski, Gene. "Join the Newest Speech Debate." Syndicated newspaper column, October 28, 2015.

Posner, Eric. "The World Doesn't Love the First Amendment." Slate.com, September 25, 2012.

Powers, Kirsten. *The Silencing: How the Left is Killing Free Speech*. Washington, DC: Regnery Press, 2012.

"Re-Birth of Confederate Flag Controversy Poses Problems for Educators." Associated Press report, February 8, 2016.

Reider, Rem. "Campuses Need First Amendment Training." *USA Today*, November 29, 2015, p. 7-A.

Reynolds, Glenn Harlan. "PC Culture is Killing Higher Education." Syndicated newspaper column, March 30, 2016.

Salamone, Rosemary C. "Free Speech and School Governance in the Wake of Hazelwood." *Georgia Law Review*, Winter 1992, p. 253.

Schmidt, Peter. "Colleges are Divided on Need for New Speech Policies." *Chronicle of Higher Education*, March 10, 2014.

"Schools Fail Free Speech 101." *USA Today*, February 12, 2007, p. 8-A.

Shahzad, Erum H. *First Amendment Constraints of Public School Administrators to Regulate Off-Campus Student Speech in the Technology Age*. Doctoral dissertation, University of North Texas, 2003.

Shepherd, Alicia B. "Uncivil War." *American Journalism Review,* June 2002.

Shiffrin, Steven H. "The Dark Side of the First Amendment." *UCLA Law Review*, 61 UCLA L. Rev 1480, 2014).

Silverglate, Harvey A. "A Campus Crusade Against the Constitution." *The Wall Street Journal,* September 19, 2014, p. 11-A.

Smith, Craig R., and David M. Hunsaker. *The Four Freedoms of the First Amendment*. Long Grove, IL: Waveland Press, 2004.

Smolla, Rodney A. *A Year in the Life of the Supreme Court*. Durham, NC: Duke University Press, 1995.

Stains, Laurence R. "Speech Impediment." *Rolling Stone*, August 5, 1993, pp. 46-48.

Stephens, George E, and John B. Webster. *Law and the Student Press*. Ames, IA: The Iowa State University Press, 1973.

Stern, Mark David. "Judges Have No Idea What to Do About Student Speech on the Internet." Slate.com, February 18, 2016.

Street, Scott. "Promoting Order or Squelching Campus Dissent." *Chronicle of Higher Education*, January 12, 2001, p. 38-A.

Strossen, Nadine. "Regulating Racist Speech on Campus: A Modest Proposal." *Duke Law Journal*, 1990, pp. 484-573.

Taylor, John. "Are You Politically Correct?" *New York,* January 21, 1991, p. 34.

Terry, Carolyn. "The First Under Fire." *Presstime*, September 1995, pp. 36-42.

"The First Amendment vs. School Safety." *SPLC Report*, Spring 2000, pp. 18-21.

Trager, Robert L., and Donna L. Dickerson. *College Student Press Law*. National Council of College Publications Advisers, 1976.

———. *Freedom of Expression in the 21st Century*. Thousand Oaks, CA: Pine Forge Press, 1999.

———. "Prior Restraint in High School: Law, Attitudes, and Practice." *Journalism Quarterly*, vol. 57 (1980), pp. 135-38.

Turley, Jonathan. "Courts Kill Student Rights." See also *USA Today*, March 4, 2014, p. 9-A.

Van Alstyne, William W. *The First Amendment: Cases and Materials.* Westbury, NY: Foundation Press, 1995.

"What Every Student Journalist Should Know." *Quill*, September 1997, pp. 44-49.

Wheeler, Lydia. "Colleges Are Restricting Free Speech on Campus, Lawmakers Say." TheHill.com, June 2, 2015.

Wigal, Grace. "Hazelwood East School District v. Kuhlmeier: The Death of No Prior Restraint in an Official High School Newspaper." *West Virginia Law Review*, Vol. 91, (1989), pp. 635-663.

Will, George F. "A Freedom From Speech." Syndicated newspaper column, November 14, 2015.

———. "Thanks For the Laughs, America." Syndicated newspaper column, November 29, 2014.

Zimmerman, Jonathan. "Let Students Keep Their Opinions on Their Chests." *USA Today*, March 17, 2003, 11-A.

Index

About the Author

Dr. Randy Bobbitt is a visiting lecturer at the University of West Florida and a veteran of three decades of teaching courses in journalism, media law and ethics, and public relations. Prior to joining the faculty at UWF, he taught at the University of North Carolina Wilmington, Marshall University, and the University of South Florida. He earned a PhD in communication law and policy from Bowling Green State University and is a frequent speaker at student and professional conferences. *From Barnette to Blaine* is his eighth book. His two previous Lexington titles are *Lottery Wars: Case Studies in Bible-Belt Politics, 1986–2005*; and *Us Against Them: The Political Culture of Talk Radio*.